"From the first time I read a Mark Batterson book (*In a Pit with a really long title, you know the one I'm talking about*), I've loved the way he looks at life and faith. He doesn't say *if only* and settle for regret. He says *what if* and leans into adventure. Read this book and you will too!"

—**Jon Acuff**, *New York Times* bestselling author
of *Do Over: Rescue Monday, Reinvent
Your Work, and Never Get Stuck*

"Mark Batterson brings God to life in ways that change us. IF:Gathering exists because of the power of this little word and the way God moves through dreams rather than fear. Whatever is holding you back, lay it down. You don't want to miss the stories God has for you. Because *if* God is real, what do we have to lose?"

Jennie Allen, visionary of IF:Gathering
and author of *Restless*

"Mark Batterson has the extraordinary gift of making inspiration seem contagious. His new book *If* will motivate and encourage you in a way that is genuinely entertaining and solidly biblical."

—**Eric Metaxas**, *New York Times* bestselling author
of *Miracles* and *Bonhoeffer*

"Finally, a book that shows you how and why we should all take the risks that lead to a life of genuine and faithful purpose."

—**Judah Smith**, *New York Times* bestselling author
of *Jesus Is*

"Pastor Mark has a gift for making spiritual truths accessible and actionable. His writing is informative, enlightening, educational, and a pleasure to read. It will leave you filled with the peace that comes only from renewed faith. Pastor Mark's books have provided more spiritual guidance for me than anything else, except for the Bible, of course! *If* will remind you of God's promises, reinforce the key principles of your faith, and reinvigorate your spiritual walk. I am inspired, strengthened, and encouraged, ready to take on life's challenges and continue in pursuit of my dreams. Thank you, Pastor Mark!"

—**Mara Schiavocampo**, correspondent, *Good Morning America*

"What if God really does want what's best for us? That's the intriguing question Mark Batterson encourages us to ask—and it's the one that can change our whole lives."

—**David Green**, CEO, Hobby Lobby

"There is no better storyteller than Mark Batterson. His insights will stop you cold in your tracks and help you discover a great *what if* for your life."

—**Ben Arment**, author of *Dream Year* and creator of the Story conference

"Forget regret! Give up guilt! Do away with doubt! Mark Batterson shows us how to move forward with confidence and enthusiasm, knowing that God is not just right by our side but on our side."

—**Hugh Freeze**, head football coach, University of Mississippi

if

Trading Your *If Only* Regrets
for God's *What If* Possibilities

Mark Batterson

BakerBooks
a division of Baker Publishing Group
Grand Rapids, Michigan

© 2015 by Mark Batterson

Published by Baker Books
a division of Baker Publishing Group
P.O. Box 6287, Grand Rapids, MI 49516-6287
www.bakerbooks.com

Printed in the United States of America

Library of Congress Cataloging-in-Publication Data
Batterson, Mark.
    If : trading your if only regrets for God's what if possibilities / Mark Batterson.
        pages cm
    Includes bibliographical references.
    ISBN 978-0-8010-1600-4 (cloth)
    ISBN 978-0-8010-1604-2 (ITPE)
    1. Christian life. 2. Risk taking—Religious aspects—Christianity. 3. Regret—Religious aspects—Christianity. 4. Dreams—Religious aspects—Christianity. I. Title.
BV4501.3.B3874 2015
248.4—dc23   2015016916

Unless otherwise indicated, Scripture quotations are from the Holy Bible, New International Version®. NIV®. Copyright © 1973, 1978, 1984, 2011 by Biblica, Inc.™ Used by permission of Zondervan. All rights reserved worldwide. www.zondervan.com

Scripture quotations labeled ESV are from The Holy Bible, English Standard Version® (ESV®), copyright © 2001 by Crossway, a publishing ministry of Good News Publishers. Used by permission. All rights reserved. ESV Text Edition: 2007

Scripture quotations labeled KJV are from the King James Version of the Bible.

Scripture quotations labeled NASB are from the New American Standard Bible®, copyright © 1960, 1962, 1963, 1968, 1971, 1972, 1973, 1975, 1977, 1995 by The Lockman Foundation. Used by permission.

Scripture quotations labeled NEB are from The New English Bible. Copyright © 1961, 1970, 1989 by The Delegates of Oxford University Press and The Syndics of the Cambridge University Press. Reprinted by permission.

Scripture quotations labeled NIV 1984 are from the Holy Bible, New International Version®. NIV®. Copyright © 1973, 1978, 1984 by Biblica, Inc.™ Used by permission of Zondervan. All rights reserved worldwide. www.zondervan.com

Scripture quotations labeled NKJV are from the New King James Version. Copyright © 1982 by Thomas Nelson, Inc. Used by permission. All rights reserved.

Scripture quotations labeled NLT are from the Holy Bible, New Living Translation, copyright © 1996, 2004, 2007 by Tyndale House Foundation. Used by permission of Tyndale House Publishers, Inc., Carol Stream, Illinois 60188. All rights reserved.

The author is represented by Fedd & Company, Inc.

15 16 17 18 19 20 21   7 6 5 4 3 2 1

Contents

The Third *If:* *What If?*

The Fourth *If:* *No Ifs, Ands, or Buts about It*

1

The Power of *If*

☑ Kiss my wife on top of the Eiffel Tower.

It was a picture perfect day in Paris. After climbing 669 steps to the second floor, we hitched a very scary elevator ride to the top of the Eiffel Tower. Then, with France as my witness, I kissed my wife. Life goal #102? Check!

And it all started with *if*.

I'll explain, but first, let's have a little fun. How was that goal accomplished? Well, that depends on how you look at it. You could simply say that I puckered my lips, took an approach path from the left, closed my eyes at the last second, and voilà—a kiss in France, not to be confused with a French kiss.

That's how it happened, but there's more to it than that. That simple kiss was the result of a rather complex itinerary. We flew out of Dulles International Airport on an Airbus A320, made it through French customs, took the regional RER train to Paris, hailed a taxi whose driver enjoyed saying *mademoiselle* a little too much for my taste, and got walking directions from a French lady

7

with a dog in her purse. Not even kidding! Classic as a croissant! But that too is just a fraction of the story.

You could argue that our Eiffel Tower Kiss originated the moment I set life goal #102. And that's partially true. You won't accomplish 100 percent of the goals you don't set. But the true origin of our kiss traces all the way back to the 1889 World's Fair in Paris when more than a hundred artists submitted plans to design the centerpiece, the masterpiece of the Exposition Universelle.

The winner was an engineer named Alexandre Gustave Eiffel, who proposed a 984-foot tower, the tallest building in the world at that time. Skeptics scoffed at his design, calling it useless and artless. Eiffel called her *La Dame De Fer*—the Iron Lady.

It was Gustave Eiffel's *if* that made our romantic rendezvous atop the tower possible, but Eiffel himself thanked seventy-two scientists, engineers, and mathematicians on whose shoulders he stood. Their names are inscribed on the tower, and without their collective genius, our kiss is cancelled. So I guess we owe our kiss to each of their *ifs* as well.

Then there are the three hundred riveters, hammermen, and carpenters who put together the 18,038-piece jigsaw puzzle of wrought iron in two years, two months, and five days. Oh, and don't forget the acrobatic team Eiffel hired to help his workers maintain balance on very thin beams during strong gusts of wind. We have each of them to thank—as well as the Paris city council that voted in 1909 *not* to tear down the tower despite the fact that its twenty-year permit had expired. We owe our kiss to each councilmember and to each of the voters who put them in office.

It's starting to sound like all of history revolves around and conspired for our kiss, so let me stop there and make my point. Every moment, like our kiss atop the Eiffel Tower, is created by millions of *ifs* that combine in a million different ways to make that moment possible.

And if you need to read that sentence again, no shame. It's complicated—as complicated as the sovereignty of God. Yet as simple as *if*.

Gustave Eiffel did not build his tower so Lora and I could kiss on top of it. Nevertheless, his *if* made it possible. And it's your *ifs* that open doors of opportunity for others, most of whom you won't meet on this side of eternity. But make no mistake about it, every little *if* makes an exponential difference across time and eternity.

History is like an intricately interwoven tapestry with infinite patterns that only the Omniscient One can see and foresee—but *if* threads the needle. Your *ifs* don't just change the trajectory of your life; they change the course of history.

Our kiss atop the Eiffel Tower is part of a chain reaction that started when I wondered if Lora would go out with me. Then I acted on that *if*—well, actually I dialed and hung up a few times first. You could get away with that before caller ID.

Long story short, one *if* led to another *if*, which led to *I do*. The net result? Twenty-two years of marriage and three *ifs* named Parker, Summer, and Josiah.

If you stop and think about it, everything begins with *if*.

Every achievement, from the Nobel Prize to the Oscars, begins with *what if*? Every dream, from landing a man on the moon to the moon pies created to commemorate it, begins with *what if*? Every breakthrough, from the internet to iTunes, begins with *what if*?

There are 1,784 *ifs* in the Bible. Most of those *ifs* function as conditional conjunctions on the front end of God's promises. If we meet the condition, God delivers on the promise! So all that stands between your current circumstances and your wildest dreams is one little *if*.

One little *if* can change everything.

One little *if* can change anything.

WHAT IF?

On August 15, 1987, Howard Schultz was faced with the toughest decision of his life—whether or not to buy a small chain of coffeehouses with a strange name: Starbucks.

Knowing what we know now, it seems like a no-brainer. But to Schultz, the $3.8 million price tag felt like a case of the salmon swallowing the whale. In his memoir, *Pour Your Heart into It*, the architect behind the Starbucks brand reflects on his *what if* moment.

> *This is my moment*, I thought. *If I don't seize the opportunity, if I don't step out of my comfort zone and risk it all, if I let too much time tick on, my moment will pass.* I knew that if I didn't take advantage of this opportunity, I would replay it in my mind for my whole life, wondering: *What if?*[1]

Howard Schultz made a defining decision to give up the safety net of his $75,000 salary to pursue his passion for all things coffee. Starbucks stock went public five years later, on June 26, 1992. It was the second most actively traded stock on the NASDAQ that day, and by the closing bell its market capitalization stood at $273 million. Not bad for a $3.8 million investment!

Starbucks now has 16,580 stores in 40 countries, with revenues topping $4.7 billion, and their 137,000 employees totals twice the population of Greenland. By conservative estimates, Starbucks sold 3,861,778,846 cups of coffee last year.[2] Not to mention the other 87,000 possible drink combinations![3]

And every sip of every drink started with *what if*.

For the record, my favorite drink at Starbucks is a caramel macchiato. Just because we own and operate an independent coffeehouse on Capitol Hill doesn't mean I'm antiestablishment. Listen, if I'm nowhere near Ebenezer's coffeehouse, I'll take caffeine wherever I can get it. Which, thanks to Starbucks, seems like every other street corner in America!

If you reverse engineer Starbucks all the way back to its humble origins, it started with Howard Schultz's *what if*. That's true of Ebenezer's too—*what if* we built a coffeehouse where our church and our community could cross paths?

A million customers later, *what if* is making lots of dreams come true. Every penny of net profit, more than $1 million now, has been reinvested in a wide variety of kingdom causes. And every penny traces back to *what if*.

What's your *what if*?

If you don't know yet, keep reading.

I want you to know that I've been praying for you. While I may not know your name or your circumstances, God does. And I've been asking Him to put this book in the right hands at the right time. That's my prayer for every book I write. So when someone apologizes for having not read one of my books, apology accepted. I trust God's timing.

Of course, the flip side is true. The fact that you hold this book in your hands is evidence that you're ready for *what if*. I'm praying that God will reveal it as you read.

If is more than a book.

It's your *what if*.

But first, you have to get past *if only*.

YOUR GREATEST REGRET

One of the saddest epitaphs in the Bible is hidden away in Jeremiah 46:17. It reminds me of an old headstone in an old cemetery, overgrown with weeds. The prophet exclaims,

> Give Pharaoh of Egypt the title King Bombast, the man who missed his moment. (NEB)

Pharaoh Hophra was the fourth king of the twenty-sixth dynasty of Egypt. As the political and religious leader of one of the most advanced civilizations on earth, the pharaoh had so much potential, so much power. History was his for the taking, his for the making. But he missed his *what if* moment. The opportunity isn't identified, but Pharaoh Hophra ruled for nineteen years, so he probably missed more than one! And because he missed his *what if*, he took his *if only* regrets with him to his tomb.

Let me make a rather bold prediction.

At the end of your life, your greatest regret won't be *the things you did but wish you hadn't*. Your greatest regret will be the things *you didn't do but wish you had*. It's the *what if* dreams that we never act upon that turn into *if only* regrets.

That prediction is backed up by a study done by two social psychologists, Tom Gilovich and Vicki Medvec.[4] According to their research, time is a key factor in what we regret. In the short term, we tend to regret *actions* more than *inactions* by a count of 53 to 47 percent. In other words, we feel acute regret over the mistakes we've made. But over the long haul, we regret *inactions* more than *actions*, 84 to 16 percent.

That doesn't mean we won't have some deep-seated regrets about things we wish we hadn't said or done, but our longest-lasting regrets will be the opportunities we left on the table. Those are the *if onlys* that haunt us to the grave and beyond.

Now let me translate that study into theological terms.

We fixate on sins of commission far too much. We practice holiness by subtraction—don't do this, don't do that, and you're okay. The problem with that is this: you can do nothing wrong and still do nothing right.

Righteousness is more than doing nothing wrong—it's doing something *right*. It's not just resisting temptation—it's going after God-ordained opportunities. Holiness by subtraction is playing not to lose. Righteousness is going all in with God. It's playing to win. It's living as if the victory has already been won at Calvary's cross. And it has.

In my opinion, it's the *sins of omission* that grieve the heart of our heavenly Father most—the wouldas, couldas, and shouldas. Why? Because no one knows our God-given potential like the God who gave it to us in the first place!

Potential is God's gift to us.

Making the most of it is our gift back to God.

Anything less results in regret.

COUNTERFACTUAL THINKING

Little-known fact: I wanted to be a history teacher when I was in high school. I've settled for armchair historian, but I'm still a history junkie.

Technically, history is the study of past events—what actually happened. But there is a branch of history, counterfactual theory, that asks the *what if* questions. It considers the alternate realities that might have emerged if the hinges of history had swung the other way.

It's been said that *what if* is the historian's favorite question.[5]

What if one of the four musket balls that passed through George Washington's coat during the Battle of Monongahela in 1755 had pierced his heart?

What if the D-Day invasion by Allied forces on June 6, 1944, had failed to halt the Nazi regime?

What if the confederates had won the Battle of Little Round Top at Gettysburg on July 2, 1863?

History is full of *what ifs*, and so is Scripture.

What if David had missed Goliath's forehead?

What if Esther had not fasted, thereby finding favor, thus saving the Jewish people from genocide?

What if Joseph and Mary had not heeded the angel's warning to flee Bethlehem before Herod's henchmen showed up?

Let's stay in that vein.

Counterfactual theory is simply an exercise in counterfactual thinking. And it's not just a helpful exercise for historians; it's a healthy exercise for anyone and everyone. Counterfactual thinking is a critical dimension of goal setting and decision making. It's thinking outside the box. It's going against the grain. It's the divergent ability to reimagine alternatives.

And that's what this book is designed to do. It's not just history or Scripture that are full of *what if* moments. They are the turning points, the tipping points in our lives too!

13

Neuroimaging has shown that as we age, our cognitive center of gravity shifts from the imaginative right brain to the logical left brain. At some point, most of us stop living out of imagination and start living out of memory. That's the day we stop creating the future and start repeating the past. That's the day we stop living by faith and start living by logic. That's the day we stop dreaming of *what if* possibilities and end up with *if only* regrets.

But it doesn't have to be that way!

LIFE PLAN

I recently spent two days with a life coach crafting a life plan.

Those two days will pay dividends for the rest of my life. I only wish I hadn't waited as long as I did to do it. Honestly, I'd spent more time planning vacations than planning my life! I had some life goals, like goal #102. But I wasn't living with the kind of intentionality it takes to turn possibilities into realities.

I went through nineteen exercises with my life coach, each one aimed at reimagining my life. The focus was my future, but we looked at it through the prism of my past. It was like a connect-the-dots puzzle, with the letters spelling out God's faithfulness.

By the time we were done, my sense of destiny was off the charts. One of those exercises involved storyboarding my life by identifying turning points. Next, we titled the chapters of my life. Finally, we pinpointed what are called "life gates"—the defining moments that change the trajectory of our lives. They are the *what if* moments when a dream is conceived, a decision is made, or a risk is taken.

One of the revelations I had during that life plan process is that I am my own historian. It's God who ordains our days, orders our steps, and prepares good works in advance. But we have to be students of our own history, including our *if only* regrets. We have

14

to learn the lessons and leverage the mistakes. We have to connect the dots between cause and effect. And we have to reimagine our future through the frame of God's promises.

No matter how many regrets you have, God is the God of second chances. No matter how deep-seated those regrets are, He can turn your *if only* regrets into *what if* possibilities.

This book is full of stories about people just like you who have done just that. Jesus puts a hyphen in history. If you give Him complete editorial control, the Author and Finisher of our faith will write *His-story* through your life. I can't promise a fairytale without any pain or suffering, but I can promise that it will end with happily ever after. Even better, happily *forever* after.

And that brings us to the eighth chapter of Romans.

THE GREAT EIGHT

When it comes to the eighth chapter of Romans, even wordsmiths are at a loss for words. Not many adjectives can do justice to its mystery and majesty.

Theologian and pastor John Piper calls the eighth chapter of Romans the greatest chapter in the Bible. In shorthand, "the Great Eight."[6]

Who am I to argue with him?

Martin Luther called it "the clearest gospel of them all."[7] William Tyndale, who was martyred for translating the Bible into English, called it "the most excellent part of the New Testament."[8] And Douglass Moo, a professor at one of my alma maters, calls it "the inner sanctuary within the cathedral of Christian faith."[9]

I've always thought of it as "The *If* Chapter." The ten *ifs* in Romans 8 add up to infinite possibilities. One last label—"Super 8." Like a good film, Romans 8 has got it all—action, adventure, story line, even some special effects.

It's Michelangelo's *David*.
It's da Vinci's *Mona Lisa*.
It's Beethoven's Symphony No. 5.
It's Lincoln's Gettysburg Address.

The Great Eight starts with a big bang:

There is now no condemnation for those who are in Christ Jesus.[10]

It has a fairytale finish:

For I am convinced that neither death nor life, neither angels nor demons, neither the present nor the future, nor any powers, neither height nor depth, nor anything else in all creation, will be able to separate us from the love of God that is in Christ Jesus our Lord.[11]

Right in the middle, it crosses the Brooklyn Bridge of the Bible:

All things work together for good to them that love God, to them who are the called according to his purpose.[12]

Then there's the subplot:

In all these things we are more than conquerors through him who loved us.[13]

I'll touch on all of those truths, but the touchstone is a little two-letter word in the middle of the chapter. It's the linchpin, the kingpin. It's the hinge on which the greatest chapter turns.

If God is for us, who can be against us?[14]

That's the game changer, the life changer. But you've got to settle the issue. If you have subconscious doubts about God's good intentions, they'll manifest in a thousand forms of fear. If you believe with every fiber of your being that God is for you, an alternate reality awaits you.

That's the goal, but first, one disclaimer.

This book is not a systematic theology, which is an oxymoron anyway!

If is *not* a commentary; it's more of an impressionist painting.

It's not about parsing thirty-nine verses with left-brain logic. It's about painting a landscape of faith, hope, and love with right-brain brushstrokes. I loved the Great Eight when I started writing, just like I loved Lora the day we got married. Twenty-two years later, our love is deeper, longer, and stronger. That's how I felt about the Great Eight when I finished this book, and that's my prayer for you. May you fall in love with the God of *what if* all over again! May your pulse quicken as you turn the pages of this book and, more importantly, *the* Book.

I hope you start reading and can't stop, but let me offer a suggestion if I may. *If* has thirty chapters for a reason. I'd recommend one chapter a day. Think of it as thirty days to *what if*. And why not read it with a friend, a small group, or a book club? *If* loves company!

What's your *what if*?

Let's find out.

What if you are one decision away
from a totally different life?

The First *If*

If Only

Regrets.
We all have them, no exceptions.
But what we do with them is up to us.
Don't play the victim.
You are more than a conqueror.
Don't let regrets hold you ransom.
Learn to leverage them.
There is no regret God cannot redeem.
The best is yet to come.

2

The Most Terrifying Fact

If God is for us, who can be against us?

Romans 8:31

I was seated in the Grand Ballroom of the Washington Hilton hotel on February 2, 2012, along with 3,500 of my closest friends.

Since 1953, the National Prayer Breakfast has been a fixture on the first Thursday of February. The guest list includes ambassadors, diplomats, and heads of state from a hundred countries. The guest of honor is the president of the United States.

Then there are the average joes, like me. To be honest, the pomp and circumstance is a little distracting. I was more focused on figuring out who was who than listening to what was being said from the stage. Then that year's keynote, Eric Metaxas, said something that resulted in a eureka moment. I'm not sure why it struck me the way it did, when it did. But one sentence struck a dominant seventh chord.

He said, "Everything I rejected about God was not God."[1]

It was like tectonic plates shifted with that one seismic statement, and I still feel the aftershocks. Most people who reject God
are really rejecting religion, without knowing it. They aren't really
rejecting God for who He *is*. They are actually rejecting God for
who He *isn't*.

Eric pushed the envelope even further: "Everything I rejected
about God was not God. It was religion. . . . It was people who
go to church and do not show the love of [Jesus], people who
don't practice what they preach, people who are indifferent to
the poor and suffering. . . . I had rejected that, but guess what?
Jesus had also rejected that. . . . Jesus was and is the enemy of
dead religion."

Let me pull that thread.

The most insidious lie we can believe about God is that He is
somehow *against* us. It's the very same lie that planted seeds of
doubt in Eve's spirit in the Garden of Eden.

We've doubted God's goodness ever since, and it's the root cause
of a thousand other problems. If the enemy can get us to buy into
that original lie, we posture ourselves against God because we think
God is against us. Then we reject God for all the wrong reasons.

No. No. A thousand times no!

God is *for* you.

God is *for* you in every way imaginable.

God is *for* you for all eternity.

There is a simple rule of thumb in journalism: don't bury the
lead. So here's the lead: *God is for you.* The rest of this book is
sequential—we'll take the Great Eight one verse at a time, from
1 to 39. But the leading question is this: *If God is for us, who can
be against us?*

It's doubly important, so I'll double back to it again.

Back to Eric Metaxas.

Along with identifying what he'd rejected that wasn't really
God, he profiled the good God he had rediscovered by seeking
Him from a place of honesty rather than religiosity. He detailed

God's most applaudable attributes, and then he asked a brilliant question: "Who would reject that?"[2]

It was a rhetorical question, but let me answer it anyway. The obvious answer is, no one! No one would reject a God like that.

I have a theory: *If you don't love God, it's because you don't know God.*

I hope that doesn't come across as condescending in any way, shape, or form. I just believe it. *To know God is to love God.* Not the God who *isn't*; the God who *is*.

What is there to not love? After all, God *is* love. Those who reject God because they believe God is *against* them are rejecting who God *isn't*.

THE LAW OF THE LEVER

Archimedes of Syracuse is famous for jumping out of his bathtub, running naked through the streets, and yelling, "Eureka!" after discovering the principle of water displacement. That is likely an ancient urban legend, but Archimedes certainly ranks as one of the most brilliant minds in antiquity. In the second century BC, he came very close to pinpointing the value of pi, showing it to be greater than $^{223}/_{71}$ and less than $^{22}/_{7}$.

The world's first seagoing steamship with a screw propeller was the SS *Archimedes*, named in honor of Archimedes's screw pump. He even has a moon crater, a lunar mountain range, and an asteroid, *3600 Archimedes*, named in honor of his astronomical achievements. But he is perhaps most famous for one oft-quoted quip: "Give me a place to stand, and I will move the earth."[3]

Archimedes didn't invent the lever, but he did coin the law of the lever. Simply put, a lever amplifies input force to provide a greater output force. The longer the lever, the greater the leverage.

The concept of leverage has been, well, leveraged in a thousand ways. But let me zero in on systems thinking. In any system, a leverage point is the place in a system's structure where a solution element can be applied. A high leverage point is a place where *a small amount of change force can cause a large change in the system's behavior*. It's a 1 percent change that makes a 99 percent difference.

There is no higher leverage point than the two-letter word *if*.

It defines our deepest regrets: *if only*.

It defies impossible circumstances: *as if*.

It's pregnant with infinite possibilities: *what if*.

And it overcomes all refutations: no *ifs, ands, or buts* about it.

Biblically speaking, *if* is the conditional conjunction that turns God's eternal promises into our present realities. Each of those promises is a high leverage point, but perhaps no promise in the Bible has more leverage than Romans 8:31:

> If God is for us, who can be against us?

That one little *if* can change your life!

If God is for you, it doesn't matter what comes against you. And it doesn't matter what comes against you, if God is for you. No weapon formed against you will prosper.[4] He that is in us is greater than he that is in the world.[5] We can do all things through Christ who strengthens us.[6]

Oswald Chambers coined one of my all-time favorite words: *unconquerableness*. "No power on earth or in hell can conquer the Spirit of God in a human spirit," he said. "It is an inner unconquerableness."[7]

It might not pass spell-check, but it spells *what if*.

Religion is all about what you can do *for God*. Christianity is all about what Christ has done *for you*. But it starts with this kernel of truth: God is *for* you.

If the Father is on our side, game on.

If Christ is in our corner, the fight is fixed.

And if the Holy Spirit is our tag team, Katy, bar the door!

THE TIPPING POINT

In his breakout bestseller, *The Tipping Point*, Malcolm Gladwell defines the tipping point as "the moment of critical mass, the threshold, the boiling point."[8] It's the moment when an idea, trend, or social behavior passes the point of no return and gains acceptance. Gladwell shares some brilliant examples in his book, but let me borrow the concept and broaden it.

In the realm of physics, a tipping point is when an object is displaced from a stable state of equilibrium into a new state.

In economics, it's the point at which an emerging technology becomes the industry standard.

In sociology, it's when a quorum of people adopts a behavior so that it reaches critical mass and goes viral.

And in sports, it's the moment when momentum shifts.

Spiritually speaking, the tipping point is when you believe, without any reservation, that God is for you. It's the revelation that God doesn't just *love* you, He *likes* you. He loves you enough to die for you, and He likes you enough to spend eternity with you. Yet some of us remain skeptical.

We project our self-contempt onto God, assuming that God must be as angry with us as we are with ourselves. Or we fall into the performance-based trap of thinking that our behavior determines God's posture toward us—whether that is *for* or *against*.

Listen, the fact that God is *for* you was proven at Calvary's cross.

Let me be succinct.

God is good + God is love = God is *for* you

It's as simple and as amazing as that.

What is the first thing the angels tried to convince the shepherds of when they announced the birth of Christ? After telling them not to fear—a feeling that comes from a faulty understanding of God's intentions or the false assumption that God is against us—they announced glad tidings of great joy. And what else?

Good will toward men.[9]

It's a small statement with a long lever.

It was the angels' way of saying, God is for you. It's a positioning statement—God is on our side. God is in our corner. It also establishes that *God's will is good will*. His will is only good, always good. And He never holds out on us. No good thing will God withhold from those who walk uprightly before Him.[10]

Go ahead and reject God for who He *isn't*.

Then accept Him for who He *is*.

God *is* for you.

THE MOST TERRIFYING FACT

I recently read an issue of *Wired* magazine guest edited by film producer Christopher Nolan. It was devoted to the physics of film, including some of Nolan's mind-benders—*Memento*, *Inception*, and *Interstellar*. I read it from cover to cover, thoroughly enjoying everything about it except for one thing. And that one thing, I couldn't disagree with more.

As much as I liked that issue, I disliked the Stanley Kubrick quote on the back cover. He may be regarded as one of Hollywood's greatest film directors of all time, but I don't like the way his script reads. He said,

> The most terrifying fact about the universe is not that it is hostile but that it is indifferent. But if we can come to terms with this indifference, then our existence as a species can have genuine meaning.[11]

In my humble opinion, Kubrick's eyes were wide shut. I believe the polar opposite, and it's the antidote to indifference. The Oscar goes to the Great Eight. It's the first word and the final word. God is for you every day, in every way! That is the most terrifying fact in the universe—terrifyingly wonderful.

The crucifixion spells the end of *if only* regrets.

The resurrection spells the beginning of *what if* possiblities.

And when this life ends, infinite *what ifs* await us.

What if you rejected everything about God
that wasn't God and accepted Him
for who He is—God **for** *you?*

3

Can't Forget

There is now no condemnation.

Romans 8:1

Pick a date, any date, after February 5, 1980.

Jill Price can instantly tell you what day of the week it was, what she did that day, and any major event that took place. She can even tell you what the weather was like. For most of us, our problem is remembering. For Jill Price, it's forgetting. She has a condition called hyperthymestic syndrome—automatic autobiographical recall of every day of her life from the age of fourteen on.

For the average person, autobiographical memory is highly selective. We tend to remember emotional experiences or significant events like a first kiss, a big game, or an epic adventure. Unfortunately, we also remember highly embarrassing moments—like falling in the mud during recess and having to wear itchy wool pants with an ugly plaid pattern, provided by the school nurse, while classmates mercilessly tease you. I wish that was hypothetical, but

28

it's my longest lasting memory from the fourth grade. Not that I'm scarred or anything!

Studies suggest that just 3 percent of life events are highly memorable. So over the course of an average year, approximately seventeen experiences will make it into long-term memory. The other 97 percent of life doesn't make the cut. Most of life fades to black—the black hole called the subconscious.

But that's not true for Jill. Jill remembers *everything*.

She remembers that the final episode of *M*A*S*H* aired on February 28, 1983. She remembers that it was a Monday. She also remembers that it was a rainy day and her windshield wipers stopped working.

That might seem like a gift, and it is, if you're trying to remember names or birthdays or happen to be on *Jeopardy!* But there is a downside, a dark side.

In her memoir, *The Woman Who Can't Forget*, Jill says,

> Imagine being able to remember every fight you ever had with a friend; every time someone let you down; all the stupid mistakes you've ever made; the meanest, most harmful things you've ever said to people and those they've said to you. Then imagine not being able to push them out of your mind no matter what you tried.[1]

For Jill, the emotions aren't dialed down by time. They are just as potent as the day she experienced them. "As I grew up and more and more memories were stored in my brain," Jill says, "more and more of them flashed through my mind in this endless barrage, and I became a prisoner to my memory."[2]

A prisoner to my memory.

In that respect, Jill isn't alone. Consciously or subconsciously, most of us are prisoners of our past. Even if we've confessed our sin, we still feel condemned. And that feeling of condemnation undermines the fact that God is *for* us. We keep beating ourselves up. We keep sabotaging ourselves. We keep believing the self-defeating lies that come from the enemy and become self-fulfilling

29

prophecies. The only exit is fully accepting, understanding, and believing the life-changing truth that there is *no* condemnation for those who are in Christ.

None. Nada. Zilch. Zero. Not a trace. Not a whiff. Not a hint.

And that's just the first note in this Symphony No. 8.

SCARLET LETTER

I believe that consciously or subconsciously, most people are held hostage by one or two or three mistakes in their past. And if it's a secret sin, it feels like solitary confinement. We can't get on with our lives because we can't get past the past. Instead of living in the here and now, we're living back then and back there.

We define ourselves by what we've done wrong, instead of defining ourselves by what Christ has done *right*. Or we define ourselves by the hurtful things done *to us* instead of what Christ has done *for us*.

In 1850, Nathaniel Hawthorne published his magnum opus, *The Scarlet Letter*. In this novel, a young woman, Hester Prynne, is found guilty of adultery. She is required to wear a scarlet *A* on her dress—the symbol of shame. We do the same thing, don't we? We are quick to label people by the categorical mistake they've made or one dimension of their identity. I'm afraid that is just as true of the church as it is of the culture.

Whether it's an *A* for adultery, a *D* for divorce, or a *G* for gay—that isn't how God sees us and labels us. He takes off our graveclothes of sin and clothes us with garments of salvation.[3] He gives us a new name, a new identity, a new destiny. He puts a different *A* on us—apple of His eye.[4]

There is a story line in John's Gospel that is not unlike Hawthorne's *Scarlet Letter*. A woman is caught in the act of adultery. The religious mob is ready to stone her to death when Jesus steps up and steps in. Jesus doesn't defend her adultery, but He does defend this adulteress. And His defense is pure brilliance: "He who is without sin among you, let him throw a stone at her first." One by one, they drop their stones and walk away until it's just Jesus and this woman. Then Jesus labels her *F* for *forgiven* and says, "Go and sin no more."[5]

I can't help but wonder, would I have come to this woman's defense, or would I have picked up a stone?

I honestly don't know, but I'll tell you this. Whenever I hear about a high-profile failure, I try to never respond in a holier-than-thou fashion. The first thing that fires across my synapses is John Bradford's famous adage: "But for the grace of God, there go I."

I live by the maxim, *love people when they least expect it and least deserve it*. That's how you change someone's life forever. When the Pharisees were writing people off, Jesus was writing them in. When everyone else was showing them the door, Jesus was showing them grace.

This woman walks off the pages of Scripture, but not before Jesus totally changes her trajectory. Grace is the catalyst that turns guilt into gratitude. One act of grace can turn the worst moment into the defining moment of someone's life. You can be that agent of grace.

This is that moment for this woman. It turns her greatest *if only* regret into a wonderful *what if* possibility: "Go and sin no more!"

381 MILES

God got Israel out of Egypt in one day, but it took forty years to get Egypt out of Israel. It happened at a place called Gilgal, 381 miles northeast of Egypt. The Israelites thought like slaves, acted like slaves. After all, it's tough to break the cycle after four hundred years of slavery.

Technically, the Israelites were set free at the exodus. Practically, it took forty years to fully exorcise their demons. It wasn't until they

31

reached Gilgal that they finally left the past in the past. God said, "Today I have rolled away the shame of your slavery in Egypt."[6]

Sometimes it takes forty long years to bring closure to the feelings of condemnation. Sometimes you have to travel 381 miles just to get the past out of your present. But no matter how long it's been or how far you've traveled, God can still roll away your *if only* regrets. It's never too late to be who you might have been. We'll get to *what if*, but every path to the Promised Land must go through Gilgal.

If you are in Christ, you are no longer defined by what you've done wrong. You are defined by what Christ has done right. You are a new creation, but sometimes it takes some time for your new nature to become second nature.

God can deliver you in one day, but it may take years to break old habits or build new habits. And for the record, the key to one is the other. If you want to break the sin habit, you'd better establish a prayer habit.

Jesus came to put the past in its place—the past.

We just need to leave it there.

When I was ten years old, I remember my older brother, Don, throwing away a board game that had become an unhealthy obsession in his life. He packed it up and threw it in the garbage. I remember wondering why he didn't *sell* it, but that decision made a profound impression on me. It was a Gilgal moment.

If you want to leave the past in the past, it helps if you bury it, burn it, flush it, or delete it. Isn't that what Christ has done with our sin? He crucified our sin by nailing it to a cross. Don't resurrect it!

NO CLAW

Every word in the first verse of Super 8 is significant, but the word that may be the most overlooked is *now*.

Full forgiveness is our present-tense reality. Right here. Right now. And it's not just a theory that Paul is floating here. How many times must Paul, who was once known as Saul, have had sinful flashbacks to Stephen's stoning? Or the countless other Christians he hunted down like animals?

Paul was an eyewitness, which means those snapshots were seared into his visual cortex. When he closed his eyes, those images could have haunted him the rest of his life. By today's standards, Saul was a terrorist—then he had an encounter with Christ that blinded him. He regained his physical sight after three days, but the grace of God enabled him to turn a blind eye to sin forever.

If God turns a blind eye to confessed sin, shouldn't we?

That doesn't mean we deny our sin or ignore it. If you underestimate your sinfulness, you depreciate the grace of God. Paul called himself the chief of sinners.[7] He freely admitted that he was the worst of sinners, and perhaps that is why he appreciated the grace of God most.

The reason many of us label others by their sin is because it makes us feel better about ourselves. We may be sinners, but at least we haven't done this or that or the other thing!

But Paul is explicit: all have sinned and fallen short of the glory of God.[8] There is no gradation.

We're either *in sin* or *in Christ*.

We're either *guilty* or *forgiven*.

We're either *sinners* or *saints*.

Even after his conversion, Paul could have allowed sinful memories to hold him hostage. Residual feelings of condemnation could have kept him from going on his missionary journeys, kept him from preaching the gospel, kept him from writing half of the New Testament.

But Paul knew that his sin was nailed to the cross, and the hammer of God's mercy has no claw. Before you step into *what if*, you have to get past *if only*. And the crossroad is the cross of Christ. It's the cross that turns *if only* regrets into *what if* possibilities.

HIGHLIGHT TAPE

At Calvary's cross, Jesus broke the chains, broke the curse, and broke the code. It's history's greatest accomplishment, but sometimes we shortchange it. My sin debt is paid in full, and I'm fully forgiven. But that's only half the gospel—the *glass-half-empty gospel*.

We tend to focus on the penalty being paid, which is wonderful beyond words. But the righteousness of Christ has been credited to your account. So the glass isn't half empty; it's full of the righteousness of Christ.

This half-empty mindset causes us to focus on forgiveness, but Jesus didn't die on the cross just to *forgive* you. His aim is much higher than that. He died to *change* you. And He didn't die on the cross just to keep you *safe*. He died to make you *dangerous*—a threat to the enemy. He died so that you could make a difference for all eternity.

Let me change metaphors and paint a picture.

When I was in seminary, I had an eighty-year-old friend named Wiley. He'd occasionally pick up some Whoppers from Burger King, come over to campus, and we'd have conversations that covered the gamut. The Whoppers were always cold by the time he arrived, which makes me queasy—but it was a change of pace from ramen noodles!

One day I pulled out an old highlight tape from my basketball-playing days that my dad had spliced together. Those were the VHS days, so it was a third-generation rough cut. But on that sacred tape was every three-point shot, every dunk, and every round mound of rebound from my high school basketball career.

My dad made copies and sent it to recruiters, but the tapes must have gotten lost in the mail. It's the only reason I can think of as to why they wouldn't come knocking—yeah, even *begging*. At least Wiley was impressed, as we watched with our cold Whoppers in hand. At one point he said, "Mark, you never miss."

Now, what Wiley failed to realize is that this tape wasn't one game! Evidently he didn't notice that I was wearing our red home jersey on some shots and white away jersey on other shots, and the opponents kept changing jerseys!

For one moment in time, one person on the planet thought I was the greatest basketball player on the planet. Reality check: my dad made me look way better than I really am.

Isn't that exactly what the heavenly Father does with our game tape? All the turnovers are deleted. Right? Every missed shot is edited out. It doesn't show up on the video; it doesn't show up in the box score. Why? Because it's been edited out by the Author and Perfecter of our faith!

When you're confessing, God is editing. And it's not just our sin that is edited out. It's His righteousness that is edited in. What's left is a human highlight reel that would make *SportsCenter* proud.

What if you started acting like an agent of grace—looking for opportunities to love people when they least expect it and least deserve it?

4

Double Jeopardy

For those who are in Christ Jesus.

Romans 8:1

Every tennis legend who has played on Centre Court at Wimbledon, from Arthur Ashe to Serena Williams, has walked under an inscription on the players' entrance with a prophetic message to both winner and loser:

> If you can meet with Triumph and Disaster
> And treat those two imposters just the same[1]

That's it—an incomplete yet powerful thought, cut and pasted from a poem by British Nobel Laureate Rudyard Kipling. The one word title? "If—." It's an ode to self-discipline, and the BBC named it Britain's favorite poem a century after it was penned. Its enduring magnetism is a testament to the power of that two-letter word.

Not unlike the inscription over the players' entrance at Wimbledon, there is an inscription over the entrance to the Great Eight:

There is now no condemnation for those who are in Christ Jesus.[2]

I've devoted two chapters to this one verse because it deserves a double take. That first verse should be our first thought every morning—no better way to start the day. It's the emergency exit from *if only* and the main entrance to *what if*. And if you want to understand the other truths in the Great Eight, you've got to walk under that inscription on the way in and the way out.

The Jewish people leveraged their door frames as a daily reminder of God's sovereignty. A specially trained scribe used indelible ink and a special quill pen to inscribe on parchment the Shema—the most important prayer in Judaism.[3] The parchment was then rolled up and placed inside a special case called the mezuzah. Not only was it dangled over the front door, it was hung on every door—a constant reminder, a sacred reminder.

Why did we stop doing that?

We need to surround ourselves with sacred reminders. That's why I have dozens of my own unique mezuzahs in my office. I have the liquor bottle we found in the walls of the crack house that we turned into Ebenezer's coffeehouse—a reminder that nothing is beyond God's redemptive reach. I have the men's restroom sign from the movie theaters at Union Station where our church met for thirteen amazing years—a reminder that God can open and close any door He wants to. I have a picture of the cow pasture in Alexandria, Minnesota, where I felt called to ministry—a reminder that God doesn't call the qualified, He qualifies the called. And I have the cowboy hat I wore while hiking the Grand Canyon rim-to-rim with Parker—a sweat-stained reminder of the 130-degree temperatures we endured going after a life goal.

You can mezuzah your world in a hundred different ways. I have friends who use tattoos to do it and others who prefer Pinterest. Of course, the most literal application might be inscribing Scripture over your doors! I can't think of a better welcome or sendoff than the one-liners from the Great Eight.

GAME FILM

I recently did a chapel for the then-reigning Super Bowl champions. I've spoken at quite a few NFL chapels, but this one was different because they let me sit in on their team meeting!

I heard the head coach's pep talk. I listened to the offensive coordinator script the first fifteen plays of the game, which felt like a foreign language class and advanced algebra class wrapped into one. Lots of Xs and Ys with numbers, names, and angles.

I knew players and coaches spent lots of time in the film room, but it was enlightening to see it up close and personal. The special teams coach spotlighted their opponent's tendencies by replaying parts of the film over and over again. He exposed their weaknesses and game-planned how his team would exploit them.

The highlight? Watching the coach draw up a fake field goal during the meeting, then seeing them execute it in the game just the way he drew it up.

The enemy of our soul knows our weaknesses, and he tries to exploit them. His goal? To take you out of the game any way he can. The good news, of course, is that God is on our side. And it doesn't matter who is against us, if God is for us!

The way you overcome the adversary is by flipping the script, and the script is Scripture. The enemy doesn't have any unscouted looks. In fact, his tactics are as old as Eden. If you study the game film in Genesis 3 and Luke 4—the temptation of the first Adam and the temptation of the Second Adam—you'll discover that the enemy is as predictable now as he was then. Of course, we can't afford to be ignorant of his devices, or we give him an unfair advantage.[4]

Satan is a complex personality, but one of his monikers is "the accuser of our brethren."[5] Condemnation is his native tongue. He tries to remind us of everything we've done wrong over and over again like a broken record. Why? So that all of our emotional energy is spent on past guilt. That way we have no emotional energy left over to dream God-sized dreams or pursue God-ordained passions.

The irony of his accusations is this: he leaves our *unconfessed* sins alone. Why wake a sleeping dog? He'd rather you don't deal with unconfessed sin at all. So he doesn't touch it with a ten-foot pole. His accusations pinpoint *confessed* sin, sins that have already been forgiven and forgotten. That's why they are false accusations—those sins have already been acquitted.

DOUBLE JEOPARDY

Let me make a critical distinction.

Condemnation is feeling guilty over *confessed sin*.

Conviction is feeling guilty over *unconfessed sin*.

Conviction is healthy and holy, and it comes from the Holy Spirit. It's the way we get right with God and get on with our lives. If you don't listen to His convicting voice, you won't hear His comforting voice, His wise voice, or His GPS voice either. Hearing the voice of God is a package deal. If you don't listen to *everything* the Holy Spirit has to say, it's difficult to hear *anything* He has to say.

So you've got to tune in to the convicting voice of the Holy Spirit, but you also need to tune out the condemning voice of the enemy.

The voice of condemnation is enemy subterfuge meant to discourage and disorient. It's the little voice in your head that keeps reminding you of what the heavenly Father has forgotten. You need to turn the dial to Romans 8:1 and stay tuned. Here's one more tactic: the next time the enemy reminds you of your past, remind him of his future. His failure is as certain as your forgiveness.

There are thousands of promises in the Bible, and as I've already mentioned, the vast majority come with an *if* attached to the front end. One of the most amazing *ifs* is 1 John 1:8–9, but it's a two-edged sword that cuts both ways.

> If we claim to be without sin, we deceive ourselves and the truth is not in us. If we confess our sins, he is faithful and just and will forgive us our sins and purify us from all unrighteousness.

If we plead innocent, we're guilty as charged. Even the advocate can't come to our defense. But if we plead guilty as charged, we're found innocent and we come under God's protective custody. Our record of wrong is completely expunged. And there is no double jeopardy—you cannot be tried twice for the same sin. The force of the *no* in "no condemnation" cannot be overstated. It's an absolute negation that has no limit on time, scope, or cost. Once confessed, sins are forgiven once and for all. The sinless Son of God took the blame, took the hit, and took the fall for fallen sinners.

2,232 LIFETIMES

There is a saying born of baseball: three strikes and you're out.

It's so ingrained in our psyche that we play life the same way we play ball. We give people three chances, no more. But God never gives up on us. It's not in His nature.

When Peter asked Jesus how many times he should forgive his brother, Jesus set the gold standard. Peter answered his own question by saying *seven*, and I'm sure he thought he was being generous, but Jesus ups the ante to *seventy times seven*. Then He ups the ante even more with a story about a master who forgave his servant a ten-thousand-talent debt.

Let me do the currency exchange.

One talent equaled 60 minas.

One mina equaled three months' wages.

So one talent totaled 180 months of wages. That's fifteen years! And that's just *one* talent. A ten-thousand-talent debt totaled 150,000 years of wages! Using today's average life expectancy, it would have taken this servant 2,232 lifetimes to pay off the debt. Of course, the average life expectancy in the first century was less than half of what it is now, so it would have taken twice as many lifetimes to pay off the debt.

Let's have a little more fun with the numbers. Instead of years, let's put this debt into dollars. The federal minimum wage is $7.25. Let's take a nine-to-five, Monday-to-Friday job. That's an annual income of $15,080, just above the poverty line for a single taxpayer in the United States. That might not seem like much, but when you multiply it by 150,000 years, it totals $2,262,000,000. Three commas means *billions*.

Now here's the amazing thing: by virtue of what Christ accomplished on the cross, your debt is paid in full. And not just down to the dollar—right down to the red cent. As the old hymn says,

> My sin, oh, the bliss of this glorious thought!
> My sin, not in part but the whole,
> Is nailed to the cross, and I bear it no more,
> Praise the Lord, praise the Lord, O my soul![6]

PAID IN FULL

Just minutes before his final breath, Jesus cried out, "*Tetelestai!*" from the cross. In English, it translates as "It is finished."

It was the same word that was written on ancient receipts in New Testament times, indicating that a debt had been paid in full. Jesus' death on the cross was the final installment on sin. The entire $2,262,000,000 debt was paid in full at Calvary.

Where sin abounds, grace does much more abound.[7]

Did you catch it? *Much more.*

I recently bumped into someone from National Community Church who waitresses at one of my favorite restaurants. She asked me what I wanted and I asked her how she was doing. Her teary eyes told me, *not good*. She said she made a mistake, and I could sense the acute regret. I have no idea what mistake she made, but God gave me a one-sentence sermon. She was serving other customers, so that's all I had time for. I simply yet sincerely said, "His grace is sufficient." That's it. It doesn't matter how big or how bad the mistake, those four words are always true.

The mercy bank is never closed. And there are never insufficient funds. The supply of grace is always greater than the demand of sin. The split second we confess our sin, a miraculous transaction happens. All of our sin is transferred to Christ's account and paid in full. But as good as that is, that's only half the gospel. There is a second wire transfer. All of His righteousness is credited to our account. Then our gracious God says, "Let's call it even!"

To be *in Christ* means we stand in His righteousness. So when we stand before the judgment seat of God, we won't have to account for our sin, because it was already accounted for at the cross. The Father will see the righteousness of His Son that has been credited to our account.

That's good news.

That's the gospel truth.

What if you tuned out the voice
of condemnation and tuned in
to the voice of conviction?

5

A $100 Million Fast

It was weakened by the flesh.

Romans 8:3

Would you fast for twenty-two days if you knew it would net $100 million for a cause you care about? Of course you would. Who wouldn't?

Hold that thought.

Shortly after moving to Washington, DC, I heard rumors of a bipartisan, multiracial prayer meeting hosted by Congressman Tony Hall. I was intrigued enough to check it out. I've since written a book or two on prayer, and we've hosted our fair share of prayer meetings at National Community Church, but that inaugural prayer meeting was a defining moment for me.

I knew that prayer, not politics, would be the thing that changes our city from the inside out. Afterward, I greeted Congressman Hall and went on my way. It had been nearly two decades since that prayer meeting when Tony and I caught up over a cup of coffee at Ebenezer's.

43

After serving twenty-four years in the United States House of Representatives, Tony Hall was appointed the United States Ambassador to the United Nations Agencies for Food and Agriculture in Rome. Following his ambassadorship, Tony moved back to Washington to lead the International Alliance to End Hunger.

You can't get within ten feet of Tony Hall without feeling his pulsing passion to end world hunger. That is Tony's *what if*. That is what wakes him up in the morning and keeps him up at night.

The genesis of Tony's passion was a trip to Ethiopia during a severe famine nearly thirty years ago. The congressional delegation visited a number of sites, including a small medical outpost run by two nuns. While they were there, thousands of refugees, looking like walking skeletons, appeared on the horizon. They had walked hundreds of miles to get food—food that the nuns did not have.

When they discovered there was no food, many of them lay down on the ground and waited to die.

Their moaning will echo in Tony's ears forever. Some mothers handed Tony their children, hoping he could help. He could not. "I watched twenty-four children die in fifteen minutes," Tony said. "And I never got over that."

Tony's heart broke, and it's still an open wound. But it's our woundedness that God uses to help and to heal others.

UNTO GOD

If that experience in Ethiopia was the genesis of Tony's passion, the revelation happened the day Congress cut all funding for the Select Committee on Hunger, the committee Tony chaired. With one stroke of the pen, his cause became a lost cause.

The *New York Times* had called the Select Committee on Hunger "the conscience of the Congress." But as Tony so poignantly points out, "The poor cannot afford lobbyists."

When the committee was cut, Tony was tempted to quit Congress altogether. Then his wife, Jan, said, "Have you ever thought about fasting?" Sometimes the Holy Spirit speaks in a voice that sounds just like your spouse!

That one question changed the trajectory of Tony's life. It was the catalyst that caused him to ask *what if*.

Tony and Jan read Isaiah 58. Then they rolled the dice on that *what if*.

> Is this not the fast that I have chosen:
> To loose the bonds of wickedness,
> To undo the heavy burdens,
> To let the oppressed go free,
> And that you break every yoke?
> Is it not to share your bread with the hungry?[1]

The next day, Tony stood before a bank of dozens of microphones and announced his fast for hunger. "I was afraid of looking like a fool," Tony told me. "I figured it might even cost me my seat in Congress." But that's what walking after the Spirit looks like, feels like. It felt like one man against the world, but Tony knew that if God was for it, nothing could stop it.

The next twenty-two days would prove to be the most difficult yet most amazing days of his life. His body weakened, with nothing but water to sustain it. But his resolve strengthened like carbon steel forged at 2,246 degrees Fahrenheit. Ten thousand high schools joined the fast. The major networks across the country and around the world documented what Tony was doing.

Then, on day twenty-two, the breakthrough happened. The World Bank told Tony they wanted to convene a world conference on hunger. After the conference, more than $100 million was pledged to the cause Tony cares so much about. Mohammed Yunus, winner of the Nobel Peace Prize for his work on microcredit and microfinance, later told Tony that the fund had multiplied many times over, totaling nearly half a billion dollars.[2]

"You can't fast unto hunger," Tony was quick to caution, "or any other cause for that matter. You have to fast unto God."

The *cause* is not the cause. It's the effect. God is the catalyst for every righteous cause! "But when you fast and pray," Tony said, "God leans in a little closer." So true!

THE RABBIT HOLE

There is an iconic scene in the cult classic *The Matrix* that makes for a great metaphor. Morpheus gives Neo a choice between two pills:

> You take the blue pill and the story ends. You wake up in your bed and you believe whatever you want to believe. You take the red pill and you stay in wonderland and I show you how deep the rabbit hole goes.[3]

The red pill is *what if*. It's the rabbit hole of faith. And one way you pop the pill is by practicing the spiritual discipline of fasting. The full benefit of fasting is beyond the scope of this book, but it's one of the best ways to break the power of the flesh. If you can say no to food, you can say no to just about anything. No matter what addiction you struggle with, fasting is the way you break the yoke of bondage. No matter what cause you care about, fasting invites the favor of God. In God's kingdom, fasting is the way you go faster, go further. It's not a shortcut, but it is a moving sidewalk.

When you abstain from food, it shows God you're serious. And God takes that seriously, if the cause honors Him. The reality is this: some spiritual breakthroughs are only possible with the combination of prayer and fasting. When you fast and pray, the synergy is more than the sum of its parts.

So let me ask the question again: Would you fast for twenty-two days *if* you knew it would net $100 million for a cause you care about?

The catch, of course, is that fasting doesn't come with a money-back guarantee. If it did, it wouldn't require faith. But fasting is one way we ask *what if*. If you fail to fast, you're popping the blue pill. You're maintaining the status quo and thereby missing out on supernatural breakthroughs. You'll never know what God would have or could have done. You're only left with *if only*.

We waste 83.2 percent of our emotional energy on things we cannot control. All right, I totally made that percentage up, but I think it's a ballpark number. Don't worry about what you cannot control. Don't even worry about doing something grand or glorious. Just do what you know is right. And make sure you do it for God.

Have you ever thought about fasting?

All that stands between you and a $100 million miracle may be one little *if*.

THE "NO" MUSCLE

Fasting is one of the best ways to *what if*.

If you feel like your dream is in a holding pattern, try fasting.

If you feel like your marriage is maintaining the status quo, try fasting.

If your heart is breaking for your kids, try fasting.

If you need a breakthrough, try fasting.

If you need to make a big decision, try fasting.

When I look in the rearview mirror, it's amazing how many defining moments trace back to seasons of fasting. It was a forty-day media fast that netted my first book. It was a ten-day Daniel fast that led to the miraculous purchase of our Capitol Hill campus. During a twenty-one-day New Year's fast, a $1 million gift to National Community Church came out of nowhere. And that's the tip of the iceberg.

I wasn't fasting unto a book, unto a campus, or unto $1 million.

I was fasting unto God, and God leaned in.

This is so important, let me drill down on it.

We have more than 600 skeletal muscles in our body. For what it's worth, if all of them pulled in one direction, you could lift 25 tons![4] The hardest-working muscle is the heart. It pumps 2,500 gallons of blood through 60,000 miles of veins, arteries, and capillaries every single day, and it has the capacity to beat more than three billion times without skipping a beat.

The largest muscle is the gluteus maximus. Despite what you've probably heard, the strongest muscle is *not* the tongue. By weight, it's the masseter muscle in your jaw that can clench the teeth with a force as great as two hundred pounds on the molars.

The muscles in the eye may be the most active. If you read a book for an hour, the eyes make ten thousand coordinated movements. And then there are forty-three muscles in the face, most of which are controlled by the seventh cranial nerve. According to one study, it takes forty-three muscles to frown and seventeen muscles to smile. So in this one instance, I recommend the path of least resistance!

Of all the muscles, the most important, in my opinion, is the "no" muscle. It's the muscle you have to flex anytime you say no to dessert because you're on a diet or no to sex because it's a sacred covenant between a husband and a wife or no to the snooze button because it's time to get up and get into God's Word. When you say no to temptation, you are flexing your "no" muscle.

The obvious question is: How do you exercise the "no" muscle? You know how to work out your heart muscle—you get in a good cardiovascular workout. You know how to exercise your pectorals— hit the bench press. You know how to exercise your quads—do some squats.

So how do you exercise your "no" muscle? Fasting.

Spiritually speaking, nothing will take you further, faster than fasting. You must fast unto God, but it breaks strongholds and yields breakthroughs. At its core, fasting is the way we declare to God that we need Him and want Him more than food itself.

It takes tremendous discipline to give up food, but doing so cultivates discipline in other areas of our lives. It's the discipline that begets discipline. If you can say no to food, you can say no to anything. And that will cut down on *if only* regrets!

The best way to kill sinful desires is by starving them to death. That's precisely what fasting does. It doesn't just weaken your physical body; it weakens your sinful flesh. And it simultaneously strengthens your spirit.

WORD OF THE YEAR

One of my New Year's routines is choosing a word of the year and verse of the year. I had broken so many resolutions I had to try something else!

Last year, the word was *no*, as in, no! I knew I had to say no more than I was. And it wasn't easy, because my default setting is yes.

My word of the year is one way I put the boundary stones back where they belong. It also becomes a focal point for the year. So one of the things I did was determine that I wouldn't do more than twelve overnight speaking trips. The motivation was pretty simple—my kids are at an age and stage where I want to be there for them. At the end of the day, I want to be famous in my home. And it's tough to be famous in your home if you're never home!

A few years ago I read a little book by Andy Stanley titled *Choosing to Cheat*. One sentence was a game changer for me. It's become one of my most-quoted quotes. "To say *yes* to one," says Andy, "is to say *no* to the other."[5] Of course, the opposite is true as well. Saying no to one thing is saying yes to something else.

Fasting isn't just saying no to food.

It's saying yes to God.

Most of us keep a to-do list, but it might be even more beneficial to start a *stop doing* list. You need to curse the barren fig tree! Remember the tree that wasn't producing fruit? Jesus cursed it.[6] You have some barren fig trees in your life—things that are simply

49

taking up time, taking up space. It's hard to say no to anything, even those things that aren't working. But that's how you make room for *what if*.

While I'm not necessarily prescribing you follow my annual "one word" ritual, you might want to give it a try. And if you're not sure what word to choose, why not start with *if*? Again, there are 1,784 *ifs* in Scripture.[7] That'll keep you busy for a while!

What if you tried a food fast,
media fast, or complaining fast
for ten, twenty-one, or forty days?

6

Muscle Memory

Walk not after the flesh, but after the Spirit.

Romans 8:4 KJV

During the NCAA basketball tournament, I often get the urge to shoot hoops. March Madness brings out the ex-athlete in me. And for the record, the older you get, the better you were! I played four years of collegiate basketball and earned First Team All-American honors my senior season.

Of course, it was the NCCAA, not the NCAA. The extra C stands for *Christian*. I know, not quite as impressive!

During a recent Final Four, I decided to see how many free throws I could hit in a row. I was just under an 80 percent free throw shooter in college. Good, but not great. That was two decades ago. Plus, I hadn't shot a basketball in at least six months.

So I was a little surprised when I hit thirty-three in a row. I was on a roll, so I decided to keep going and see how many I could hit out of a hundred. You'll have to take my word for it, but I made the next fifty-nine shots. Then I missed two in a row, hit the last five, and finished ninety-seven out of a hundred. I'm not sure I could do that again, especially if you were watching me. But it wasn't pure luck either.

When I was in the seventh grade, I started playing basketball. For the next decade, I played two hours a day, every day. I grew up in Chicago during the Michael Jordan era, so I would mimic his moves after watching Bulls games. Before I had the necessary vertical leap, I used a trampoline to dunk on the Detroit Pistons. Even during the dead of winter, I practiced on my driveway hoop, in a parka. Along with the standard game of horse, we invented a shooting game called swish. If the ball hit the rim, it didn't even count. And, of course, I'd shoot free throws for hours on end.

My point? Hitting ninety-seven out of a hundred free throws wasn't luck. It was—and it wasn't. It's called muscle memory. Shooting free throws is a little like riding a bike. Once the skill is learned, it's never forgotten.

Despite the connotation, muscle memory isn't stored in your muscles. It's a procedural memory that is stored in your brain anytime you repeat a muscle movement. Whether it's putting a golf ball, playing the violin, or performing a dance routine, the muscle memory becomes stronger the more it is repeated.

It has its detractors, but I subscribe to the 10,000 Hour Rule. Introduced by psychologist K. Anders Ericsson and popularized by author Malcolm Gladwell, the 10,000 Hour Rule purports that the minimum amount of time it takes to become an expert at anything is roughly 10,000 hours. That's both encouraging and discouraging, isn't it? Encouraging because anyone can do it if they set their mind to it. Discouraging because there are no shortcuts, no matter how smart or gifted you are! Of course, some Olympic athletes, chess grand masters, and virtuoso violinists might argue that it takes even more time than that. But it's a baseline, a timeline for greatness.

LEARNING CURVE

Just like a foreign language or martial art, spiritual disciplines have a learning curve. Can you imagine getting frustrated the first day of a foreign language class because you aren't fluent? Or getting upset because you wanted a black belt week one?

Yet that's how we often feel when we aren't fluent in prayer or worship. Just as it takes time to conjugate verbs, it takes time to conjugate praise.

The spiritual disciplines are art forms. Your first prayer will probably look like a kindergartener's painting. Of course, God still puts it on His refrigerator! But if you keep practicing prayer, your faith will become fluent.

Living a Spirit-led life is a steep learning curve. It takes time—and by time, I mean decades, not days. You have to grow in the spiritual disciplines little by little. That's how you go from strength to strength. You keep benchmarking. Your faith ceiling becomes your faith floor. And make no mistake about it, those spiritual disciplines accrue compound interest.

I don't start from scratch every time I study the Word of God. When I pick it up, I pick up where I left off. I'm standing on the shoulders of what I studied the day before, the week before, the year before.

I recently attended the wake of a ninety-four-year-old preacher named Charlotte Hall. Her son and my friend, Pastor Michael Hall, showed me one of her old Bibles. It was well used, well lived. Michael said that she had read the Bible cover-to-cover fifty-two times! I promise you this: she wasn't just starting over every time. With each reading, she reinvested the dividends of previous revelation. With each reading, her faith increased exponentially.

What's true of Scripture is true of worship. Most worship songs last about four minutes and thirty-seven seconds. Total guess, but it's ballpark. When I sing that song, I'm singing for four minutes and thirty-seven seconds. But it's really forty-four *years* of worship condensed into the length of the song! If I'm worshiping God with all of my heart, it must include every heartbeat I've ever had. The older you get, the greater your potential for worship. Why? Because you have a longer track record with God. You have more memories to draw on—memories of His miracles, His love, His faithfulness. But no matter what your age, your sound waves of worship will reverberate for all eternity!

So when you get frustrated with your praying or worshiping or any other spiritual discipline, remember that this is just the practice round. We'll have all of eternity to perfect our praise. In the meantime, keep climbing the learning curve.

THEORY OF EVERYTHING

In the realm of physics, an all-encompassing theoretical framework that fully explains and links together all physical aspects of the universe is called a *theory of everything*. It's also called a master theory, ultimate theory, or final theory. Here's my theory of everything: the answer to every prayer is *more of the Holy Spirit*.

Stop and think about it.

Need to make a critical decision? You need the *Spirit* of wisdom and revelation. Need the right words for a business proposal or marriage proposal? The Holy Spirit is our teleprompter—He gives us the right words at the right time. Or do you need a little love? Well, that's the first fruit of the Spirit. So what you really need is more of the Spirit. The same is true with joy, peace, patience, and every other fruit of the Spirit. Need to overcome an addiction? You need the last fruit of the Spirit—self-control. Of course, that's an oxymoron because it doesn't come from you. It's the Spirit who manufactures it. So it's really Spirit-control.

Whatever it is you need more of, you need more of the Holy Spirit. And for the record, the Spirit of God doesn't just want to fill you. He wants to stretch you—to increase your capacity!

If you feel like your life is in chaos, the Spirit of God is hovering—just like He did at the dawn of creation. He specializes in bringing order out of chaos, light out of darkness, beauty out of nothingness.

No matter what question you have, the Holy Spirit is the answer. No matter what problem you face, the Holy Spirit is the solution.

Here's what I know for sure: I need the Holy Spirit more today than I did yesterday. And I need as much of Him as I can get. Or maybe I should say, I need to yield as much of me as I can to Him. When we do that, the Holy Spirit doesn't make us any better than anybody else. He makes us better than ourselves![1] He gives us wisdom beyond our knowledge, power beyond our strength, and gifting beyond our ability. With the help of the Holy Spirit, we become better than our best effort, better than our best thought. We become the best version of ourselves possible. Of course, it takes time—a lifetime.

Since we're on the subject of the fruit of the Spirit, let me put this in agricultural terms. Sin is a seed. If you plant it and water it, it will grow. If you starve it, it'll die. And the same is true of holiness: It's a harvest. So is wealth. So is health. So is everything else!

Let us not become weary in doing good, for at the proper time we will reap a harvest if we do not give up.[2]

It's hard to imagine a farmer planting beans, then being surprised that it doesn't come up corn. Why? Because you reap what you sow. Yet some of us seem shocked when the seeds of sin yield their crop.

The same is true of holiness. It's not a crapshoot. Holiness is a harvest. Are you planting love or hate? Joy or ingratitude? Patience or impatience? Self-control or self-indulgence? You cannot break the law of sowing and reaping. It can only break you. Or make you, if you keep sowing the right seeds.

Want a bumper crop? Then you need more of the Holy Spirit. But the Holy Spirit can't fill you if you're full of yourself. The list of the nine fruit of the Spirit doubles as a wish list. Deep down inside, it's all we want, all we need. But what we really want, really need is more of the Holy Spirit Himself.

It's the Holy Spirit who dispels *if only*.

It's the Holy Spirit who spells out *what if*.

If you want God to do something new, you can't keep doing the same old thing. You've got to do something different. Then you've got to turn it into a righteous routine that you do over and over and over again.

One word of caution: Practice doesn't make perfect. Practice makes *permanent*. The key is practicing the presence of God every day in every way. And when you get into God's presence, it's game on.

THE SECRET TO SUCCESS

When I was in my rookie year as a pastor, I spent one of the most formative weeks of my life with author and pastor Jack Hayford. It's still paying dividends nearly two decades later.

I don't have many heroes. In fact, I can count them on one hand. My dad is certainly one of them—I can't remember a single instance of my dad complaining. Not one. My father-in-law, Bob Schmidgall, is certainly another. My friend and spiritual father Dick Foth ranks right up there. In fact, we tag-teamed on a book titled *A Trip around the Sun*. I'm forever indebted to the pastor who gave me an opportunity to pastor, Bob Rhoden. And then there's Jack Hayford.

That's my personal hall of fame.

I first met Jack when I was a teenager. My father-in-law invited him to speak at Calvary Church in Naperville, Illinois, and there was quite a buzz. His radio program was broadcast in Chicago, so many people knew and loved his teaching. It was a packed house that night, and it turned into one of the funniest preaching moments ever because Jack left the barn door open.

When Jack gets in a preaching groove, he puts one hand in his pocket, then two. Not helping! Oh, and did I mention that the stage was about five feet high? Not helping either! Every lady in the audience had her head buried in her Bible! Of course, Jack had no idea until my father-in-law jotted a note and put it on the pulpit mid-sermon: "Jack, your zipper is down."

Like an Olympic ice-skater doing a single Lutz, Jack spun around, zipped his zipper, and completed the 360-degree maneuver so beautifully that the Russian judges would have given him a ten. What's even funnier is that Jack said at dinner after the service that he didn't think anyone noticed. Uh, we were all Peeping Toms that night.

Seven years later, I was in my first year of pastoring at National Community Church. I had never been on a church staff, let alone pastored a church. Jack's nuances of language and leadership left an indelible imprint on me. NCC was fewer than a hundred people at the time, but the lessons learned that week helped our church—helped *me*—grow.

Jack is now in his eighties, and he's as wise and witty as ever. He recently spent two hours with a handful of pastors in Washington, DC. That two-hour talk revolved around the secret to his success. And by success, I simply mean stewardship. It's doing the best you can with what you have where you are. Jack's secret? *Make decisions against yourself.*

Jack is transparent to begin with, but the aging process has resulted in total transparency. At some point, you're too old to settle for clichés or platitudes. So Jack shared about some of the near-miss mistakes that could have cost him his ministry and his reputation. The thing that saved him? Making decisions against himself.

I'll come back to Jack in a moment, but stop and think about it. Do you know someone who has six-pack abs? That person made a decision against themselves. They went to the gym when the rest of us went back for seconds. Or how about the person who earned their JD, MD, or PhD? They went to the library when the rest of us turned on the TV! It was that decision against themselves, made day after day, that helped them earn that degree. It doesn't matter whether it's a world-class athlete or world-class musician; they got there by making decisions against themselves.

What decision do you need to make against yourself?

That one decision could save you from a hundred *if onlys*. It could also domino into a thousand *what ifs*!

GOOD ENOUGH

Back to Jack. Some of the decisions Jack made against himself involved resisting temptation—the lust of flesh, the lust of the eyes, the pride of life.[3] They were black-and-white, right-and-wrong issues. But others were simply personal convictions. They weren't wrong for anyone else, just for Jack. For example, the distinct moment when Jack felt like God told him to give up chocolate.

Jack would be the first person to say that there is nothing wrong with chocolate. In fact, let's take a moment right now to thank God for chocolate—dark chocolate, milk chocolate, and white chocolate. And don't forget chocolate-coated peanut butter, chocolate-and-marshmallow s'mores, and mint-chocolate fudge. In my book, chocolate is irrefutable evidence that God loves us and has a wonderful plan for our lives!

For nearly thirty years, Jack hasn't eaten chocolate. Not because it's wrong, but because it's a personal conviction. He'd never impose that personal conviction on others—that's called legalism. He simply made a decision against himself, and it's helped him exercise self-control in every other area of his life as well. After all, if you can say no to chocolate, you are pretty close to complete sanctification!

If you really want God's best, you won't just say no to what's wrong. You'll also say no to second best. Good isn't good enough any more!

Success in any endeavor has its perks, no question about it. But success also involves risk beyond what most of us are willing to take, sacrifice beyond what most of us are willing to make. In other words, more success equals more risk plus more sacrifice.

The larger National Community Church grows, the harder it gets. I'm not complaining. I've embraced the fact that the blessings of God complicate our lives, and I thank God for those complications! But the stakes are much higher with every decision we make because it affects far more people than it did a decade ago.

Occasionally, an aspiring author will ask me the key to writing. My short answer is this one: set your alarm clock for very early in the morning! If that isn't making a decision against yourself, I don't know what is. The next time you're tempted to hit the snooze button, realize that you're delaying your dream nine minutes at a time.

In the Great Eight, Paul says, "walk not after the flesh."[4] The best translation, in my opinion, is Jack Hayford's secret sauce: *make decisions against yourself.* Paul says it this way in 1 Corinthians 10:23:

Everything is permissible—but not everything is beneficial.[5]

This one little distinction between *permissible* and *beneficial* can take you from good to great.[6] Don't settle for what's permissible—not doing anything wrong. That's the path of least resistance. Go after greatness, and by greatness I mean being great at the Great Commandment. It's giving God everything you've got—*my utmost for His highest.*[7] It's not just choosing what's right; it's choosing what's best.

This one decision establishes a trend line in your life. The permissible trend line is a one-way to *if only* regrets. If that's how you've been trending, it's time to make a U-turn. The beneficial trend line is the road less traveled, but it's the only way to *what if* possibilities.

You have to make this defining decision: *permissible or beneficial?* Then it must be backed up by daily decisions against yourself. God can deliver you from anything in a single day, but you've got to back it up with daily disciplines.

If you don't practice spiritual disciplines day in and day out, that deliverance will be short-lived. You'll fall back into whatever it was that God delivered you from. Anybody can say "I do" at the altar; the hard part is saying "I do" every day thereafter. Anybody can set a life goal; the hard part is going after it every day. Anybody can say no to any addiction for a day, but you have to say it day after day after day.

You get into shape one workout at a time.

You get out of debt one paycheck at a time.

You read through the Bible one verse at a time.

Whatever goal you're going after, you've got to take it one step at a time, one day at a time!

BREAKING BAD

If you want to break a bad habit, you have to build a good one. It's the law of displacement.

Again, the only way to break the sin habit is by establishing a prayer habit. And, I might add, a fasting habit might just double your chances! Notice that Paul doesn't just say "walk not after the flesh." He also says to walk "after the Spirit."[8] Making a decision *against* something is only half the battle. The other half is making a decision *for* something.

The eminent Dallas Willard once said, "Not going to London or Atlanta is a poor plan for going to New York." That's pretty obvious, but that's how many of us approach spiritual formation. We try to not sin by not sinning. But that's like me saying, "Be spontaneous!" You can't do it, can you?

In psychology, it's called a double bind. If you're focused on what you *shouldn't* do, you probably won't do what you should.

It's holiness by subtraction, and it doesn't add up to righteousness. Goodness is not the absence of badness. After all, you can do nothing wrong and still do nothing right.

Would you rather be *right* or *righteous*? They are not one and the same.

Righteousness isn't just *being* right; it's *doing* something right. It's not just breaking even; it's going all in and all out for Christ.

Too many Christ followers are playing not to lose, and that's what results in *if only* regrets. It's like a prevent defense in football, which in my opinion, doesn't prevent anything except a touchdown by the other team.

We're called to advance the kingdom, not hold the fort.

It's the difference between *why* and *why not*.

It's the difference between *if only* and *what if*.

Jesus said, "I will build my church, and the gates of hell shall not prevail against it."[9]

First of all, Jesus didn't say *you* will build *your* church. It's not yours; it's His. And that goes for your business, your school, or your team too. It's not yours; it's His. So the pressure's off you. If we are walking in obedience, He will fight our battles for us!

Secondly, gates are defensive measures. So by definition, we're called to play offense. You need a vision that is bigger than the temptations you face. You need a yes that is bigger and better than your no. The most effective way to overcome *if only* regrets is going after *what if* dreams that simply overwhelm them.

What if you made a decision against yourself by setting your alarm clock for thirty minutes earlier so you had time to read the Bible from cover to cover this year?

7

Factory Reset

In order that the righteous requirement of
the law might be fully met in us.

Romans 8:4

I'm a regular at Apple Genius Bar. If shaking my phone violently doesn't fix the problem, well, I know where to turn for help!

When my iPhone started misbehaving a while back, one of the geniuses told me there were two ways to reset my phone. Who knew? Evidently, just about everybody except me! A soft reset closes applications and clears your cache, but the data stored on your hard drive is not affected.

That didn't do the trick, so we did a hard reset. It's also known as a factory reset because the iPhone is restored to the original manufacturer's settings it had when it left the factory floor. It reinitializes the core hardware components and reboots your operating system. And all the settings, applications, and data are wiped clean. It's a fresh start. It's a new phone.

You are a new creation.[1] Not new as in soft reset. New as in *factory* reset. It doesn't mean *like new*. It means *brand new*! It's new in time, new in nature.

It means mint condition, right off the assembly line, latest and greatest.

When you put your faith in Christ, it's a hard reset. It doesn't just clear the cache. It completely clears your history, as if it never happened. That's what the word *justified* means—*just as if I'd never sinned*.

That's more than a mnemonic device. It's more than a paradigm shift. It's a factory reset.

At the cross, Jesus turns *if only* regrets into *what if* possibilities. He sets us free from sin and the shameful feelings that go with it. The prison doors of past guilt and future fear fly wide open. If you fear God, you have nothing else to fear. All other fears are served an eviction notice. They cannot coexist with God's perfect love. His love reboots our heart, our soul, and our mind so that we can be fully alive, fully present.

God forgives *and* forgets.[2] Amazing, isn't it?

He remembers everything you've done right while forgetting everything you've done wrong. Yet while God cannot remember our confessed sin, we have a much harder time forgetting it.

We tend to remember our mistakes more readily than our successes. That's why it's harder to forgive ourselves than it is to receive God's forgiveness. We tend to remember what we should forget and forget what we should remember.

That inability to forget the sin we've confessed is part of our sin nature itself. The fall fractured the image of God in us, including in the amygdala. That's the part of the brain responsible for storing emotional memories. The strength of the memory is dictated by the strength of the emotion. We quickly forget the moments that don't make a blip on our emotional radar. But strong emotions, like shame, take sinful snapshots and poster-size them. They get blown out of proportion in the darkroom of the mind.

There is an old adage: *the battle is won or lost in the mind*. I believe that's true, but let's be more specific. When it comes to *what if* possibilities, the battlefront is the imagination. When it comes to *if only* regrets, our memory can become no man's land.

A BEELINE FOR THE CROSS

When I graduated from Bible college, my graduation gift was an eighty-six-volume set of Charles Haddon Spurgeon's sermons that must have weighed five hundred pounds. Of course, if I had known that Google would enable me to search those sermons a few years later, I would have asked for something else!

Spurgeon ranks as one of history's greatest preachers. If he were alive today, I'm sure his one-liners would trend on Twitter. Almost every sermon has a brilliant maxim, but my personal favorite is this one: "I take my text and make a beeline for the cross."[3]

There are 31,102 verses in the Bible, and all of them point to the cross somehow, some way. The Old Testament points forward while the New Testament points backward. But either way, the cross is the reference point.

Just as this is true of every text, it is true of every circumstance. Make a beeline for the cross! It outranks every adage, outlasts every axiom.

Hold that thought.

The word *remember* is repeated no less than 148 times in Scripture.[4]

Remember the sabbath day, to keep it holy.[5]

Remember the days of old.[6]

Remember the wonders he has done.[7]

Remember Lot's wife![8]

We must find creative ways to remember the vows we have made. We can't afford to forget the promises of God. And when God proves faithful, we must build altars of remembrance. But the thing we must remember most, the thing we can least afford to forget, is the cross of Jesus Christ.

One of my earliest church memories is of the communion table that stood front and center at Trinity Covenant Church in Crystal, Minnesota. Inscribed on the face of it were these words in a gothic font:

Do This in Remembrance of Me

We recite those words every time we celebrate communion, so they almost become an afterthought. But when Jesus spoke them, it was a hard reset for the disciples. The Israelites had celebrated the Passover for thousands of years as a way of commemorating their exodus from Egypt. The evening before the exodus, the Israelites were instructed to sacrifice a lamb without defect and to mark their doorframe with its blood. Then when the death angel passed through Egypt, he would pass over their home.

Little did the disciples know that they were eating the Passover meal with the Passover Lamb who would sacrifice Himself.

Jesus rebooted their understanding of the bread and the cup, telling the disciples they represented His body, His blood. And because of what He accomplished at Calvary's cross, we come under the protective custody of the blood of the Lamb. Like the Passover, communion is a commemoration of our exodus from slavery. We were slaves to sin, but Christ set us free. Whenever we go to the Lord's Table, we make a beeline to the foot of the cross—the place where sin met its match. We remember that our sin is nailed to the cross. We remember that the Father remembers it no more!

In all my years as a pastor, the most powerful communion experience I've ever been part of involved a written confession of sin. There was something cathartic about putting my sin on paper. Then we instructed people to visit one of the Stations of the Cross where there was a hammer and nails. I'll never forget the sound of the hammer hitting the nail or the sight of the confession-plastered cross.

One of our fundamental problems is living as if Christ is still nailed to the cross. He's not. He's seated at the right hand of the Father, in power and glory. The only thing nailed to the cross is our sin. And once your sin is nailed, it's nailed.

THE POWER OF CONFESSION

God has a remarkable memory.

The Omniscient One doesn't just know everything; He *remembers* everything. In fact, He remembers it before it happens! Every moment of your life was ordained in God's imagination before it became a memory—every laugh, every dream, every sacrifice. Nothing is lost on God, not even your tears. He doesn't just remember them; He collects them in a bottle.[9]

There is only one thing that God can forget, will forget—confessed sin. That is the power of confession. It's our factory reset.

You aren't just forgiven.

Your *sin* is forgotten.

So when you confess sin that's already been confessed, you're reminding God of something He's already forgotten. The reason we bring it back up is that despite the *fact* that we are forgiven, we don't *feel* forgiven. And the reason we don't feel forgiven, in my opinion, is because of our generic confessions.

"Dear Lord, please forgive me for everything I've ever done wrong."

Can God do that? Absolutely, if you mean it. But it's still weak sauce. We don't even let our kids get by with that! It's not enough to be sorry; you need to know exactly what you're sorry for. The goal of confession isn't forgiveness; it's change. Too often we say we're sorry, but we keep making the same mistake over and over again.

Imagine going to the doctor and simply saying you don't feel well. It'd be awfully difficult for the doctor to give a diagnosis or a prognosis. You need to be a little more specific than that! You start with symptoms and work your way to the root problem. And that's true of our confession. When it comes to confession, I believe in *name it, claim it*. You have to name your sin so you can claim God's mercy!

NUANCED MERCY

A number of years ago, I found myself in Wittenberg, Germany, on Reformation Day. That's where a parish priest named Martin Luther nailed his Ninety-Five Theses to the doors of the Castle Church. Before the trip, I read a rather detailed biography of Luther. He certainly had his blind spots, like the rest of us. But one thing that struck me was that Martin Luther would spend up to six hours in a single session confessing his sin. The reason it struck me is that I rarely spent more than six minutes!

Perhaps that's why we don't feel like the righteous requirements of the law have been fully met in us. We haven't fully confessed our sin.

Luther's biographer noted, "Every sin, in order to be absolved, was to be confessed. Therefore the soul must be searched and the memory ransacked and the motives probed."[10]

When was the last time you searched your soul, ransacked your memory, or probed your motives?

Just as a nebulous confession will result in a nebulous feeling of forgiveness, a nuanced confession will result in a more nuanced sense of forgiveness.

One of my best practices, when it comes to worship, is putting songs on repeat—it helps me meditate on the nuances of the lyrics. Eventually, that song gets downloaded to my spirit. One of the songs I put on repeat this past year was Hillsong's "From the

Inside Out." The opening line of the lyrics is powerful: "A thousand times I've failed, still your mercy remains." That line reminds me of one of my most-quoted verses, Lamentations 3:22–23 (ESV):

> His mercies never come to an end;
> they are new every morning.

The English word *new* is the Hebrew word *hadas*. It doesn't just mean again and again, as amazing as that would be. It's new as in *different*. It means *never before experienced*. Today's mercy is different from yesterday or the day before or the day before the day before. Just as the seasonal flu vaccine changes from year to year, God's mercy changes from day to day. It's a new strain of mercy.

Why? Because you didn't sin today the way you did yesterday!

Try this little exercise: Figure out how old you are—not in years but in days. Whatever number you come up with isn't just your age in days; it doubles as the sum total of different kinds of mercy you've received life-to-date. By the time you're twenty-one, you've experienced 7,665 unique mercies. When you hit midlife, it numbers 14,600. And by the time you hit retirement, God has mercied you 23,725 times!

His mercy for you is different than it is for anyone else. It's a tailored mercy that perfectly fits your sin, your shortcomings, your needs, and your mistakes. His mercy fits like a glove! But a nuanced appreciation of God's mercy begins with a nuanced confession of our sin.

While we're on the subject of nuance, *mercy* and *grace* are not the same thing.

Mercy is not getting what you do deserve.

Grace is getting what you don't deserve.

That nuance doubles my appreciation for both. And within each, there are infinite varieties. That's why it's called "the *manifold* grace of God."[11] Like snowflakes, God's grace never crystallizes the same way twice. That's what makes it so amazing!

Leverage Your Regrets

Before leaving our *if only* regrets behind, one last thought: God wants to do so much more than simply forgive your sin. He wants to leverage your past regrets for His eternal purposes!

Have you made a mistake that cost you your reputation? Help others avoid it. Overcome an addiction? Help someone else who struggles with the same thing. Been through a bad breakup? Help someone get through what you went through.

Wherever you've been hurt, that's where God wants you to help others, to heal others! Don't just leave the past in the past. With God's help, leverage those *if only* regrets and turn them into *what if* possibilities.

That's what Craig DeRoche did.

Craig DeRoche climbed the political ladder all the way to the top rung, becoming Speaker of the Michigan House of Representatives. Then Craig was arrested on DUI charges, and his house of cards came crashing down. What no one but Craig knew was that he had battled an alcohol addiction for twenty-nine years. In one fell swoop, he lost his job, lost his paycheck, and lost his reputation. It was the proverbial fall from grace, but that is often where we discover the grace of God.

I met Craig in rather random fashion. I was walking through Ebenezer's coffeehouse on the way to my office, like I do every workday, when I bumped into Craig. He thanked me for *The Circle Maker*, which he happened to be reading at the time. Then he gave me the condensed version of his testimony.

Craig wasn't just arrested; he was humiliated.

Helicopters hovered over his house. Five hundred newspapers ran his story. When he finally went to trial, the judge let the media sit in the jury box. It was a high-stakes, high-profile mistake.

That's how Craig came to the end of himself, and that's when he voluntarily checked himself into a rehab facility. It was there, on June 29, 2010, that Craig surrendered his life to the lordship of Jesus Christ. At that moment, God rolled away the shame of his three-decade enslavement to alcohol.

At the end of our conversation, Craig handed me his business card. I was a little surprised by the title on the card. Craig is now the executive director of Justice Fellowship and serves as the leader of criminal justice reform advocacy at Prison Fellowship. Why? Because no human life is irredeemable—no one is beyond the reach of God. They believe in justice with an adjective in front of it: restorative justice. Their mission is to see prisoners transformed from the inside out by the grace of God, even as they are punished by the letter of human law.

Over the last decade, I've received hundreds of letters from inmates who have read one of my books, and they tell a common story. Time and time again, I've heard how God has leveraged their worst mistakes. While they wish they could go back and undo what they did, one after another has testified to the way God has turned the worst thing they've done into the best thing that ever happened to them. It wasn't until they were behind bars that God set them free from sin and the shame that goes with it. If God hasn't given up on them, then neither should we. In fact, God is raising up a generation of preachers in the most unlikely of places—prison!

Craig's story could have ended very poorly, with him in a drunken stupor. Instead, God is leveraging Craig's mistakes for His purposes. And He can do the same for you.

That's who God is.

That's what God does.

He's the God who turns *if only* regrets into *what if* possibilities!

Maybe you've struggled with an addiction that traces back to your teen years. Perhaps your first marriage ended in divorce. Or maybe you're in prison right now for a crime you committed.

The enemy wants to leverage it *against* you—blackmailing you with feelings of shame. God wants to leverage it *for* you. Don't let regret stalk you the rest of your life. Repentance is a restraining order against regret. It'll still come around now and then, but that's when you make a beeline for the cross!

The cross is our high leverage point. Leverage your regrets by learning the hard lessons, the painful lessons. Bitter or better? That's up to you! Leverage your regrets by making the most of your second chance, your second marriage, or the second half of your life.

God doesn't just leave our regrets on the cross. He resurrects those regrets in glorified form. If you let Him, God will leverage your *if only* regrets for His glory!

*What if you set aside an entire day
to search your soul, probe your
motives, and confess your sin?*

The Second *If*

As If

What is real versus what is imagined—
the brain does not distinguish between them.
Therein lies the power of as if.
Therein lies the power of faith.
It sees the invisible.
It believes the impossible.
As if *bridges the gap between* if only *and* what if.
It's the way we defy our circumstances.
It's the way God's promises become our reality.

8

Reaction Time

Those who live according to the Spirit set
their minds on the things of the Spirit.

Romans 8:5 ESV

By the end of his distinguished career as a pioneering neurosurgeon, Dr. Wilder Penfield had performed brain surgery on 1,132 patients. Many of them suffered from epileptic seizures, and Dr. Penfield wanted to know why. With the help of local anesthesia, the tops of patients' skulls were removed but they remained conscious during the surgery so they could converse with Dr. Penfield.

During one of those open-brain operations, Dr. Penfield made a fascinating discovery. When he used a very mild electrical current to stimulate different parts of the cortex, some of Dr. Penfield's patients experienced flashbacks—vivid memories from past events replayed in their mind's eye. One patient recalled every note from a symphony she had heard at a concert many years before. Another patient recalled sitting at a train stop as a child, and she gave a detailed description of each train car as it went by in her memory.

Another patient visualized a childhood comb and was able to recount the exact number of teeth it had.

Beyond the detailed recollection, the thing that struck Dr. Penfield about these memories was the fact that many of them were all but forgotten. In fact, some of them predated his patients' earliest memories. Dr. Penfield concluded that every sight, every sound, every experience, every conscious thought and subconscious dream is recorded on our internal hard drive, the cerebral cortex.

Here is how the complex process works, in simplified terms. When you hear a song, see a picture, or read a verse of Scripture, an engram is traced on the surface of the cerebral cortex. That encoding is also called a memory trace, and it's how we walk down memory lane. Almost like a deluxe Etch A Sketch, songs and pictures and words get traced and retraced. With each repetition, the engram gets inscribed deeper and deeper until it's literally engraved on the surface of the cerebral cortex.

Now juxtapose that with this:

Let this mind be in you which was also in Christ Jesus.[1]

Simply put: the mind of Christ is the Word of God.

Just as Jesus is the embodiment of the Word, the Bible is Jesus in words. He is, after all, "the Word."[2] So when you pray or meditate or memorize the Word of God, you're engraving Jesus on your brain. Neurologically speaking, you are recruiting new neuronal connections and rerouting old neuronal connections. Slowly but surely, your brain is being rewired, renewed. Think of it as a mind sync. You are downloading the very words, the very thoughts of God. And over time, those downloads are upgrades that form the mind of Christ in us.

That's how we set our minds on the things of the Spirit.

That's how we tap into the power of *as if*.

One surefire way to be filled with God's Spirit is to be filled with God's Word. It was the Spirit of God who inspired the original writers of Scripture, so when we read Scripture, we are inhaling what the Holy Spirit exhaled thousands of years ago.

COVER TO COVER

In ancient Jewish culture, formal education began at six years of age. Jewish boys enrolled in the local synagogue school called *bet sefer*, which means "house of the book." By the time they graduated four years later, they would have memorized the entire Torah—every jot and tittle of Genesis, Exodus, Leviticus, Numbers, and Deuteronomy was engraved on their cerebral cortex via memorization. There goes our excuse, right?

According to tradition, the rabbi would cover their slate with honey on the first day of class. Then the rabbi would instruct his class to lick the honey off their slate while reciting Psalm 119:103: "How sweet are thy words unto my taste! yea, sweeter than honey to my mouth!" (KJV).

That was the first and perhaps most important lesson in their entire education. The rabbi wanted his students to fall in love with the Word of God. He wanted them to taste and see that the Word is good.

In a sense, the Bible is the land of milk and honey. It is our Promised Land. There are thousands of promises in Scripture, and each of those *what ifs* is there for the taking.

A decade ago, I was profoundly challenged by something J. I. Packer said: "Every Christian worth his salt reads the Bible from cover to cover every year." I couldn't argue with it, but to be honest, I wasn't doing it.

So I made a decision that I would attempt to read through a different version of the Bible every year. Have I succeeded every year? No. But that's my goal year in and year out: to read all 66 books, all 1,189 chapters, all 31,102 verses.

The goal isn't to get through the Bible.

The goal is to get the Bible through me.

Of course, the key to accomplishing that yearly goal of getting through Scripture is establishing a daily discipline. In fact, daily disciplines are the key to just about any long-range goal. You get there one day at a time.

KEEPERS OF THE WORD

If I could wave a magic wand, ensuring absolute adherence to one command of Scripture, Deuteronomy 17:19 would make my short list. In the presence of the Levitical priests, the kings of Israel were required to make a copy of the law in their own handwriting. They were required to keep it on their person at all times. And they were required to read it every single day. My advice? Act like a king!

Make a vow to get into God's Word every single day.

> And it shall be with him, and he shall read therein all the days of his life: that he may learn to fear the Lord his God, to keep all the words of this law and these statutes, to do them. (KJV)

The key word here is *keep*, so let me drill down on it. The Jewish rabbis said that every word of Scripture has seventy faces and six hundred thousand meanings. This is one of those kaleidoscopic words in Hebrew.

The word *keep* means *keepsake*, as in treasured possession.

It means to *guard something*, as if your life depended on it.

It means to *keep track of*, like a courtroom stenographer.

It means to *watch over*, like an air traffic controller.

It means to *keep watch*, like a night watchman.

It means to *preserve*, like a taxidermist.

It means to *examine*, like a forensic scientist.

It means to *cross-examine*, like a prosecuting attorney.

It means to *put in a vault*, like a banker.

It means to *put a contract on something*, like a real estate agent.

It means to *decipher secrets*, like World War II code talkers.

To keep the Word of God in our hearts, to keep our minds set on the Spirit, requires that kind of due diligence. Few things are as exhausting as intentionality, but the payoff is always worth the price. You pay the price by getting into God's Word daily. Then the Holy Spirit brings it to memory when we need it. Almost like Wilder Penfield using his electrode to elicit memories buried deep within the cerebral cortex, the Holy Spirit brings to memory what we need to know, when we need to know it.

And He doesn't just remind us of things we've learned or things buried deep within our subconscious. The Holy Spirit also reveals things that bypass the conscious mind, things that are beyond the ability of our five senses to perceive. Ever had a thought come out of nowhere, a thought that is beyond your intellectual capacity? I call them *God ideas*. Those God ideas come from the Holy Spirit who both *seals* things in our memory and *reveals* things to our imagination.

QUICKEN

The Bible wasn't meant merely to be read. It was meant to be prayed through, meditated on, and lived out. If all you do is read it, all you've done is audit the Word of God. And you don't get credit for an audit. You've simply been educated beyond the level of your obedience. The key is the *quickening* of the Holy Spirit.

Before I zoom in, let me zoom out on this part of the Holy Spirit's portfolio. There is an amazing *if* in Romans 8:11:

> If the Spirit of him that raised up Jesus from the dead dwell in you, he that raised up Christ from the dead shall also quicken your mortal bodies by his Spirit. (KJV)

In this instance, *quickening* refers to our bodily resurrection from the dead. When Christ returns, the dead in Christ will rise first. Bodies that have been buried six feet deep will be unearthed, hearts that stopped beating millennia ago will pump holy adrenaline, and cremated ashes will rematerialize. What a moment that will be! One for the ages!

But the Holy Spirit quickens us in more ways than one. Sometimes it's a God idea that fires across our synapses. Sometimes it's a prompting to step up, step in, or step out in faith. Sometimes it's a word of wisdom in a difficult situation. When the Holy Spirit quickens you in that way, don't hesitate. Act on the idea, seize the opportunity, speak the word.

In my experience, the quickening of the Holy Spirit happens most often when we are meditating on the Word of God. In the words of the Psalmist: "Quicken thou me according to thy word."[3]

Psalm 119 is the longest chapter in the Bible by a long shot. It's a poem with twenty-two stanzas, each stanza beginning with one of the twenty-two letters of the Hebrew alphabet. It's an A-to-Z ode to the Word of God. The psalmist references "The Word," or one of its ten synonyms, no less than 174 times.

A wide variety of commands are given, including the command to "keep the Word" twenty-two times. The word *quicken* is repeated half as many times, eleven, but it's no less important. Keeping and quickening are double majors.

It's a little gruesome, but let me paint a word picture you probably won't forget. I was flipping channels recently when I came across a rerun of *Mission Impossible III*. I landed there right when a micro-explosive device was shot through the nose and implanted in the brain of IMF agent Ethan Hunt, played by Tom Cruise. I won't tell you what happens after the bomb is detonated, but he's the good guy, so you know he survives! The quickening of the Holy Spirit is like a truth bomb that blows up in your spirit. It can be one word, one phrase, or one verse that jumps off the page and into your mind, into your heart, into your spirit.

Here's how it works for me.

I open my Bible to wherever I am in my reading plan and start reading. I continue until I come to any verse that may suggest pausing. It's often something I need to think about or pray about.

Sometimes it's the conviction of the Holy Spirit, and I need to have a conversation with God before I continue.

That's the quickening of the Holy Spirit. When I come to one of those verses, I do three things. First, I underline it or circle it in my Bible. Second, I write it out longhand in my journal. Third, I journal thoughts, confessions, and ideas associated with it. Then, when I feel like the Holy Spirit brings closure, I go to the next verse.

GO SLOW

When I was ten years old, I got my first digital watch with a timer that measured to the hundredth of a second. I used to pass the time testing my reaction time until my thumb would go numb. I don't think I ever beat .05 seconds between start and stop.

Whether you're a baseball player in the batter's box or a basketball player on a breakaway, it's the quick-twitch muscles that enable you to hit a home run or dunk a basketball. In the realm of gaming, it's your quick-twitch reactions that enable you to get to the next level.

Spiritually speaking, it's our quick-twitch reactions that make us or break us at critical moments. The split second after someone insults you, offends you, or cuts you off in traffic, what's your reaction? What's your reaction time?

Or how about the promptings of the Holy Spirit? What's your reaction time? Your *reaction time* is the time lapse between God's command and your obedience. And it's one of the best measures of spiritual maturity.

The apostle James said, "Be quick to listen, slow to speak."[4] That little piece of advice has the potential to solve some of our biggest problems! Along with being quick to listen, I want to be quick to forgive, quick to help, and quick to give God glory.

When it comes to the Word of God, I want to be a quick study. But in order to be a quick study, you have to *go slow*. The more you pray through or meditate on a passage, the longer it will take you to get through the Bible. But the Word will have a longer-lasting effect on you. And the slower you go, the quicker your reaction time will be to the prompting of the Holy Spirit.

Let me come right out and say it: delayed obedience is disobedience.

Remember the ten spies who doubted God's ability to deliver on His promise and dissuaded the Israelites from entering into the Promised Land? Their doubt was so offensive to God—because He had already revealed His power to them through the exodus from Egypt and the parting of the Red Sea—that God executed judgment on the spot. The very next day, the Israelites did an about-face.[5] They changed their minds, but it was too little, too late. One day's delay cost them forty years! They missed out on the Promised Land because their reaction time was too slow.

Now, that doesn't mean you should live in fear of missing out. After all, God is the God of second chances. But please understand this: inaction *is* an action, and indecision *is* a decision.

I, for one, don't want to waste forty years because I'm slow on the draw. I certainly don't want to get ahead of God by trying to manufacture my own miracle. I've done that a time or two! But I do want to seize God-ordained opportunities as quickly, as decisively, and as boldly as I possibly can.

THE POWER OF WORDS

It's a little embarrassing to admit, but I once read through a Webster's dictionary. I only made it to Q, as in *quirky*, but that still qualifies me as a wordophile. I spend way too much time on Thesaurus.com. And when I can't find the right word, I often make one up.

I know I've already dissected the word *keep*, but allow me to do it one more time with *quicken*. It'll help you understand a key role that the Holy Spirit plays in our lives.

The word *quicken* means *to catalyze*. Think chemistry. Hebrews 4:12 says that the Word is living and active. The KJV says *quick*. Every other book in my library is made of dead trees, most of them written by dead authors. The Author of Scripture is alive and well. The same Spirit who inspired Moses, David, Peter, and Paul as they *wrote* inspires us as we *read*. And when the living Word is catalyzed by faith, a supernatural reaction takes place that forgives sin, relieves fear, inspires ideas, and births dreams.

Quicken also means *to transfer possession*. Think real estate. You can't just put a contract on a home; you have to go to settlement. By faith, we take ownership of the Word and the Word takes ownership of us. When the Word is quickened, it seals the deal.

It means *to sustain life*, as in life support.

It also means *to bring back to life*, as in defibrillation.

Every time you read the Word of God, a little resurrection happens. It's the way the Holy Spirit brings our God-ordained dreams back to life. It revives faith, hope, and love. It resurrects *what if*.

One final meaning, and perhaps the most powerful, is *to conceive*.

Is anything more miraculous than the moment of conception? All the potential in the world is contained in that single-celled life. Encrypted in each cell is a complete genetic code.

When the Word of God is conceived in you through the quickening of the Holy Spirit, it impregnates us with possibilities. It changes your deepest desires, eradicates your worst fears, and fulfills your wildest dreams.

The quickening of God's Word makes your heart break for the things that break the heart of God. It forms the mind of Christ in you. And when the Word comes to full term, it gives birth to *what if.*

*What if you made a vow to get into
God's Word every single day?*

83

9

The Anchoring Effect

For the mind set on the flesh is death, but the
mind set on the Spirit is life and peace.

Romans 8:6 NASB

The mission of the San Francisco Exploratorium is to ignite curiosity, encourage exploration, and change the way the world learns. In
keeping with their mission, the Exploratorium conducted a secret
study with unsuspecting guests. Randomly selected participants
were asked two questions:

1. Is the height of the highest redwood more or less than 1,200
   feet?
2. What is your best guess about the height of the tallest
   redwood?

A second group of participants was asked the same question
with different numbers:

1. Is the height of the highest redwood more or less than 180 feet?

2. What is your best guess about the height of the tallest redwood?

The two different heights—1,200 feet and 180 feet—are called anchors. Those anchors greatly affected the answers from each group. Those who were given the high anchor of 1,200 feet guessed an average height of 844 feet. Those who were given the low anchor of 180 feet guessed an average height of 282 feet. That is a 563-foot difference!

The 55 percent difference is the result of something psychologists call the "anchoring effect."[1] Simply put, we tend to rely too heavily on the first fact, first price, or first impression. Once we "anchor" to it, it becomes the baseline for decision making.

In case you're curious, redwoods rank as the tallest tree species on the planet. Their root system goes down 13 feet with an 100-foot radius. They can measure up to 22 feet in girth and 360 feet in height, and they can live up to 2,000 years!

I can tell you from personal experience, few things are more awe-inspiring than standing at the base of one of these giants and gazing skyward.

Back to anchoring.

It happens every day in a thousand different ways.

Parents use anchoring to outwit their teenagers. If your teen wants to stay out till midnight, but you want them home by 11:00 p.m., start out by offering them 10:00 p.m. Then when you meet in the middle, they think it's a compromise! Nope, just an old anchoring trick.

Savvy retailers do the same with sales. If you buy a $50 item for $50, you don't feel good about it because you paid full price. Even if the full price is a fair price! Retailers know this, so they put things on sale. If you get a $50 item for 20 percent off, you feel great, even if the sale price is artificially inflated.

Even the serpent used an anchoring technique to get Adam and Eve fixated on forbidden fruit. They were free to eat from every tree, save one. But he got them focused on the one tree they were commanded not to eat from, the Tree of the Knowledge of Good and Evil.

The implications and applications of anchoring are profound. If the battle is won or lost in the mind, then where you drop anchor will dictate the outcome.

The writer of Hebrews refers to hope as an anchor,[2] and it's a powerful *as if*. A ship's anchor doesn't just keep it from drifting. An anchor can also be thrown in front of a ship and used to navigate through treacherous channels. The nautical term is *kedging*, and it's the picture the writer of Hebrews is painting. Hope is anchoring ourselves to the *what if* promises of God as we navigate through Class V rapids. Peace is found the same way. So is joy! For better or for worse, your focus determines your reality. That's the power of *as if*.

There is an old acronym for fear: False Expectations Appearing Real. Fear gives weight to things that don't deserve it—and it weighs us down.

Faith is the exact opposite—it's being sure of what we hope for.[3] If gratitude is thanking God for things *after* they happen, then faith is thanking God for things *before* they happen.

It Is Well

In 1873, a wealthy Chicago businessman named Horatio Spafford was planning on joining his famous friend D. L. Moody for an evangelistic campaign in England. He sent his wife and four daughters ahead, but their ship sank in the middle of the Atlantic, and his four daughters died. When his wife telegrammed the news, Horatio boarded a ship with a heavy heart. As their vessel neared the spot where his daughters had died, Spafford penned the words to the hymn "It Is Well with My Soul":

> When peace like a river, attendeth my way,
>> When sorrows like sea billows roll;
> Whatever my lot, Thou hast taught me to say,
>> It is well, it is well, with my soul.[4]

Horatio Spafford dropped anchor in the middle of the Atlantic. Like Job, he chose to trust God's heart when he couldn't understand his circumstances.

Our family did the same thing when my father-in-law, Bob Schmidgall, died at fifty-five from a heart attack. This song was one of his favorites, so it's the song we sang at his graveside. It was our way of anchoring to a hope that is beyond the grave.

If your emotions are anchored to your circumstances, they'll look like a stock chart that goes up and down daily. You'll have lots of bear markets and probably a crash or two. If your emotions are anchored to the cross, it becomes your fixed point of peace. If you've made peace with God, peace is the order of the day. But like with all of God's good gifts, you still have to work at it. That's how we work out our salvation with fear and trembling.[5] If you want the peace that passes understanding to guard your heart and mind,[6] you've got to stay anchored to the right things.

> Whatever is true, whatever is noble, whatever is right, whatever is pure, whatever is lovely, whatever is admirable—if anything is excellent or praiseworthy—think about such things.[7]

MINDSET

I have a habit of dividing words. *Responsibility*, for example, makes more sense with a hyphen: *response-ability*. It's the ability to choose your response in any set of circumstances. Taking responsibility doesn't mean taking the blame or taking the credit. In my dictionary, it means being accountable for your response no matter what.

In the same way, I like combining words. The two words *mind set* in Romans 8:6 might as well be one word, *mindset*. The Greek word *phronema* means to fix one's mind on something. Sounds an awful lot like anchoring doesn't it? And it doesn't happen by happenstance. It involves a great deal of *as if* intentionality.

Our family has four values: gratitude, generosity, humility, and courage. Those four values are like four cardinal points on the compass rose. And it's my job, as a husband and a father, to model those values for my family. So I work hard at them.

This past year, gratitude may have been my best practice. I've kept a gratitude journal off and on for many years, but I decided to number the blessings this year.[8] Year to date, I'm on #537. That simple act of numbering may be the best way to count your blessings! It also has an anchoring effect—it keeps me focused on the things I'm grateful for, not frustrated about.

Gratitude is a mindset.

So is humility.

So is generosity.

So is courage.

So is everything else!

Nearly a decade ago, we incorporated an organizational practice of sharing wins at the beginning of every staff meeting at NCC. Sometimes it only takes ten or fifteen minutes. Other times, our staff meetings turn into prayer meetings. An hour later, we'll find ourselves on our faces thanking God for who He is and what He's done. But no matter how long it takes, the positive energy is palpable.

No better way to start the workweek!

Sharing wins keeps our team focused on the positives. Honestly, I can't imagine too many churches our size with fewer problems. And I can't imagine too many staffs our size with better chemistry. The formula is simple: anchor yourself to the wins!

The biblical word for *win* is *testimony*. It's the way we borrow faith from others—if God did it for them, He can do it for me. And the way you pay back a testimony is by loaning your faith to someone else.

Our testimony is our secret weapon. Of course, you can't keep it secret. It's the way we share the win with others and overcome the enemy![9]

THE LOSADA RATIO

Marcial Losada is an organizational psychologist who studies the power of positivity. He argues that we need a *negative feedback loop* to survive. Without midcourse corrections, we mindlessly make the same mistakes. And that adds up to lots of *if onlys*.

But if you want to thrive, you need a *positive feedback loop*. Simply put: celebrate what you want to see more of. His studies have produced what is known as the Losada ratio: it's the ratio of positive feedback to negative feedback in a system. It doesn't matter whether the system is a church, a family, or your workplace, there needs to be at least 2.9 positive feedbacks for every negative feedback.

What's your ratio as a spouse, as a parent, as a friend?

Part of the reason for the disparity is that negative feedback tends to carry more weight and last longer. So it has to be counterbalanced. A pretty good rule of thumb is this: dish out three compliments for every complaint. And I would suggest that it starts with a mindset: *catch people doing things right*. You've got to stay focused on the positive.

I'm not lobbying for Pollyannaism. I'm advocating for an optimism that is anchored to the thousands of *what if* promises God has given us. And living *as if* they're true!

Pick a promise, any promise. Then drop anchor!

If you want to stay positive, here are a few simple tactics. First and foremost, get into God's Word on a daily basis. That's the most obvious, most practical way of anchoring yourself to the promises of God.

Start keeping a gratitude journal. It's a high leverage point for positivity. Of course, a gratitude journal is for personal gratification. If you want to share the love, cultivate the habit of writing

Spirit-led, heartfelt thank-you notes to the people you appreciate. It'll only take you two minutes, but it can make someone's day, someone's year! I recently got a handwritten note from the afore-mentioned Jack Hayford. I know he's too busy to write thank-you notes, but that's what makes it even more meaningful.

Next, find a way to share wins in your family or in your workplace. It has the power to shift the focus, shift the culture. It'll also anchor you to your kids or to your colleagues in a powerful new way.

Last but not least, worship is a powerful way of anchoring to the reality of what's happening in heaven. When we worship, that heavenly reality invades our area code, our zip code!

One of my rituals is putting a song on repeat while I'm running or writing. It helps me get in a groove. While writing, I use songs without lyrics so I can concentrate on the words I'm writing. In case you care, I listened to "Raising the Sail" from the *Truman Show* soundtrack thousands of times while writing *The Circle Maker*. For *If* it was "Revive" by NCC Worship and "Lord, I Need You" by Chris Tomlin. When I put a worship song on repeat, it gets into my spirit. I sing it till I believe it. Then it becomes second nature.

ANCHORS

One of the ways I keep myself grounded in God's grace is by collecting mementos—mezuzahs—that remind me of God's goodness and faithfulness. The Israelites would often use stones to build altars. I use just about anything and everything you can imagine. I've already mentioned a few of my mementos that serve as mezuzahs. Here are a few more.

My grandfather's Bible is my most prized possession. It was a well-used, well-lived 1934 Thompson Chain-Reference Bible. I love looking at the verses he underlined and the notes he wrote in the margin. That Bible somehow anchors me to my grandfather's legacy and fuels my faith.

I have a taxicab topper that was found at one of the properties we miraculously purchased, an old auto shop that used to repair DC taxis. It not only anchors me to that miracle but helps me believe God for the next one.

And I have a miniature spear that is a memento from the first stop on my first book tour for my first book, *In a Pit with a Lion on a Snowy Day*. It's a reminder that the God who began a good work is the same God who will carry it to completion.

I've got nearly a hundred mementos, and whenever someone visits me in my office, I do a little show-and-tell. Each one of those anchors keeps me grounded spiritually.

What are you anchored to? What pictures, signs, or symbols do you need to hang on the walls of your house, the walls of your heart?

The purpose of those mementos isn't just to look back. It's to see the faithfulness of God that fuels our faith moving forward. Those mementos keep me anchored to *what if.*

I admit it, I'm a pack rat. So collecting mementos comes naturally to me. But even if you aren't particularly nostalgic, you need to find ways to anchor yourself. It can be building an altar or making a vow—but no matter what it is, it helps if there is a physical reminder.

SIXTY THOUSAND THOUGHTS

I know that studies are a dime a dozen, and it's very difficult to quantify the information I'm about to share. After all, 67.2 percent of statistics are made up. Yes, I'm being facetious. But even if these numbers are ballpark, they are game changers. When it comes to the human mind, experts estimate that we have fifty to seventy thousand thoughts per day. I'll use sixty thousand as a happy medium.

Now let me cite four game-changing statistics.

Psychologists posit that 98 or 99 percent of our thoughts are habitual.[10] In other words, they're the same thoughts we had yesterday, and the day before yesterday, and the day before that.

If you want to anchor yourself to *what if*, that won't cut it. Your mind must be renewed day by day. You can't keep thinking the same things and expect a different outcome, a different outlook. One simple way of overcoming habitual thinking is taking on a learning mindset. Make it your goal to learn something new every day. It can come from a book or a TED talk. It can come from a conversation or a class. It can come from a walk down the street.

The French poet Jacques Réda used to walk the streets of Paris with the intention of seeing one new thing each day. It's the way he renewed his love for his city. It also kept him from falling into the trap of habitual thinking, a death trap if you're a poet.

Second, only 12 percent of our thoughts are focused on the future. Now, that's good if your future-focused thoughts range from low-grade anxiety to full-fledged fear. Too often we misuse our imagination to rehearse the wrong *what if*. But by definition, faith is future oriented. It's being sure of what we hope for. In *The Circle Maker*, I share my life goal list. Those 115 goals are anchors. It's the way I kedge into the future. It's the way I stay focused on *what if*.

Third, a Harvard University study found that the average person spends 46.9 percent of their waking hours thinking about something other than what they are presently doing.[11] According to psychologists Matthew Killingsworth and Daniel Gilbert, "A wandering mind is an unhappy mind." It's the opposite of anchoring. And it's the reason we're physically present yet emotionally absent. Of course, the most obvious culprits are the digital devices that keep us disengaged. Nothing dumbs down our ability to daydream like our so-called smartphones!

Finally, the Cleveland Clinic estimates that 80 percent of our thoughts are negative.[12] That's 48,000 negative thoughts per day!

And when we verbalize those negative thoughts, it compounds the problem. For what it's worth, I have a friend who makes a habit of reading Scripture *out loud*. I don't think the volume matters, but there is something about using your vocal cords to speak the Word that is powerful.

The tongue has the power of life and death.[13] It's not some abracadabra incantation, but sometimes you have to say it like you believe it. Jesus literally spoke to the wind and the waves, right? He rebuked storms. He rebuked demons. He rebuked fevers. He even told us to tell mountains to move! When you verbalize faith, you give it power, you give it weight, you give it credence. So say it, or sing it, like you really believe it.

Of course, the opposite is true as well. There are some things you should *not* say. When Jeremiah used his age as an excuse, the Lord rebuked him: "Say not, I am a child."[14] In other words, don't disqualify yourself if God has called you! I want to speak life-giving, faith-filled, grace-laced words. There are some things I refuse to say because it gives them power. I call it my "Say Not" list.

What words need to go on your "Say Not" list?

I'm not just talking about four-letter words. Jesus said we'd give account for every idle word. The word *idle* means *unemployed*. An idle word is a useless, worthless word—a word that doesn't accomplish anything.

Let me share one last story that I hope inspires you as much as it did me. In *The Circle Maker*, I share the story of R. W. Shambach, who prayed in 1960 that God would close down a movie theater and turn it into a church. That hundred-year-old theater is now our Capitol Hill campus. That's the short version.

I recently met R. W.'s daughter, Donna, and she shared something that inspired me to no end. Unfortunately, some pastors' kids share stories that cast a shadow of doubt on their preacher parent's integrity. Not Donna. She said that sometimes the family would hear her dad preaching and giving altar calls in his sleep! But the most powerful thing she said was this: "I never heard my father speak a negative word about anyone or anything—not one negative word."

Out of the overflow of the heart the mouth speaks,[15] so our words are X-rays of what's on the inside. That's where the battle is won and lost. If we want our words to reflect His Word, that's where we've got to drop anchor. And when we do, the mind of Christ becomes our mindset.

What if you stopped gossiping and started bragging about people behind their backs?

10

The Power of Suggestion

If Christ is in you, although the body is dead because
of sin, the Spirit is life because of righteousness.

Romans 8:10 ESV

When I was in college, I tore my anterior cruciate ligament in the
last quarter of the last game of my sophomore basketball season.

It would be outpatient surgery now, but I spent a night in the
hospital after reconstructive surgery. I have an above-average pain
threshold, but when the general anesthesia wore off, I needed pain-
killers fast, so I hit the nurse's call button. The nurse explained that
there was morphine in my IV bag, and all I had to do was press a
little button that released it into my bloodstream.

I pressed the button and felt better—much better. In fact, I got
a little push happy! I thought I was getting morphine every time,
but once I hit my dosage limit, it cut off the morphine. I didn't
know this until after the fact, and I'm glad I didn't, because the

dummy drug worked just as effectively. This phenomenon is called the placebo effect, of course, and it's been documented in a hundred different ways. Its antithesis, the *nocebo* effect, has also been demonstrated.

I'm not sure the following would meet today's research standards, but a fascinating experiment was conducted half a century ago. Three men tested their strength on a gripping machine, with an average measure of 101 pounds of pressure. Then the participants were hypnotized. I know that doesn't sound super scientific, but the results are intriguing nonetheless.

Once they were hypnotized, the experimenter told the participants, "You *cannot* grip because you are weak." Under the power of suggestion, their average grip strength fell to 29 pounds of pressure. Then the experimenter said, "Now you *can* grip." Their average grip increased to 145 pounds of pressure.[1]

"Whether you think you can or think you can't, you're right," as Henry Ford is reputed to have said.

That's the power of suggestion. In the experiment I just cited, their strength was increased fivefold when they said "I can" versus when they said "I can't."

Juxtapose that with this:

I can do all things through Christ who strengthens me.[2]

We've already begun to explore the power of *what if*, but let's turn our attention to its second cousin, *as if*. The mind doesn't know the difference between what's real and what's imagined, which is why *as if* is so full of potential. Of course, *as if* must be anchored to the truth. A motivational speech by Matt Foley—the guy who's been living in a van down by the river—doesn't cut it. Neither do Stuart Smalley's positive affirmations! By the way, the real Stuart Smalley is Al Franken, former *SNL* comic and current senator from the state of Minnesota. He lives two blocks from me and is a regular customer at Ebenezer's.

I certainly don't mean any disrespect, but quite frankly, you're not good enough or smart enough. And doggone it, some people don't like you. The reality is this: you're a sinner in need of a Savior. But you are also more than a conqueror.

Acting *as if* is easier said than done, but it's the definition of faith. Do we believe what God says about us or not? The Great Eight says we are "more than conquerors"[3]—the problem is that I feel like a total failure half the time. I'm a pastor, but I wrestle with temptation as much as anybody. As a parent, I've done some things right, but I've also done some things wrong. And I love my wife like crazy, but I don't always feel like a knight in shining armor.

My point? I feel like a failure much of the time, but once again, the Super 8 casts me as more than a conqueror.

So which is it?

It helps to think of Scripture as a script. While the reality of our circumstances often feels like it's off script, I've got to take my cues from God's Word. I've got to live *as if* I am who God says I am. If you believe the enemy's lies, you're in deep existential trouble. If you believe you are who God says you are, it'll get you out of trouble and keep you out of trouble.

I know those who are philosophically opposed to Christianity would like to think that faith is nothing more than an emotional crutch. But the crux of Christianity is the empty tomb. If Jesus remained dead and buried, we'd be living a lie. But if Jesus did walk out of the tomb under his own power, then all bets are off. And we need to live *as if* it's true, because it is.

The resurrection isn't something we celebrate one day a year. It's something we celebrate every day in every way. It informs every reality. It validates *as if.*

When you're in trouble, take heart: He has overcome the world.[4] When you're lonely, don't forget: He will never leave you nor forsake you.[5] When you feel like you've lost your way, remember: He orders your footsteps.[6]

AS IF

Here are a few of my favorite *as ifs*.

Saint Augustine said, "God loves each of us as if there were only one of us."[7]

If you fully grasp this *as if*, it's the most liberating truth in the world. It'll set you free from all fear because that's what perfect love does. God can't love you any more or any less because He already loves you unconditionally, eternally. We just need to live like His beloved.

I write at length on the subject of miracles in one of my recent books, *The Grave Robber*. That book is framed by something Albert Einstein said: "There are only two ways to live your life. One is as if nothing is a miracle. The other is as if everything is."[8]

So which is it? Either way, you live *as if*. But when you live *as if* everything is a miracle, you discover the miracles that are all around you, all the time.

Many moons ago, I got a coffee mug from Amazon. I must have been one of their first and best customers back in the day. On the mug was a powerful *as if*, compliments of Mahatma Gandhi: "Live as if you were to die tomorrow. Learn as if you were to live forever."

My favorite *as if* statement doubles as one of my core convictions. It's tough to pin down the original source, but Augustine of Hippo may have said it first: "Pray as if everything depended on God. Work as if everything depended on you."

Here are just a few more to fuel the fire.

Our third president, Thomas Jefferson, said, "When you do a thing, act as if the whole world was watching."[9] That's what Jefferson did on July 4, 1776. He framed the Declaration of Independence, and it still frames our freedom as Americans.

William James, the first educator to offer a course in psychology, said, "If you want a quality, act as if you already had it."[10] He also said, "Act as if what you do makes a difference. It does."[11]

I know, you get the point. And forgive me if it feels like overkill, but every *as if* is an acorn, with the potential to become an oak tree. *As if* is the seed that every success is born of. The key is alignment. If those *as ifs* don't line up with the truth of Scripture, it's a house of cards. But if they do, you can move mountains.

THE ULTIMATE *AS IF*

There are ten *ifs* in the Great Eight. Verse 31 is the ultimate *what if*—"If God is for us, who can be against us?" But the *if* in verse 10—"If Christ is in you"—is the ultimate *as if*.

There is a tradition in professional sports of playing for a fallen comrade. When Myra Hiatt Kraft, the wife of New England Patriots owner Robert Kraft, lost her battle to cancer, each team member had an MHK patch sewn on his jersey. The Chicago Bears did the same when their founder, George Stanley Halas, died in 1983. The symbolism is powerful, and there is an element of *as if* in it. The team is no longer playing for themselves; they are playing for someone else. In a far more significant way, we aren't playing for ourselves anymore.

> I have been crucified with Christ and I no longer live, but Christ lives in me. The life I now live in the body, I live by faith in the Son of God.[12]

We live for the applause of nail-scarred hands.

We long to hear, "Well done, good and faithful servant."

I hesitate even using the word *placebo* because it refers to a fake. The grace of God is anything but a placebo—it's the real deal. But the word *placebo* actually has biblical roots. It's the Latin word Jerome used in his Vulgate translation of Psalm 116:9: "I shall please the Lord in the land of the living."

The word *placebo* means *to please*. And when the object of our pleasure is God, it's a panacea. I'm a people-pleaser by personality, but here's what I've discovered. The more you care about what people think, the less you really care about them. I've also learned that you can please all of the people some of the time, and some of the people all of the time, but you can't please all of the people all of the time. Of course, that isn't the goal. We don't live to please people, as if life is a popularity contest. Besides, none of them sits on the Judgment Seat. Someday I'll stand before my Creator and give account, so I live to please God and God alone.

Now let me make an observation: It's hard to get offended if you're dead. It's hard to get angry, get upset, or get depressed too. Why? Because you're dead.

The day you put your faith in Christ is the day your old self died. RIP. Your desires, your dreams, and your plans are dead in the water. And I mean that literally, as in baptism. The person who goes under the water is not the same as the person who comes up. You are a new creation in Christ.

Of course, you have to step into this identity on a daily basis. First Corinthians 15:31 has become a motto of mine: "I die daily" (NKJV). Jesus said it this way: "Whoever wants to be my disciple must deny themselves and take up their cross daily."[13] The key word in both verses is *daily*.

There is great freedom in this daily death. When you wake up each morning, it's like a little resurrection. And you know you'll die to self once again, so it's the first day and last day of your life.

You live *as if* Christ was crucified yesterday, rose from the dead today, and is coming back tomorrow.[14]

THE POWER OF *AS IF*

A few years ago, a school district in San Francisco pulled off a rather ingenious experiment. Three teachers were chosen to pilot a special program. They were told by administrators, "You are the best we have. We want you to teach ninety high-IQ students. We'll let you move at their pace and see how much they can learn in a year."

By the end of the school year, those specially selected students had achieved 20 to 30 percent more than the rest of the school district. That's when the principal called the three teachers into his office and told them, "I have a confession to make. You did not have ninety high-IQ students. They were run-of-the-mill students randomly selected."

As you can imagine, the teachers felt pretty good about what they pulled off. Then the principal said, "I have another confession. You were not the best teachers we have. Your names were the first three out of the hat."[15]

The obvious question is: If they were average students taught by average teachers, how did they achieve above average results? The answer is, as you can guess by now, the power of *as if*.

Let me share one of the most powerful *as ifs* I've ever encountered. The German poet and playwright Johann Wolfgang von Goethe said, "Treat a man *as he is* and he will remain *as he is*. Treat a man *as he can be and should be* and he will become as he can be and should be."[16]

No one modeled that better than Jesus.

The Pharisees treated people *as they were*. Jesus treated people *as they could be*. And that only makes sense. After all, no one knew their God-given potential like the One who gave it to them in the first place.

Have you ever noticed how some of the nicknames Jesus gave to his disciples seemed like misnomers?

Peter was impetuous, yet Jesus called him the Rock.

James and John were mama's boys, yet He called them the Sons of Thunder. They lived up to those nicknames. James would become the first of the disciples to be martyred. John would live the longest, penning both the Gospel that bears his name and the final book in the Bible, Revelation.

What if Jesus had treated them as they were? I think they would have remained as they were. But Jesus saw who they could become and treated them *as if*.

At some point in our lives, we all need someone who believes in us more than we believe in ourselves. That's who Jesus is. That's what Jesus does. The faith the disciples put in Jesus isn't that remarkable—after all, they were eyewitnesses to His miracles. What's remarkable is the faith Jesus put in the disciples and the faith He puts in us!

I know it's not easy to see past people's problems, much less their personalities. But that's what prophets do. Parents, if all you ever do is point out what your kids do wrong, you'll probably see more of the same. Remember the Losada ratio? Kids need more compliments than criticisms. So do adults!

And that's what Jesus models. He certainly put the disciples in their place when the occasion called for it. Like the time he said to Peter, "Get behind me, Satan!"[17] Ouch! But it was his constant affirmations that opened the door to an occasional exhortation. That's how healthy relationships grow. They require a high dosage of both grace and truth.

Grace means I'll love you no matter what.

Truth means I'll be honest no matter what.

No one was more graceful and more truthful than Jesus. He was full of both.[18] When those two elements combine, you're loving people the way Jesus did.

What if you started treating your friends and family as they should be and as they could be?

11

Cross-Eyed

Therefore, brothers and sisters, we have an obligation—
but it is not to the flesh, to live according to it.

Romans 8:12

Before the thirteen colonies became a country, four-fifths of Americans had heard George Whitefield preach in person.

More accurately, they heard him loud and clear. Without amplification, he spoke to crowds numbering in the tens of thousands. Earwitnesses claimed that his voice could carry a country mile. Whitefield didn't preach in a church from behind a pulpit; he preached in fields and fairgrounds. And when he did, entire towns closed up shop. Whether he was preaching at the crack of dawn or the stroke of midnight, people got up early and stayed up late.

Whitefield made thirteen trips to America, tallying 782 days at sea crisscrossing the Atlantic Ocean. In total, he preached 18,000 sermons during his thirty-four-year preaching career.[1] That's a batting average of more than 500 sermons per year, or if you prefer, 1.369863 per day. Hey, if you preach that many sermons, you deserve all the decimal credit you can get!

The First Great Awakening in America had many generals, but George Whitefield was five-star. In total, he proclaimed the gospel to more than ten *million* people. And the question is: What drew the crowds? One thing is certain; it wasn't Whitefield's good looks.

My apologies if that sounds a little uncouth, but the surviving portraits aren't pretty, even with the classic colonial wig. Whitefield was cross-eyed, which made eye contact an awkward experience. But if ever there was a double meaning, that's it. No one fixed his eyes on the cross of Jesus Christ more than Whitefield.

Some historians consider George Whitefield the first religious celebrity in America. I don't like that terminology, but it seems everyone was attracted to the man and the message, even those who didn't agree with him. Perhaps the most striking example is Benjamin Franklin. Franklin didn't agree with much of Whitefield's doctrine, but he became Whitefield's publicist and printer. He even admitted to emptying his pockets in response to one of Whitefield's offerings.

How did Whitefield have that effect? What drove him? And what drew the crowds?

Simply put, he preached *as if* it were true. He said it like he believed it. And he was driven by a powerful *therefore*.

THUNDER AND LIGHTNING

It might be a bit of an overstatement, but most nineteenth-century preachers were as dynamic as, say, someone who had undergone a lobotomy. Sermons were sedatives—then along came George Whitefield.

While his collared contemporaries read dry moral essays from the pulpit, Whitefield preached like a cage fighter. And he had the nickname to match: "Thunder and Lightning."[2] It wasn't happenstance either; it was a defining moment, a defining decision. One story that he shared in one of his sermons doubled as Whitefield's *as if* moment.

In the year 1675, the Archbishop of Canterbury was acquainted with an actor named Mr. Butterton. One day the Archbishop said to Butterton, "Tell me, Mr. Butterton, what is the reason you actors on stage can affect your congregations with the speaking of things imaginary, as if they were real, while we in church speak of things real, which our congregations only receive as if they were imaginary?"

"Why, my Lord," said Butterton, "the reason is very plain. We actors on stage speak of things imaginary as if they were real, and you in the pulpit speak of things real as if they were imaginary."[3]

That *as if* statement hit Whitefield's bulls-eye—*speaking of things real as if imaginary*. Whitefield resolved to revive real Christianity. Upon telling that story, Whitefield is said to have shouted, "Therefore, I will not be a velvet-mouthed preacher."[4] He was never accused of such!

Did you catch it? *Therefore*. Therefore is where *as if* begins.

It's a one-word manifesto, a God-ordained passion, a God-given dream. It defines who you are and who you're not. It's your defining moment, your driving motivation. It's the *why* behind every *what*. It's the thing you'd go to your grave fighting for.

What's your *therefore*?

For Whitefield, it was "to preach, as Apelles painted, for all eternity."[5] For Whitefield, *therefore* started at the Tower of London, where he preached to a captive audience of prisoners. He often wept during his sermons, urgently pleading with people to come to Jesus. His last sermon was delivered in Newburyport, Massachusetts, on September 29, 1770. Barely able to stand, Whitefield preached for two hours, until 2:00 a.m. Later that morning, he literally ran out of breath, dying of an asthmatic fit. His friend and colleague John Wesley eulogized Whitefield this way: "Oh, what has the church suffered in the setting of that bright star which shone so gloriously in our hemisphere. We have none left to succeed him; none of his gifts; none anything like him in usefulness."[6]

In 1941, the Nobel Prize–winning poet T. S. Eliot posed a poetic question: "Can all of a life represent one motive?" If he didn't succeed at it, George Whitefield came close.

ROW 22, SEAT 12

It's impossible to predict when or where *therefore* will be revealed. It often happens in the most inconspicuous and innocuous circumstances. For me, it was row 22, seat 12 in the rear left floor section of Willow Creek Community Church.

I was a twenty-two-year-old seminary student attending their leadership conference for credit. I thought I'd get three credits, but I got extra credit. I discovered my *therefore*. I can only describe it as a holy dare—it was like the Holy Spirit dared me not to just plant a church but to do it *differently*.

It still gives me goose bumps two decades later. It will always be the MO of my ministry. In a sentence:

There are ways of doing church that no one has thought of yet.

That's what gets me up early and keeps me up late.
That's my *therefore*.

If the kingdom of God had departments, I'd apply for Research and Development. Part of it is a function of personality. I'm a trailblazer, according to the StrengthsFinder test. Which is a positive way of saying that I get bored easily. I'm not into "been there, done that." Part of it is a function of theology—I believe the church ought to be the most creative place on the planet. We also have this core value: everything is an experiment. Perhaps the best descriptor of National Community Church is this: we're orthodox in belief yet unorthodox in practice.

As a writer and preacher, this *therefore* drives me. I try to say old things in new ways. I believe every *ology* is a branch of theology, and I love juxtaposing different disciplines. It's my way of turning

106

the kaleidoscope to reveal new combinations of truth, because all truth is God's truth.

In my opinion, every revival begins with *therefore*. And by revival, I mean personal and societal. For Whitefield, it was a Great Awakening that swept America. For me, it was a moment that defines every other moment of my ministry. It was a dare to be different. Either way, *therefore* involves throwing down the gauntlet. It's the point of no return.

1,220 THEREFORES

There are 1,220 *therefores* in Scripture. They are the theological bridges across which some of Scripture's greatest truths travel. And none has a longer span than the very first word of the Great Eight. Like every preacher who has taken hermeneutics, I learned a simple axiom: *whenever you come across a therefore, find out what it's there for.*

This book revolves around the eighth chapter of Romans, but there are sixteen songs in Paul's album to the Romans. The Great Eight is the title track, but one word ties them all together. You guessed it: *therefore*. If the first seven chapters are the *cause*, the Great Eight is the *effect*. It's the consequence of everything Paul has said so far. *Therefore* tees up the sum total of truth in the first seven chapters, and then Paul swings for the fences.

The first *therefore* in the Great Eight is the most significant connective clause in Romans, but it's not the only one. The first eleven verses are a chorus of *what God has done for us*. The next few verses are the refrain of *what God expects from us*, starting with verse 12:

> Therefore, brothers and sisters, we have an obligation—but it is not to the flesh, to live according to it.

Obligation.

It's not your favorite word, is it? But that's because we interpret it, or rather misinterpret it, in a negative light. Don't think of it as something you *have to do*; think of it as something you *get to do*. Our greatest obligation doubles as our greatest opportunity—surrendering our lives to the lordship of Christ. Can you think of any greater privilege than being used for God's eternal purposes?

The word means to be legally or morally bound, and the best picture might be marriage. When you say "I do" at the altar, you are obligating yourself for better or for worse, for richer or for poorer, in sickness and in health, till death do you part. I've officiated lots of weddings, and I've never seen anyone enter into that obligation with anything other than joyful anticipation.

When we enter into a covenant relationship with God, we tend to focus on the fact that we are legally and morally bound to God, but God is also legally and morally bound to us. The gospel demands that we give all of ourselves to God, but when we do, God gives all of Himself to us. I'll make that trade seven days a week, and twice on Sundays! It's a covenant of blessing, and every blessing belongs to you *in Christ*.

Every promise is *yes* in Christ.

THE BARTER KING

I recently came across a rather interesting reality show, *Barter Kings*. It's all about trading something of lesser value for something of greater value. Do it enough times, and you might just end up with something of significant value. Start with a toaster, for example, and trade it for a used bike; then trade the used bike for a microwave. Trade the microwave for airplane passes, the airplane passes for a horse, the horse for a used car, and the used car for Jet Skis. *Voilà!* The show tracks those trading strings, and it's full of twists and turns.

One of the most infamous trading strings involved a Canadian blogger, Kyle MacDonald, who started with one red paper clip and *what if*. It took nearly a year and fourteen very random transactions, which included a hand-sculpted doorknob, a KISS motorized snow globe, and a role in a film. By the time he was done, the red paper clip was bartered all the way to a two-story farmhouse in Kipling, Saskatchewan.

Pretty crazy, but not as crazy as the gospel.

> God made him who had no sin to be sin for us, so that in him we might become the righteousness of God.[7]

Here's the deal the Barter King puts on the table: *you trade all of your sin for all of My righteousness, and we'll call it even.* You'll never get a better barter. And that's why it's called the Good News. Salvation is the trade up. The tradeoff is giving full veto power to the Holy Spirit. But once again, that's a good obligation.

He'll take you places you can't go.

He'll set up divine appointments with people you can't meet.

And He'll do things in you and through you that are impossible.

VETO POWER

I live in a city that eats, sleeps, and breathes politics. Our local news is national news, which isn't always positive. I understand the frustration and skepticism about what happens inside the Beltway, but I'm also grateful for public servants from both sides of the aisle that I've had the privilege of serving as pastor.

I've preached to them, prayed for them, and had conversations with them. And when they let down their guard, you realize they have the same fears and faults, hopes and dreams as the rest of us. The only difference is that their decisions have far-ranging ramifications for the country at large.

One of my more memorable meetings was with a DC council-member who ran for mayor in the last election cycle. At the end of our time together, I asked him what I could pray for. I was half expecting a prayer request that he'd win the election. Instead, he said, "Pray that I don't let fear dictate my decisions."

What dictates your decisions?

It's not something we think about or talk about much, but all of us have an internal dictator. For some, it's fear. For others, it's *as if* faith.

In politics, people face a tremendous temptation to make decisions for all the wrong reasons—like trading political favors for kickbacks or changing values to win votes. We need a few more public officials who don't care about public opinion polls, a few more public officials who have the ability to discern what's right, then the moral courage to do it.

Over the course of church history, seven sins have been identified as deadly—pride, greed, lust, anger, gluttony, envy, and sloth. Each of those seven deadly sins is a dictator. They work in different ways, but they are trying to dictate your decisions.

If you lose your temper, it may be anger.

If you can't keep a diet, it may be gluttony.

If you struggle with pornography, it may be lust.

Each of the deadly sins is a dictator, and the only way to dethrone those dictators is by enthroning Jesus Christ in every area of your life. That's the defining decision. And it must be backed up with predecisions. Let me give you a simple example.

One of the dictators is greed, and greed actually comes across as a good guy. His platform? *More is better*. But it's an insidious lie because *enough is never enough*.

How do you overthrow greed? The coup d'état is the tithe. You give the first 10 percent of your income back to God. Honestly, it's the only way I know to keep greed off the throne of my life.

Over the years, Lora and I have tried to give a greater percentage of our income back to God, and what we've found is that the more we give away, the more we enjoy what we keep. If you give 20 percent, you'll enjoy the 80 percent you keep 20 percent more! We falsely assume that joy is found in the portion we keep, but it's actually found in the portion we give. The tithe is one way of giving veto power to God. It's a reminder that it's all from God and for God. It's a way of making sure that generosity dictates my decisions, not greed.

What dictator do you need to overthrow?

It starts by giving God veto power. And it leads to one more *therefore*:

> Therefore, I urge you, brothers and sisters, in view of God's mercy, to offer your bodies as a living sacrifice, holy and pleasing to God—this is your true and proper worship.[8]

What if you stopped letting fear
dictate your decisions?

12

The Scenic Route

For those who are led by the Spirit of
God are the children of God.

Romans 8:14

In 2001, four college friends who weren't sure what they wanted to do after graduation came up with a great *what if* idea. They bought an old RV, painted it green, and traveled the country interviewing people who inspired them. From a winemaker in California to a lobsterman in Maine to a Supreme Court Justice in DC, they asked an eclectic collection of people to share lessons learned on life's journey. Hundreds of interviews and 15,000 miles later, *Roadtrip Nation* aired on PBS.

Even if you don't have wanderlust, don't you wish you had done that? I wasn't sure what to do after college either, but I went the traditional route. I delayed getting a job by getting a master's degree. I still didn't know what I wanted to do, so I bought another year by doing a second master's degree. It was an academic delay tactic—a great experience, but I wonder if I would have learned as much or more by filling up my gas tank and doing what these road warriors did.

While driving through western Montana, the road trippers decided to exit I-90 and check out the picturesque Clark Fork River. That's when they noticed an eighteen-wheeler parked by the river and the truck driver skipping stones in the river. It was a strange sight because truckers are notorious for only stopping at truck stops.

When they asked him what he was doing, the trucker told them his wife had passed away the day before. "For thirty-five years, I've driven by this exit a million times," he told them. "And I've never stopped."[1]

The look on his face was part regret, part enlightenment. For the first time in thirty-five years, he had decided to exit the freeway. That little phrase, *exit the freeway*, became the motto of the Roadtrip movement. And I'm going to advocate for it. But first, a little stump speech.

We are the beneficiaries of unbelievable time-saving advances in technology. I remember when you had to practically plant the corn, shuck it, start a fire, and pop it in a covered pan. Then along came the microwave, for which we are thankful. But along with the time-saving benefits, I sometimes wonder if there is a side effect. Are we not the most impatient people in the history of humankind? I'll be the first to admit, if you don't put the pedal to the metal when the light turns green, I'm going to honk my horn. Why? Because I don't have two seconds to spare—I've got places to go, things to do! We wear busyness as a badge, like an honor roll bumper sticker.

Come on, isn't it rather ironic that we get incredibly frustrated when a cross-country flight is delayed ten minutes—a flight that travels at one hundred times the speed of a covered wagon and gets us to the other side of America with beverage service? For the love of Lewis and Clark, quit complaining about minor travel delays!

Our patience has worn thin, and it affects every arena of life. We want what our parents spent decades working for and saving for, in a fraction of the time, with a fraction of the effort. We're so driven to get ahead that one of the hardest commands to keep is keeping the Sabbath holy. After all, we can't afford to fall behind. But that's how we fall and fall behind.

Nothing slows us down like trying to get ahead of God. Remember when Moses tried to expedite God's plan by killing an Egyptian taskmaster? That little shortcut backfired into a forty-year delay!

Listen, I'm as driven as they come. I want to get as far as I can, as fast as I can, and I want to get there yesterday! But we've got to enjoy the journey too, by God's grace. After all, the journey *is* the destination.

ENJOY THE JOURNEY

When I started pastoring, I had some epic wrestling matches with discouragement. Especially during our first year. Our average attendance was twenty-five, and our average offering was right around $497 a week.

That's when I fell into the when/then trap. I thought, *When we hit a hundred people, then I'll love pastoring.* I thought, *When our offerings are $1,000 a week, then life will be good.* But it was a lie!

I had a defining moment right after one of our early services. The Holy Spirit said, in no uncertain terms, *Enjoy the journey!* From that moment on, I've done my best to thoroughly enjoy every stage of life, every stage of growth. I was bound and determined to enjoy pastoring twenty-five people, a hundred people, a thousand people, five thousand people—however many people God would bring through our doors.

No matter what stage of life you're in—enjoy the journey!

If you need what's next to make you happy—no matter what *next* is—you suffer from destination disease. We get so focused on then and there that we don't really enjoy here and now. *When I go to college, when I graduate from college, when I get a job, when I get a promotion, when I retire, when I get married, when we have kids—then I'll be happy.* No, no you won't. It's a mirage! If you aren't happy where you are, a vacation won't solve your problems. If you aren't happy with who you are, Botox won't work.

When was the last time you exited the freeway?

Took the scenic route?

Skipped stones?

As I see it, there are two proverbial roads you can take. The shortcut is the path of least resistance. It's well traveled, but it's like rush-hour traffic in DC. No fun! The scenic route is the road less traveled. It takes longer, and it's an uphill climb both ways. But the view from the top is spectacular.

How do you get there?

The same way you get anywhere: one step at a time.

A few years ago, I checked a life goal off my list by hiking Half Dome in Yosemite National Park with my son Parker. By degree of difficulty, it ranks right behind the Inca Trail to Machu Picchu and the Grand Canyon from rim to rim. It's a 15.5-mile hike with a 4,800-foot ascent, but if you're afraid of heights, the hardest part is the 60-degree slope to the summit.

On the morning of the hike, I glanced up at Half Dome from the valley floor and wondered how in the world I would get to the top. Especially because I was suffering from a severe case of plantar fasciitis! It seemed almost impossible, but the answer was quite simple. *One step at a time.* That's how you get anywhere! We fail to accomplish our goals for the same reason we mess up assembly projects: we don't take it step-by-step. We get ahead of ourselves, or maybe I should say, we get ahead of God.

I share 115 of my life goals in *The Circle Maker*, along with ten steps to setting goals. Anything less than God-sized goals constitutes a lack of faith. You've got to be sure of what you hope for—well-defined *what ifs*. But the hidden danger of goal setting is getting so focused on the goal that you forget that the goal isn't really the goal—it's the habit that helped you get there. You don't have to figure out where to go or what to do—that's God's job. He's preparing good works in advance. Your job is to simply keep in lockstep with the Holy Spirit.

10,000 STEPS

This past Christmas, Lora got me a Fitbit. It was a gift, not a suggestion. My wife knows that I love exercise and I love gadgets, and Fitbit is a combination of both. Using a three-dimensional accelerometer, my bracelet does everything from measure the number of steps I take each day to track the quality of my sleep cycle.

Is anything more mundane than sleeping or walking? Not anymore! I can't wait to wake up and check my graph. Every step I take, every calorie I burn takes on new meaning because it gets me one step, one calorie closer to my goal.

Before getting my Fitbit, I'd always wondered how many calories I burn during a sermon. Fitbit helped me find out—a thirty-minute sermon burns about one hundred calories. Of course, that varies from preacher to preacher. I'm guessing that George Whitefield probably burned a few more than me, especially with the wig on, outdoors, in the summer heat.

I know this may sound like a commercial for Fitbit, but it was a paradigm shift. My office is only 647 steps from my house, but I used to drive it both ways. With a new daily target of 10,000 steps, I actually hoof it now.

After Christmas, my least favorite chore is putting away all the Christmas gear. We live in a very vertical row house on Capitol Hill, and all of our stuff is stored in the attic. I used to dread that day, but not anymore. Why? Because each step is one step closer to my goal.

One last fun fact: I danced 8,350 steps with Lora on New Year's Eve. And I felt it the next year! That's 4.18 miles worth of running man, electric slide, and moonwalk.

I have a little maxim that I repeat to anyone who seems anxious about missing the will of God: *God wants you to get where God wants you to go more than you want to get where God wants you to go*. And God is awfully good at getting us there! So take a deep breath and relax. He is ordering your footsteps, every single one of them. Your job is simply this: "keep in step with the Spirit."[2] Sounds simple, doesn't it? About as simple as keeping in step with me on the dance floor!

There is a classic *Saturday Night Live* skit called "Do the Idiot." An average Joe, played by Jeff Goldblum, can't dance a lick. But his girlfriend, Julia Sweeney, takes him to a swanky dance club. When she gets him on the dance floor, it's a disaster. He looks like one of those inflatable air dancers with flailing arms outside car dealerships.

That's when Screaming Fat Guy, played by Chris Farley, yells, "Hey, everybody! Come on, let's do the Idiot!"[3]

That's me—the idiot! Sometimes when I get into my zone, Lora will have to remind me that she's right there!

My point? It's tough to keep in step with me. After all, I often do the idiot. Sometimes that's what it feels like trying to do the two-step with the Holy Spirit. You feel like a fool, but that's when God shows up and shows off.

You are someone else's miracle. Of that, I'm sure. All you have to do is let the Spirit lead and obey His promptings. Sometimes that means speaking a word of encouragement. Sometimes it means keeping your mouth shut. Sometimes it's inviting a stranger to join you for a round of golf.

CROSS-COUNTRY ANSWERS TO PRAYER

National Community Church is a very young congregation, so we place a premium on gray heads who have a little wisdom to offer. Dave and Lynn Weatherby fit the bill. They've been married for more than forty years, but they're still full of *what if*. One of the things I admire about them is that they seem to have divine appointments all the time, even on vacation.

They recently told me about a trip they took to California to attend a wedding. The day after, they decided to hit the local golf course. On the fourth hole, a single played up behind them, so they politely asked if he wanted to play through or perhaps join them. Much to their surprise, he joined them for the rest of the round. It actually helped their score, since he knew the course.

As they approached the ninth hole, he told the Weatherbys that he normally played with a group of men, but he didn't want to play with his buddies that day. Then he revealed why. His brother, who had served a thirty-year prison sentence for molesting his two sisters, was being released that same day. His brother had never shown remorse, so this day was incredibly difficult for him. He didn't think his usual foursome would understand, so he decided to head out by himself.

But he said to Dave and Lynn, "I prayed this morning that God would provide someone to play with who would be caring and understanding." If you knew Dave and Lynn, that's where you'd start laughing—because I don't know two people who are more caring or more understanding.

As they putted out the final green, Dave told their new friend, "God brought us more than two thousand miles from Bethesda, Maryland, to Modesto, California, to be the answer to your prayer!" Then they prayed a blessing for each other and parted ways.

The Celtic Christians had a rather unique name for the Holy Spirit. They called him *An Geadh Glas*, or the Wild Goose. I love that name. In fact, I wrote a book titled *Wild Goose Chase*. I can't think of a better description of what it's like to live a Spirit-led life. I have no idea where I'm going half the time, but God is in the business of strategically positioning us in the right place at the right time.

I call them supernatural synchronicities. And they're more than mere coincidence—they're providence!

If I believe anything, I believe that God orders our footsteps. And it's not just when we walk the line on our graduation day or walk the aisle on our wedding day. It's every step. Can we misstep? Of course! But the longer I live, the more I marvel at God's ability to choreograph divine appointments.

I had one of those moments speaking at the centennial celebration of the Assemblies of God in Springfield, Missouri. I hadn't been in Springfield in many years, but I did spend two formative years at Central Bible College. So the trip was more like a pilgrimage for me. CBC had recently closed, and the property was being sold, so I knew it was my last chance to visit my undergraduate alma mater. I really wanted to get into the gym and the chapel, my two favorite places on campus. But I knew it was a long shot because, well, the school was closed.

When I arrived, it felt like a ghost town. I only saw one car on campus, but I decided to try the gym anyway. I couldn't see inside because of the one-way glass, so I was rather shocked when someone opened the door as I approached. I was even more shocked when he said, "Hi, Mark. Come on in." I didn't know him from Adam, but he acted as if I had an appointment.

And maybe I did. Maybe this was a divine appointment. Turns out he's the custodian of the campus while it's for sale, and somehow he knew me. He let me into the chapel, so one last time I paced the balcony where I had learned to pray. And the library was like a walk down memory lane, because it was filled with CBC memorabilia—including a few pictures of me in my twentieth-century basketball short shorts.

By the time the tour was done, I felt like standing in the middle of the campus and yelling, "God is faithful!" at the top of my lungs! It felt like a twenty-year time lapse. And that half-hour tour is still fueling my faith.

As I was getting ready to leave, my chaperone said, "You know, I said to a friend this morning, 'I wonder if Mark Batterson is going to come by today.'"

I was dumbfounded. Maybe he put two and two together, knowing I was going to be in town for the centennial, knowing that I was a CBC grad, and knowing I might want to visit the campus one last time. But still, what are the chances? And if I wouldn't have walked up to the gym at that very moment, we would have missed each other altogether.

I know this isn't a life-saving or life-changing story, but it meant more to me than you can imagine. It felt like the heavenly Father's way of showing me how much He cares about every single step.

God is setting up divine appointments. All we need to do is follow His lead, exercise a little patience, and take it one step at a time.

What if you made a decision to
exit the freeway, take the scenic route,
and enjoy the journey more often?

13

The Reckoning

For I reckon that the sufferings of this present time are not worthy to be compared with the glory which shall be revealed in us.

Romans 8:18 KJV

Nick Vujicic was born without arms or legs.

There are a thousand things Nick is not able to do that we take for granted. Nick can't give a hug, a handshake, or a high five. He can't clap his hands because he doesn't have any. He can't tap his toe to music or feel the sand under his feet while walking the beach.

But instead of getting angry with God about the things he isn't able to do, Nick made a defining decision as a teenager to be grateful for the things he is able to do. And he's done some amazing things—surfing, for example. How do you do that without arms or legs?

Nick's life is a standing rebuke against self-pity. If Nick isn't making excuses, we probably shouldn't either! He refuses to be defined by his disabilities. Instead, Nick has leveraged his limitations and turned them into his testimony.

At last count, two hundred thousand people have put their faith in Christ after hearing Nick's testimony. I know very few people who have led that many people to faith in Christ. At the risk of sounding crass, I don't think Nick would have the same platform if he had arms and legs. It's the suffering Nick has endured that people identify with most.

Simply put, God has turned Nick's pain into eternal gain for thousands upon thousands. And Nick has come to terms with that fact. "I'd rather have no arms and no legs here on earth," he says, "and spend eternity with those who come to faith through my testimony!"[1]

"I reckon."[2]

Those are the words the apostle Paul uses when comparing present-tense suffering with future-tense glory. It's an accounting term, *logizomai*. Think spreadsheet or balance sheet. It's a record of debits and deposits. Almost like your checking account, your suffering will one day be reconciled. And while we may view suffering as a liability now, on the eternal ledger, it's an appreciating asset.

Faith is not logical, but it's not illogical either. Faith is theological—it adds God to the equation. It doesn't ignore a doctor's diagnosis. It simply seeks a second opinion from the Great Physician. That's what we did when my dad was recently diagnosed with not one but two forms of cancer. It was a sucker punch for sure, but we punch back with the promises of God. We certainly listen to what the doctors have to say and appreciate their expert advice. But we give God the final word.

Whatever God says, that's how we reckon.

NO TOMORROW

You can be saved without suffering, but you cannot fully identify with Christ. Suffering doesn't devalue our lives. It adds value in the form of invaluable lessons. It's also a multiplier of God's glory.

When compared to the eternal glory it yields, time-stamped suffering ranks as one of God's greatest gifts.

That doesn't mean your suffering will make sense in the present tense. But that's not how we reckon. We assess suffering through the eyes of eternity.

I'm certainly not suggesting that cancer or any other debilitating disease is good. It's not. It was cancer that claimed the life of my grandfather. Make no mistake about it, cancer and its sick cousins are by-products of the curse. And Jesus came to reverse the curse—the curse of sin, the curse of sickness, the curse of death.

Sometimes our healing happens on this side of the space-time continuum. That's what we pray when we pray, "Thy will be done on earth as it is in heaven." We are praying that the reality of heaven—a place where there is no sickness, no suffering, no pain—would invade our reality here and now. *As it is* is another way of saying *as if*. But even if our healing doesn't happen on this side, complete healing is on hold in heaven. Cancer may shorten our life on earth, but it doesn't have to devalue it. In fact, it can become the catalyst that makes the rest of our life more meaningful. Countless cancer survivors point to their diagnosis as the worst thing *and* best thing that's ever happened to them.

Peter Senge is a systems scientist and senior lecturer at the MIT Sloan School of Management. He writes and lectures on how imagining alternate futures can lead to transformational change. Sometimes those alternate futures are *what if* possibilities. Sometimes they are harsh realities. In my experience, nothing is more life-giving than a near-death experience. It's like a metaphysical wake-up call.

Peter Senge shares one of those experiences in the book he coauthored called *Presence*.[3] Senge was leading a seminar at the World Bank when an employee named Fred revealed that he had been diagnosed with a terminal illness. Fred was given only a few months to live. So he did just that. He started living *as if* there were no tomorrow.

Like anyone who gets a devastating diagnosis, Fred went through a period of denial. "Then something amazing happened," Fred said. "I simply stopped doing everything that wasn't essential, that didn't matter."[4] Important things became even more important. Unimportant things became even more unimportant.

A few months had passed when a friend told Fred he should seek a second opinion. His new doctor told him he had been misdiagnosed. Fred had a very rare but very curable disease. When the doctor delivered the news, Fred cried like a baby. Why? "Because I was afraid my life would go back to the way it used to be."[5]

Sometimes suffering is the catalyst that causes us to ask *what if*. Of course, it doesn't have to be a tragedy. It can also be a midlife crisis. When you hit your forties, you start counting down. But the ticktock of your body clock isn't a negative thing. It's a reminder to reckon.

Make each day count.

Live like there is no tomorrow.

Do things that will live on after you die.

NEAR-LIFE EXPERIENCE

Sometimes it's a miracle that helps us reckon differently.

After Jesus fed the five thousand with five loaves and two fish, the disciples reckoned differently.[6] Before the miracle happened, Philip looked at the five loaves and two fish and said, "What good is that?"

They quickly discovered that five plus two does *not* equal seven—not in God's kingdom. When you add God to the equation: $5 + 2 = 5,000$ with a remainder of 12 baskets left over. When the will of God doesn't add up, God makes it multiply!

So sometimes it's a miracle that helps us reckon differently.

Sometimes it takes some suffering to help us reckon differently.

Paul didn't write out of a vacuum.

His résumé of suffering is quite remarkable—five floggings, three shipwrecks, and at least one stoning. Like a tattoo that tells a story, each scar on Paul's body was a visible reminder of his suffering and God's faithfulness.

I don't write out of a vacuum either.

I haven't gone a week without taking an inhaler in forty years. I've spent weeks on end in the hospital. And I've had a few near-death experiences. The last time we tested lung function, my capacity and airflow were well below average. I honestly don't understand why God gave me a measure of athletic ability, enough to play college basketball—yet hasn't healed my asthma.

But this I know for sure: God has taught me some things through my suffering that could not have been learned any other way. God doesn't give honorary doctorates. He awards earned degrees from the school of suffering, the school of failure, and the school of pain. And while I wouldn't want to go through some of those experiences again, I wouldn't trade my transcript.

I've written about it before so I'll spare you the details, but my date of death should have been July 23, 2000. That's the day my intestines ruptured. I was rushed into emergency surgery at three o'clock in the morning and spent two days on a respirator. I lost twenty-five pounds in a week, and I underwent multiple surgeries to repair and reverse the damage done.

Instead of being my death date, July 23, 2000, turned into my second birthday. I literally party like it's 1999 because that would have been my last birthday had I not survived.

Two years of my life have an asterisk on them. I would never want to go through anything like that again, but I wouldn't trade it for anything in the world. It was a graduate course in gratitude. It was like an out-of-body experience that gave me a different perspective on life. The ten-inch scar on my abdomen is a line of demarcation in my life.

You *reckon* differently after an experience like that.

THE LAW OF DIMINISHING MARGINAL UTILITY

It sounds so fancy, "the law of diminishing marginal utility," but it's really quite simple. At some point, *more is less*. As you increase consumption of a product, while keeping consumption of other products constant, there is a decline in the gain you derive from consuming each additional unit of that product. I tested this theory with Haribo gummy bears for many years, and I can confirm that it's true! The more you consume, the less you enjoy.

This law has a lot to do with your measure of joy. Joy is not getting what you want; it's appreciating what you have. And in some cases, it requires wanting less! You've got to find fulfillment in the simple pleasures.

Since we're on the subject, let me make one other connection. The law of diminishing marginal utility is one more reason why fasting is so powerful, so important. And not just fasting, but *feasting*. The Bible prescribes both. The problem with our supersize culture is that we feast all the time. There's a name for that—gluttony.

If you indulge in whatever you want, whenever you want, you'll enjoy it less and less. And it'll be harder and harder to satiate your hunger pangs. If, however, you follow the biblical rhythm of fasting and feasting, you'll not only keep your appetite in check, you'll also enjoy every bite a little bit more!

Now let me get in your business.

There is a well-documented study that suggests that money stops making people happier at a family income right around \$75,000.[7] Obviously, you have to take things like cost of living and number of children into account. So that number fluctuates a little, but after you hit that magic number, a diminishing marginal utility kicks in.

Malcolm Gladwell expounds on this concept in his book *David and Goliath*, making a very interesting observation. If you don't have enough money to get what your kids want, you can simply say, "No, we can't." If you have more than enough money, you have to say, "No, we won't." Gladwell argues that *no we won't* is much more difficult to say than *no we can't*.

That, of course, requires that you have a set of values and know how to articulate them, and know how to make them plausible to your child—all of which are really difficult things for anyone to do, under any circumstances, especially if you have a Ferrari in the driveway, a private jet, and a house in Beverly Hills the size of an airplane hangar.[8]

One of my heroes is Stanley Tam, the founder of the United States Plastic Corporation. Stanley has given away more than $120 million dollars at last count. Despite the wealth at his disposal, he chooses to live a very simple lifestyle. He once said something that was so simple, so true: "A man can only wear one suit at a time."

I reckon.

In our culture, one of the toughest questions is this: *How much is enough?* It takes moral courage to ask it and to answer it. I realize that you may be struggling with college loans or credit card debt, and this question seems premature. But I pray that the day would come when you would have to put a ceiling on your income and start investing it in eternity like Stanley Tam.

If we simplified our lives, I reckon that we'd be happier, healthier, and holier. Most of us know it intuitively, but we live in a culture that screams, "More!" Enough is never enough. Last year's model is so, well, last year. We want the latest fashion, the latest feature. We can't imagine being out of date when it comes to colors or clothes or computers or cars. Listen, the only thing not out of date is eternity!

Reckon that.

THE DAY OF RECKONING

On January 30, 1956, *Time* magazine devoted its cover to five American missionaries killed with spears on the banks of the Curaray River in Ecuador by members of the Huaorani people. As tragic as their martyrdom was, it was not in vain. Their deaths inspired a generation of missionaries to devote their lives to the cause of Christ. One journal entry, belonging to Jim Elliot, contained what became one of the most-cited sentences of his generation:

> He is no fool who gives what he cannot keep to gain what he cannot lose.[9]

I reckon.

The Day of Reckoning is coming. We will all stand before the Judgment Seat of Christ. Or more accurately, we will all bow. No one stands in the presence of a King!

When we die, we are either in Christ or in sin. Those who die in their sin will have to give account for it. Those who die in Christ stand in His righteousness. They won't give account for their sin, because it was accounted for at the cross. They will be rewarded for deeds done while on earth.

On the Day of Reckoning, our singular regret will be whatever we didn't give back to God. That's it. Whatever we keep, we lose. Whatever we lose for His sake, we keep for eternity.

I used to trade options in my early twenties. Before my brokerage firm even allowed me to start trading, I had to read a document called *Characteristics and Risks of Standardized Options*. I think it was designed to scare investors into a safer strategy, but I didn't have the patience to wait for traditional stocks, bonds, and mutual funds. I wanted a get-rich-quick scheme.

My first month trading, I had the fortune and misfortune of turning $1,500 into $5,000. The next month I turned $5,000 into nothing! I learned a $5,000 lesson. Unlike traditional investment vehicles, options have expiration dates. If an option doesn't hit the strike price by the call date, it expires worthless.

You have an expiration date. Whatever you don't invest in the kingdom is an option that expires worthless. Whatever you invest in kingdom stock earns compound interest for eternity, and the dividends are out of this world. To reckon any other way is an eternal miscalculation.

C. T. Studd was one of the greatest cricket players of his generation. Fame and fortune were at his fingertips, but he chose to devote his life to missions instead. One of the Cambridge Seven, Studd spent a decade with the China Inland Mission. In 1913, he started the Heart of Africa mission, now known as Worldwide Evangelization for Christ International.

A century later, 1,800 WEC missionaries in fifty countries seek to make Christ known, loved, and worshiped among people who have yet to hear the gospel. A life well lived adds weight to C. T. Studd's famous words,

> Only one life 'twill soon be past.
> Only what's done for Christ will last.

I reckon.

What if you simplified your life
by downsizing your lifestyle?

14

Eternal Optimist

For the creation waits in eager expectation.

Romans 8:19

I have thousands of books in my library, but few are older than a vintage volume authored by Helen Keller. Copyrighted in 1903, *Optimism* has stood the test of time. I would be unimpressed by the title if it weren't for the unique circumstances out of which the author wrote.

Before the age of two, Helen Keller lost her vision and her hearing. In an instant, her world went dark, went silent. Then a godsend named Anne Sullivan broke through Helen's solitary confinement and touched her soul. Helen Keller became the first deafblind person to earn a bachelor's degree. She also authored a dozen books, including a manifesto on her philosophy of life, *Optimism*.

"No pessimist ever discovered the secrets of the stars," she wrote, "or sailed to an uncharted land." The last page of her book echoes the first page of Scripture. "Optimism is the harmony of man's spirit and the Spirit of God pronouncing His works good."[1]

If the Spirit of God is within you, optimism is the order of the day. It's part of your spiritual birthright. Optimism isn't at odds with the reality that is all around us. It simply means we're anchored to another reality—the crucifixion and resurrection of Jesus Christ—that is deeper and stronger and longer than the reality we can perceive with our five senses.

My copy of *Optimism* has changed hands a few times in the last hundred years. Different names and prices are penciled on the inside cover, but one of those exchanges must have been a gift. The hundred-year-old inscription reads,

> To my goodest friends, Mary Belle and Eugene, when you get blue or discouraged in life, think of Helen Keller, and be thankful for your eyes.

So simple. So good.

Most of us take our eyesight for granted, but even the simplest of visual processes is divinely complex. The retina alone conducts close to ten billion calculations every second, and that's before an image even travels through the optic nerve to the visual cortex. And that is the tip of the cortex. As we read, millions of electrical impulses are firing across billions of synaptic pathways, and we don't even give it a second thought.

Yet as amazing as the human eye is, there is something more amazing still. It's the mind's eye that enables us to imagine the unthinkable, believe the impossible. In the words of Helen Keller, "The only thing worse than being blind is having sight but no vision."[2]

SPECIMEN CUP

In 1979, Norman Cousins, the editor-in-chief of the *Saturday Review* for more than three decades, was given six months to live. Despite a 1 in 500 chance of recovery, he beat the odds by living another two decades. He revealed how he did it in his bestselling book, *Anatomy of an Illness*. While the doctors administered medicine, Cousins decided to fight his illness with his attitude. He employed a simple strategy—laughter.

Cousins told his friends to call him every time they heard or did something funny. He watched comedies and listened to stand-up comedians. He also pulled pranks on the hospital staff.

There was one nurse who never smiled or laughed. In fact, she made him feel guilty every time he hit the call button. During one of her rounds, she handed him a specimen cup and asked for a sample. Instead of urinating in it, Cousins poured his apple juice in. When she came to collect the cup, the nurse said, "We're a little cloudy today, aren't we?"

Cousins said, "Yep, better run it through again."

He downed the cup, explained the gag, and finally made her laugh.[3]

After surviving his own ordeal, Norman Cousins started helping patients with chronic pain. Sessions began with each patient sharing something they were grateful for. During one of those round-robins, Cousins shared this story:

> What I have to report is better than good. It's wonderful. It's better than wonderful. It's unbelievable. When I arrived at Los Angeles Airport last Wednesday, I went to the baggage claim and my luggage was the first one on the carousel.

The group erupted in applause. But it got better. Cousins said he'd never met anyone so fortunate as to have their luggage first on the carousel—he just had to phone his office and share the mini-miracle. But that's when he lost his quarter in the pay phone.

So Cousins dialed zero and explained his problem to the operator. She said, "Sir, if you give me your name and address, we'll mail the coin to you."

Cousins told the operator that this explained why AT&T had so many issues at the time. She, the operator, would take the time to write the customer's name and address on a card, then pass it on to another employee—who would go to the cash register, punch it open, grab a quarter, and make a record of the withdrawal.

Then this worker would place the quarter in a special holder and put the holder in a special envelope made just for this purpose. The envelope would be carefully sealed, addressed, and stamped to the tune of thirty-two cents, first-class mail. And all these gyrations for the purpose of returning one quarter!

Cousins politely said, "Now, operator, why don't you just return my coin and let's be friends?"

She repeated robotically, "Sir, if you give me your name and address, we will mail you the refund."

As he listened to this, Cousins checked the return plunger one more time—and it worked! Not only did it work; it began spewing out coins like a Vegas jackpot. Cousins cupped his hands, but he couldn't contain the silver landslide.

The operator heard the ruckus and said, "Sir—what is happening, please?"

"The machine has just given up its earnings for the past few months. There must be close to forty dollars in quarters, nickels, and dimes."

"Sir," said the operator, "will you please put the coins back in the phone?"

"Operator," he replied, "if you give me your name and address, I will be glad to mail you the coins."

When Cousins finished this story and his audience finally stopped laughing and clapping, he asked a question. "How many of you noticed in the last five or ten minutes that your chronic pain receded or disappeared?"

Every hand went up![4]

Cousins didn't just beat the odds. He lived another twenty years! How?

The one-word answer: *hope.*

And hope is a powerful *as if.*

133

HOPE AGAINST HOPE

I love people who defy their circumstances with their attitude. Against all odds, they hope against hope.

I think of Jana.

Jana lost her husband, Kevin, to an aneurysm at the age of forty-two. She was left to raise her four daughters as a single parent. Jana walked through the valley of the shadow of death, but she came out on the other side full of faith. Jana wears a pendant around her neck that encapsulates her philosophy of life: *So blessed.*

Some would argue otherwise, but Jana has pitched her tent in the land of hope. She lost her husband, but she didn't lose hope.

I think of Charles.

He's one of the first people I met when we moved to Washington, DC. Charles had a thick Nigerian accent, having immigrated to the United States as an adult. He had difficulty with the English language, but that didn't keep him from taking classes at the inner-city ministry I directed. I was teaching the classes, but Charles taught me far more than I taught him.

About a decade before I met him, in his early sixties, Charles suffered a stroke that left the right side of his body nearly incapacitated. I would often give Charles a ride to class, and I had to lift his leg into the car for him because he couldn't move it. Despite the physical challenges he faced, he had a more upbeat attitude than anyone I've ever met.

I'll never forget the day he walked out of his low-income housing unit with a smile on his face and a hat on his head that epitomized his outlook on life: *God is good.* Based on circumstances alone, he's probably the last person on the planet who should have been wearing that hat. But Charles defied his circumstances with his *what if* attitude.

So blessed.

God is good.

What is your philosophy of life?

What is your least common denominator?

One of mine is, *So far, so God.*

If you visit Ebenezer's coffeehouse, you'll see "I SAM 7:12" and "SFSG" printed on the coffee sleeve. Our coffeehouse is *not* named after Ebenezer Scrooge! It's a reference to the altar that Samuel named Ebenezer. It means "thus far the Lord has helped me." My translation? "So far, so God."

It's a twist on the old adage "so far, so good." We simply take *good* out and add *God* in.

I don't know what circumstances you find yourself in, but they don't have to define you. Even if you cannot change them, you can defy them with your *as if* attitude. In the words of George Bernard Shaw,

> People are always blaming their circumstances for what they are. I don't believe in circumstances. The people who get on in this world are the people who get up and look for the circumstances they want and if they can't find them, make them.[5]

CIRCUMSTANTIAL EVIDENCE

When I was in my early thirties, I spent five weeks at 500 Indiana Ave NW in DC Superior Court. I tried getting excused from jury duty by informing the judge that the country's chief law enforcement officer, the attorney general of the United States, attended our church.

I think it backfired. I was chosen as foreman of the jury.

For five weeks, we listened to evidence presented in a double homicide involving teenagers. When the prosecution rested its case and the jury retired to deliberate, the judge reminded us about presumption of innocence and reasonable doubt. He also delineated the difference between direct evidence and circumstantial evidence. Direct evidence is eyewitness testimony that carries unique weight in a court of law. Circumstantial evidence relies on inference, like a fingerprint at the scene of a crime or a ballistics report from a forensics expert. It's the smoking gun, so to speak.

When it comes to faith, we rely far too much on circumstantial evidence. Doubt is letting our circumstances dictate how we feel, what we believe. When we let our circumstances get between us and God, it creates a smoke screen of doubt. Faith is relying on the direct evidence of Scripture. Faith is putting the promises of God between you and your circumstances. It doesn't mean you deny reality. It simply means you're in touch with a greater reality—a reality that is far more real than the reality you can touch or taste or see or hear or smell.

Jesus was a realist. He said, "In this world you will have trouble." But He was also an eternal optimist: "Take heart! I have overcome the world."[6] Our optimism is anchored to the empty tomb. If Jesus walked out of the tomb, all bets are off. It's the ultimate *what if*. We just need to live *as if* it's true!

When Jesus broke the seal on the tomb, it sealed our victory.

There are seven promises in the book of Revelation that begin with the same phrase: "To him who overcomes."

I won't detail those promises, but each one describes a *what if* we need to white-knuckle. It paints a picture of our future reality, a dimension the Bible calls heaven. It reminds us of our true identity as overcomers. We aren't just conquerors. We are *more than* conquerors.[7]

And when you follow Christ, the best is yet to come.

Always and forever!

What if you pulled a holy prank to make someone smile, make someone laugh, or make someone's day?

The Third *If*

What If?

Dreams are created twice.
The first creation is spiritual.
The second creation is physical.
But they always start with what if?
What if you knew you couldn't fail—what would you do?
What if time or money weren't an object—
what God-sized goal would you go after?
If you're looking for an excuse, you'll always find one.
The same is true of opportunity.
And if you can't find one, you can make one.
Maybe it's time to quit asking why.
Why not?

15

Who If

The manifestation of the sons of God.

Romans 8:19 KJV

Every *what if* is created twice.

The first creation is an idea that is conceived in the mind, the heart, the spirit. The second creation is the physical manifestation of that *what if*, whatever it is. Some *what ifs* take blueprints plus brick and mortar. Others require a keyboard, a camera, or a chef's kitchen.

But no matter what it is, everything that exists was once an idea in someone's mind. Before becoming a physical reality, it was nothing more than an electrochemical signal firing across synapses deep within the cerebral cortex.

Let me use Washington, DC, as exhibit A.

The map of our capital city was first conceived in the mind of a French-born architect and engineer named Pierre Charles L'Enfant. He was commissioned by George Washington to survey a ten-mile square that was largely farmland and swampland. Even a decade later, the population of the capital city was only 8,144 at its first official census. While surveying, L'Enfant did spot one topographical feature, Jenkins Hill, that he thought held promise for what he called Congress House.

That's the hill where I've lived and pastored for nearly two decades—Capitol Hill.

After surveying the land, L'Enfant transferred his ideas onto a twenty-ounce piece of paper that was handed to President George Washington on August 19, 1791. That original map now sits enshrined in a 108-pound Plexiglas case breathing pressurized argon gas at the Library of Congress.

For more than two centuries, the L'Enfant Plan has framed the cityscape of Washington, DC. It has taken trillions of dollars; tons of marble, brick, and concrete; and countless hours of manual labor for that *what if* to become reality. But the reality is, whether I'm driving down Pennsylvania Avenue, rounding Dupont Circle, or even running on the National Mall, I'm navigating the map that L'Enfant dreamed up. My physical reality was once an idea in the mind of Pierre Charles L'Enfant.

That's true of everything, even you. The psalmist said it best:

> For you created my inmost being;
>> you knit me together in my mother's womb.
> I praise you because I am fearfully and wonderfully made;
>> your works are wonderful,
>> I know that full well.
> My frame was not hidden from you
>> when I was made in the secret place,
>> when I was woven together in the depths of the earth.
> Your eyes saw my unformed body;
>> all the days ordained for me were written in your book
>> before one of them came to be.[1]

You were once an idea in the mind of almighty God. And God only has good ideas! You are the physical manifestation of God's eternal plans and purposes. Simply put, you are God's *what if*. And just as God created you, you are called to create.

Just five words into Genesis, God creates the heavens and the earth. It's the first revelation of God's character. Then, when you get to the next to last chapter of Revelation, God is creating a new heaven and a new earth. From start to finish, God never stops creating. It's who He is. It's what He does. And we are most like Him when we exercise our creative capacity to serve His purposes on earth.

ONE GOD IDEA

I'd rather have one God idea than a thousand good ideas.

Good ideas are good, don't get me wrong. But it's God ideas that change the course of history. Simply put, a God idea is an idea that doesn't originate with you. It's the divine *what if*. They often start out as fleeting thoughts or crazy ideas. But it's those ideas that put God's glory on display.

Ebenezer's coffeehouse has had more than a million customers, but it was once a crazy idea that fired across my synapses: *This crack house would make a great coffeehouse.* I knew that idea was either a God idea or a bad idea. It's often tough to discern the difference, but the only way to find out is to give it a go.

After hosting a Convoy of Hope outreach at DC's RFK stadium for ten thousand people, I heard the Holy Spirit whisper, *Now I want you to do this every day!*

It took an entire year to plan for and pull off that outreach, so the idea of doing it every day seemed crazy! But by definition, a God-ordained dream is beyond your ability to pull off. That was the genesis of our Dream Center in DC.

Every book I've written was once a *what if*, including *If*.

The Circle Maker was my first book to hit the *New York Times* bestseller list, my first book to sell more than a million copies. The genesis of the book was an illustration for one of my sermons.

I told a story about Honi the Circle Maker, and the Holy Spirit said in His still small voice, *That illustration is your next book.*

My first published book, *In a Pit with a Lion on a Snowy Day*, traces back to a sermon I heard when I was nineteen years old—the first time I heard the story about King David's bodyguard, Benaiah, who chased a lion into a pit on a snowy day and killed it.[2]

And the title for *All In*, believe it or not, traces back to a poker tournament I saw on ESPN.

Each book has a unique genealogy. It begins with a genesis moment—that moment when a God idea is conceived in the spirit. The revelation is taking those ideas captive with a keyboard and making them obedient to Christ. I don't type on the keyboard; I pray with it. So when I'm finished, it's not a two-hundred-page book—it's a two-hundred-page prayer. Each book I write is a unique manifestation of what God is doing in my spirit. Then I use the twenty-six letters of the English alphabet to spell out that *what if*.

Let me say it one more time.

Everything that exists was once an idea, from Noah's ark to Solomon's temple. Long before a long alphabet of animals entered the ark or Jewish pilgrims journeyed thousands of miles to Jerusalem, the ark and the temple were divine *what ifs*.

So what's *your what if*?

If you don't know, it's okay. God will reveal it in His time, in His way. But for some of you, it might be closer than you think. You don't have to travel halfway around the world to discover your *what if*. It could be the two-foot-tall toddler who is tugging on you, the colleague who is without Christ, or someone God has brought into your sphere of influence who needs a mentor.

Your *what if* might be a *who if*.

WHO IF

What do Billy Graham, Campus Crusade for Christ founder Bill Bright, Young Life founder Jim Rayburn, Navigators founder

Dawson Trotman, and former Senate chaplain Richard Halverson have in common?

The answer is a Sunday school teacher named Henrietta Mears.

If the kingdom of God were a multilevel marketing pyramid, each of them would be Henrietta Mears's downline. Perhaps that's why *Christianity Today* dubbed her "the grandmother of us all."[3]

When Henrietta was thirty-eight years old, she moved from Minnesota to a burgeoning town called Hollywood, California. Her *what if* was the Sunday school at First Presbyterian Church in Hollywood, which Henrietta led to an astounding attendance of 6,500 students. For four decades, she faithfully devoted herself to her passion of building a cradle-to-grave Sunday school. While she was at it, she also started a publishing company called Gospel Light and a conference center called Forest Home, and she wrote a book, *What the Bible Is All About*, which has sold more than three million copies.

It's impossible to estimate how many millions of people have heard the gospel through the collective efforts of her protégés, but her kingdom influence is far greater than the six degrees of Kevin Bacon. It was her passion for Christ that fueled those pupils' fire.

Take the ministry that Bill Bright started, now called CRU. At last count, CRU had 20,000 full-time staff plus 663,000 trained volunteers in 181 countries. The ministry offshoots include Athletes in Action, Student Venture, and the Jesus Film Project. An estimated 3.4 billion people have heard the gospel through CRU.[4]

Bill Bright and his band of brothers, known as The Fellowship of the Burning Heart, shaped the twenty-first century way beyond our ability to connect the dots. Even my salvation is hyperlinked to Henrietta's influence on a young evangelist named Billy Graham. Billy Graham called her "one of the finest Christians I have ever known." It was a consultation with the teacher that turned into a defining moment in Billy's ministry. He walked away

143

from that encounter with a holy confidence in Holy Scripture, and it changed the way he preached. Several decades later, the Billy Graham Association produced a film called *The Hiding Place*. And it was after watching that film that I put my faith in Christ.

Toward the end of her life, Henrietta Mears offered what could well be considered her own eulogy:

> When I get old and decrepit, I'm going to draw myself up to a television and hear my voice speak around the world. It's just wonderful to think that what we speak and do are translated some way, in a most mystical and marvelous way, to other individuals and they in turn spread it out and out and out until the circle is so immense that we haven't any idea.[5]

You may not influence millions of people, but you may influence one person who influences millions. You might be parenting or coaching or teaching or mentoring the next Henrietta Mears, the next Billy Graham, the next Bill Bright. Whatever they accomplish for the kingdom of God is part of your spiritual downline!

At the very end of his letter to the Romans, Paul shares his *who's who* list. There are twenty-nine names—Paul's upline and downline.

Who's on your Romans 16 list?

Who's your *who if*?

My greatest legacy is not the church I pastor or the books I write. My greatest legacy is our three children. They are my *who if*. While no parent should take all of the credit or all of the blame for who their children become, children are a manifestation of their family of origin. They are the time capsules we send to the next generation. And there is no more important *what if* than the *who ifs* God entrusts to us as parents.

One last observation: As a child of God, you aren't just a manifestation of your biological family. You are a manifestation of your spiritual family—your true family of origin. If you let Him, the Spirit of God will manifest the Father and the Son through you.

STATION X

Fifty miles northwest of London, a fifty-eight-acre estate was purchased by the Secret Intelligence Service during World War II. Operating under the cover name of Station X, it was there that a very eclectic team of code breakers intercepted and decrypted enemy communications. Those encrypted codes were called "ultra secret," superseding the "most secret" classification.

The word *manifestation* means "full disclosure." More specifically, it's the disclosure of secrets. That is part of the Holy Spirit's portfolio—He's the code breaker. The Spirit manifests the secrets of the heart, the ultra secrets.[6] Over time, who you are is revealed by the manifestation of God's Spirit. The final reveal will happen when you are given a new name—a name known only to God.[7] It will be the ultimate *aha*, the full disclosure.

Back to *what if*.

Don't think that your *what if* has to be something grand and glorious. You can turn your mundane tasks and everyday routines into *what ifs*. And if you learn to approach every encounter, every person with a *what if* attitude, it adds an element of adventure. It's that *what if* attitude that the writer of Hebrews advocates.

> Do not forget to show hospitality to strangers, for by so doing some people have shown hospitality to angels without knowing it.[8]

Sometimes *what if* is as simple as acting *as if* everyone were an angel. And even if they aren't angels, they are image bearers of almighty God. Simply put, there are no ordinary people. In the words of C. S. Lewis,

> You have never talked to a mere mortal. Nations, cultures, arts, civilizations—these are mortal, and their life is to ours as the life of

a gnat. But it is immortals whom we joke with, work with, marry, snub, and exploit—immortal horrors or everlasting splendors.[9]

Only time will tell whether we become the immortal horrors or everlasting splendors that Lewis referenced. But one way or the other, our true character will be manifested over time and eternity. If you are in Christ, your trend line is *everlasting splendor*. It's your manifest destiny.

MANIFESTATION

When I moved to Washington, DC, one of the first people I met was St. Clair Mitchell. We became fast friends. We played tennis and golf together. We attempted a little business venture that went belly-up, which is quite a bonding experience. But the undercurrent of our relationship was a genuine desire to see a movement of God in our nation's capital.

St. Clair came to the states from the island of Dominica, so his Caribbean accent makes his preaching and praying much cooler than mine! There is one prayer in particular that was uniquely powerful. If he prayed it once, he prayed it a hundred times. And God has been answering that one prayer for two decades now:

Let Washington, DC, see the manifestation of the glory of God!

It helps to think of manifestation in meteorological terms.

The pressure exerted by the earth's atmosphere is commonly referred to as barometric pressure. At sea level, average air pressure is 14.7 pounds per square inch. If you climb a fourteener in Colorado, the air pressure at that altitude dips to less than 10 pounds per square inch.

When you get into the presence of God, it's like a slight yet sudden shift in barometric pressure. It takes time to acclimatize, but over time, the glory of God will manifest in any number of ways. Two obvious examples are the fruit of the Spirit and the gifts of the Spirit. The fruit is character and the gifts are capacities, but both are manifestations. It's the same word used in 1 Corinthians 12:7:

> To each one the manifestation of the Spirit is given.

Each of us is a unique manifestation of God's Spirit. We might have identical gifts, but they are exercised through different personalities, in different contexts.

I have a theory, very similar to my theory of everything. Just as *more of the Holy Spirit* is the answer to every prayer, I believe that *the solution to every problem is found in the presence of God.* If you need counseling, get counseling. I'm all for it. But you don't just need *a* counselor, you need *the* Counselor.

No matter how big or how bad the problem, the solution is getting into God's presence. How? The quickest way to get into God's presence is by getting into God's Word.

It's unlike any other book in my library. As inspiring as many of those books are, they are made of dead trees. The Word is living and active.[10] And when the Holy Spirit quickens the Word, it becomes a life-giving force. It's like a shot of adrenaline. It's like a hit of oxygen.

Pure Oxygen

A few years ago, I hiked the Inca Trail to Machu Picchu. When we got to Dead Woman's Pass, with an elevation over 13,000 feet, I got a headache because I wasn't getting enough oxygen to my brain. At that elevation, the atmosphere has 43 percent less oxygen. Fortunately, our guide pulled out a can of pure oxygen. Yes, I inhaled.

God's presence is pure oxygen.

Nothing shifts barometric pressure like worship—it changes and charges the atmosphere. And when you acclimatize, you have far more faith.

We recently did a sermon series at National Community Church based on my last book, *The Grave Robber*. We decided to end it with a five-hour night of worship and prayer. Why not? It wasn't about giving God a five-hour time limit to perform a miracle. I reckoned that even if we didn't experience any miracles that night, we'd be five hours closer to it!

It's not my job to tell God how to do His job. I simply need to get into God's presence and see what God does. It's very difficult to predict when and where and how God will manifest His glory, but worship creates the atmosphere where God's glory can become tangible.

We had a saying in the church I grew up in: "It's not about how high you jump; it's about how straight you walk." The proof is in the pudding—living out your faith Monday to Friday. But worship is what jump-starts our spiritual battery. Without it, the engine won't start. With it, our fuel efficiency is out of this world.

I'm not sure we fully understand what we're praying when we pray the Lord's Prayer: "your kingdom come, your will be done, on earth as it is in heaven."[11]

We're praying that the reality of heaven—a place where there is no pain, no sickness, no sin—would invade the reality of our family, our office, our church, our city.

We're praying that earth would become the mirror image of heaven—from the locker room to the boardroom to the classroom.

We're praying for a manifestation of God's presence, God's glory, in our zip code.

May His kingdom come!

May His will be done!

On earth as it is in heaven.

What if you were called to influence one person who would influence millions of people?

148

16

The Third Wheel

Who have the firstfruits of the Spirit.

Romans 8:23

"Why are you driving in D4?"

We were driving west on Route 66, our executive leadership team crammed into my 2006 Toyota Sienna, when Jim Tanious, our COO, asked me that question.

To be honest, it completely confused me.

For the record, I don't have a mechanical bone in my body. I owned my first car for two years before discovering I needed to change the oil, not just add oil. I once tried jump-starting my car by connecting the cables to something other than the battery. Sparks flew! Further exhibiting my lack of automotive knowledge, one of my favorite phrases used to be "hitting on all five cylinders" until someone informed me that most cars have four, six, or eight cylinders.[1]

I'm clueless when it comes to cars, but this one gets the blue ribbon. For nearly a decade, I drove our minivan in the wrong gear—D4. Perhaps that explains the high-pitched screeching noise now emanating from the engine region. We logged more than 100,000 miles, and I had no idea there was a fifth gear!

Spiritually speaking, most of us are driving in D4. We're trying so hard to steer clear of sin. And when that doesn't work, we try even harder. We're pushing the RPMs with human effort, but there is a fifth gear. His name is the Holy Spirit. And if you let Him, He'll do for you what you cannot do for yourself. He gives wisdom beyond words, stamina beyond strength, gifting beyond ability.

I certainly believe in working as if it depends on you, but without the help of the Holy Spirit, you'll get an A for effort and still fail miserably. Without the help of the Holy Spirit, I can't do a blamed thing.[2] With His help, I can do all things.

TWO-THIRDS CAPACITY

I was speaking at a conference for Hispanic pastors when I first met Cash Luna, the founding pastor of the largest church in Guatemala, *Casa De Dios*. Cash gave me a copy of his book, *In Honor of the Holy Spirit*. The title perfectly captures the tone of the book—it honors the Holy Spirit. But it's the subtitle that struck me: *He's Someone, Not Something*.

I don't know one Christ follower who would argue with that statement, yet many of us treat the Holy Spirit like He's the third wheel, not the third person of the Trinity. If you don't honor the Holy Spirit as an equal member of the Triune Godhead, you dishonor the Father and the Son. And you're operating at two-thirds spiritual capacity.

Let me let you in on a little secret: how you treat my children dictates how I feel about you. I love people who love on my kids! If, on the other hand, you treat me like a king while acting as if my kids don't exist, I'm deeply offended. I can't help but wonder if that's how the Father and Son feel about the Holy Spirit.

He is ignored in too many churches, but let's make it personal. He is ignored by too many people. When was the last time you told the Holy Spirit you love Him? Or thanked Him for what He does? When was the last time you prayed to the Holy Spirit? Or worshiped Him? Lots of genuine believers get uncomfortable at this point. We can relate to the Father and the Son, but the Holy Spirit makes us a lot more uncomfortable.

I grew up in churches that ignored the Holy Ghost—probably because the word *ghost* is a little spooky. I knew more about Casper the Friendly Ghost than I did the Holy Ghost. Whenever the Holy Spirit showed up in Scripture, it's almost like we blinked. Then when I was a teenager, our family started attending a church that actually acknowledged the existence of the Holy Spirit. In fact, it was a church that sought to be Spirit-filled and Spirit-led.

To be honest, it felt uncomfortable at first. Sometimes it even felt like a Corinthian freak show. But here's what I discovered: *if you ignore one-third of the Godhead, you function at two-thirds capacity.* It doesn't make you any less saved, and you certainly have the firstfruits of the Spirit. But there is untapped potential. There are dimensions of joy and grace and power that can only be accessed with the Holy Spirit's help. So if you ignore the Holy Spirit, you do so to your own detriment. You're the one who misses out.

Back to Cash's book.

After he handed me a copy, I asked him how long it took him to write it. Since my writing seasons are typically three to four months, I was shocked by his answer—ten years. Then Cash explained why it took a decade. After writing the first chapter, he felt a check in his spirit. He felt like he needed to get to know the Holy Spirit better before writing about Him. Then, and only then, he started writing about the One he'd spent ten years getting to know.

I'm afraid we treat the Holy Spirit like a casual acquaintance. We know His name but very little else. And I'm not even talking about His portfolio as a member of the Godhead. I'm talking about His voice, His personality, and His idiosyncrasies.

I was so convicted by what Cash said that I embarked on an experiment. You may want to do what I did. I felt like I needed to rediscover the Holy Spirit, so I read, studied, and meditated on every snapshot of the Holy Spirit in Scripture—from Genesis 1 to Revelation 22. It took me several months, but I fell in love with the Holy Spirit all over again.

FIRSTFRUITS

The Great Eight says we have the "firstfruits" of the Spirit.[3] Interesting word choice. Its etymology is agricultural, referencing Israel's two harvests. After the first harvest, the Israelites would take a firstfruits offering to the temple. According to Levitical law, if they honored God with the firstfruits, then God would bless the second harvest.

That principle of firstfruits is a high leverage point.

God doesn't want your leftovers. He wants the firstfruits. The tithe isn't any 10 percent; it's the *first* 10 percent. And when we honor God by giving the firstfruits back to Him, it invokes a blessing on the latter harvest. It's our 100 percent money-back guarantee, complete with lifetime warranty.

Twenty-two years ago, Lora and I made a defining decision that we would never *not* tithe. We've had our lean years, but God has proven faithful time and again. The old saying is true: you can't out-give God. But it sure is fun trying! I'm absolutely convinced that God can do more with 90 percent than I can do with 100 percent. And you can take that to the bank.

The apostle Paul takes the concept of firstfruits and applies it to the Holy Spirit. He says we have the firstfruits. I wonder if that is what some of us settle for. I'm not sure it's meant to be interpreted literally, but some of us are operating at 10 percent capacity.

No matter how greatly you've been used by God, He has new anointings, new giftings for you. The Holy Spirit doesn't just want to fill you—He wants to stretch you. And when He stretches you, you never return to the original shape.

Let me go back to the idea of guarantee. It's spelled out in fine print:

> He anointed us, set his seal of ownership on us, and put his Spirit in our hearts as a deposit, guaranteeing what is to come.[4]

Did you catch the last phrase? It's full of promise, full of hope. *What is to come* equals *what if*. It comes with a guarantee, but we've got to take it to settlement.

Can you imagine selling something and settling for a 10 percent deposit? Yet that's what we do when we invite the Holy Spirit to take up residence within us, then act as if He isn't there. Like a family member who is present physically yet absent emotionally, the Holy Spirit becomes a stranger in the house. The irony is that He owns the house because He paid for it.[5] So you're the renter!

We let Him in the front door when we put our faith in Christ, but He wants us to open every door—the basement door, the bedroom door, the closet door.

Ephesians 5:18 exhorts us: "Be filled with the Spirit."

First things first: *you cannot be filled with the Holy Spirit if you're full of yourself*. An emptying process needs to happen through confession and repentance. And like the infilling of the Holy Spirit, it's not one and done. "Be filled" is a present imperative verb, which indicates continuous action. Like a gas tank that needs to be filled and refilled, we need to pull into "Station X" and pump some high-octane Holy Spirit into our tanks.

VACUUMS

The last phrase in the last verse of Ephesians 1 reveals a unique dimension of God's personality. It describes Him as the God who "fills everything in every way."[6] That's the nature of God: God fills vacuums.

That is one of our mantras as a multisite church. When we went multisite and launched our second campus, we were concerned about losing half of our leaders to the new location. It's often our best leaders who sign up for the launch team because they have an entrepreneurial streak. We were afraid that the original campus would function at 50 percent capacity, but we learned very quickly that launching new locations created a vacuum, and God fills those vacuums with new people.

Seven campuses later, we intentionally create vacuums so that God can fill them. Is it easy fielding seven worship teams every weekend? Nope. But we wouldn't have hundreds of gifted drummers, guitarists, and vocalists if we had one band. But because we created a vacuum, God has filled it with amazing musicians.

When we give or serve, it creates a vacuum of time, talent, and treasure. Now, I know that none of us has *extra* time or money. Right? But maybe that's because we're saving rather than giving. Conserving rather than serving. In my experience, God fills the vacuum with more of what we gave, plus joy. The next time you have a need, try sowing a seed at your point of need. Then watch the way God supplies all of your needs, according to His riches in glory.[7]

If you give God the firstfruits, you'll reap a second harvest.

Where do you need to create a vacuum so that God can fill it?

There is an old axiom: nature abhors a vacuum. That famous postulate traces all the way back to the Greek physicist-philosopher Parmenides. I would slightly amend it: nature's *God* abhors a vacuum. In terms of quantum mechanics, I believe God is the mysterious fifth force. God is the gluon that holds everything together at a molecular level.

Colossians 1:17 says: "In him all things hold together."

It's God who keeps the planets in orbit. He spins planet Earth around its axis. And He makes thoughts fire across synapses.

I know, I know. Isn't it the forces of nature that do that? Yes and no. It's the forces of nature's God.

Perhaps you're recently divorced. Maybe you've lost a job or lost a loved one this year. Or maybe your last child went off to college or your athletic career ended. In each of those scenarios and a thousand others, a vacuum was created. God wants to fill that vacuum with His Spirit. The same Spirit who hovered over the void is hovering over you. He can bring beautiful order out of utter chaos.

One final footnote.

More than a hundred years ago, General William Booth, the founder of the Salvation Army, said, "The chief dangers which confront the coming century will be religion without the Holy Ghost, Christianity without Christ, forgiveness without repentance, salvation without regeneration, politics without God, heaven without hell."[8]

That's as true of the twenty-first century as it was the twentieth. Religion without the Holy Spirit is a lifeless, listless religion. It's a religion without power. It's legalism without legs. And frankly, it's downright boring.

If you go after the Holy Spirit, you'll discover that the Holy Spirit is coming after you. All you have to do is open the door to your heart and He'll open the door to opportunity—the door to *what if.*

*What if you started giving God the firstfruits
of your time, talent, and treasure?*

17

And It Came to Pass

But if we hope for what we do not yet
have, we wait for it patiently.

Romans 8:25

A quarter-century ago, Richard Thaler published a seven-page letter in a relatively obscure economics journal posing a simple question:

Would you prefer one apple in one year or two apples in one year plus one day?

Seems like a strange hypothetical, right? If you have the patience to wait one whole year for one apple, why not just wait one extra day for two apples? Even if it's the most famous and scrumptious of apples—a crisp Red Delicious!

The survey found that most people would wait one extra day. Then Thaler changed the equation:

Would you rather have one apple today or two apples tomorrow?

Most of the people who would wait one extra day for a second apple in the first question would not wait for a second apple in the second question.[1]

This is the kind of conundrum that gets researchers grants!

Thaler, the mastermind behind this particular study, is a professor of behavioral science and economics at the University of Chicago. He's also the coauthor of *Nudge*, a fascinating exposé on choice architecture and the way small decisions have large and long ramifications.

We'll explore that topic further, but first, the apple enigma.

Thaler was puzzled by our time-inconsistent preferences, so he employed lots of algebraic equations to explore our natural yet sometimes illogical tendencies. His conclusion? We become more impatient with shorter time frames. That's why being put on hold for two minutes seems like phone purgatory and waiting for two seconds at a red light seems like the unforgivable sin.

By the by, if you live in a city with a population of more than a million people, like I do, a pause will seem twice as long as it does to someone who lives in a small town.[2] It's called time-warping. We all have an internal metronome, and it ticks a little faster in the city that it does in the country.

In the grand scheme of things, a two-minute wait or two-second delay are no big deal, right? But in short time frames, we are incredibly impatient. Now, that is actually good news because the opposite is also true: *the longer you wait, the easier it is to wait a little longer*. Why? You're strengthening your patience muscle! And that is Paul's point. In a phrase, *wait for it*. Or for effect, triple it up like the movies do with a dramatic pause and higher pitch in between each *wait for it*.

Plotlines don't go from conflict to climax without rising action. You'd walk out of that movie. Of course, it's much easier to enjoy the *wait for it* in a two-hour film about someone else's life! It's much more difficult if you're, say, Caleb, one of the twelve spies who had to wait for forty-five years for the fulfillment of the promise—his piece of the Promised Land.

But isn't that what makes his life so epic? We want success without the compound interest called patience, but that isn't a movie worth watching or a life worth living. We want success at the speed of light instead of the speed of a seed planted in the ground. We want two apples yesterday. But success in any endeavor takes time, and then it takes more time.

GET RICH QUICK

When I was in my twenties, I wanted to get rich quick, so I started trading options. Looking back, I wouldn't call it investing. Not when you know as little as I did. Frankly, it was gambling. The problem is that I hit the jackpot my first month, tripling our portfolio. Of course, I lost all those net gains the next month. I rode that roller coaster for several years until I realized that it wasn't healthy for my heart. So I quit before it became a full-fledged addiction.

I wish I could say that my bad investments ended there, but I was just getting started. Around that time, I got some inside information about a potential merger, so I bought as many shares of that company as I could. That's how I learned a painful financial lesson: if you're an "outsider" who is supposedly getting "inside" information, it might not be inside information; it might in fact be *bad* information. I invested our life savings in that stock, which fortunately wasn't much money eighteen years ago, because we lost the whole nest egg. The big news wasn't a merger; it was Chapter 11 bankruptcy!

Oh, and then there was the time I invested in a fund with amazing monthly returns. So amazing that the fund manager is now in prison! After years of court proceedings, we got back a fraction of our original investment.

The common denominator in each of those instances was good old-fashioned greed, and greed is financial impatience. Far be it from me to tell you what financial instrument to invest in, but I do want to advocate for patience. It goes by another name: compound interest.

For the record, if your great-grandparents had purchased one share of Coca-Cola stock in 1919 for $40, and simply reinvested the dividends, that one share would have split into 4,608 shares by the year 2000 and be worth $7 million.

If your great-great-great-grandparents had purchased one of Asa Candler's original Coca-Cola shares in 1892, that $100 investment would have been worth $7.34 billion a hundred years later.

That is the power of compound interest.

That is the power of patience.

And it's more than just a financial concept.

Lora and I have been happily married for twenty years, and we'll celebrate our twenty-third anniversary this year. I'll let you do the math. We had a few tough years in there! But there is a compound interest with each anniversary. Our love hasn't just stood the test of time; it has accrued interest. That's what happens when you reinvest the dividends!

That compound interest, whether it's financial or relational, is called patience. And it leads to some amazing miracles.

DAY-TIGHT COMPARTMENTS

Sir William Osler was the most famous physician of his generation. He organized the Johns Hopkins School of Medicine and served as Regius Professor of Medicine at Oxford University. Considered the father of psychosomatic medicine, his textbook, *The Principles and Practice of Medicine*, was the principal reference book for medical students for three decades.

But Osler's medical career almost ended as soon as it had started because of a nervous breakdown. He was trying to finish his academic requirements, start a medical practice, and make ends meet—all at the same time. It nearly killed him. Then he came across something that Thomas Carlyle wrote: "Our main business is not to see what lies dimly at a distance, but to do what lies clearly at hand."[3] Those words revolutionized Osler's life.

In a commencement address at Yale University, Osler told the students that he owed his success to a simple principle he learned from Thomas Carlyle. He called it: *living in day-tight compartments.*[4] He told the students that they needed to let go of dead yesterdays and unborn tomorrows. "The load of tomorrow," he said, "added to that of yesterday, carried today, makes the strongest falter."[5]

In *The Screwtape Letters*, C. S. Lewis demonstrates that God wants humankind to attend chiefly to two things: "to eternity itself, and to that point of time which they call the Present. For the Present is the point at which time touches eternity."

In light of that truth, Screwtape, the veteran demon, advises a novice named Wormwood with these words: "Our business is to get them away from the eternal, and from the Present. With this in view, we sometimes tempt a human . . . to live in the Past."

Screwtape then advises Wormwood about another demonic tactic—getting people to live in the future. "We want a whole race perpetually in pursuit of the rainbow's end, never honest, nor kind, nor happy *now*, but always using as mere fuel wherewith to heap on the altar of the future every real gift which is offered them in the Present."[6]

Whether we're overcoming lifelong addictions or going after life goals, one key to accomplishing things is breaking them down into manageable and measurable steps. A goal is a dream with a deadline, and without that deadline, the dream is dead in the water!

Overcoming addictions is typically two steps forward, one step back. And when you have the setback, the temptation is to give up and cash out. But the reality is, you'll win some and lose some. The key is not letting a loss turn into a losing streak. Then you need to turn a win into a winning streak.

I've never met anyone, no matter how addicted they are, who doesn't believe they can defeat their demon for a day. And if we focused all of our attention on today, we'd probably win more than we lose! It's when we focus on forever that we lose the will to fight one more day.

The bottom line is this: *if you want to break a habit, break it down.* Just like boxing, you'll win some rounds and lose some rounds. But you've got to fight one day, one round at a time. Before you know it, your winning streaks will get longer and your losing streaks will get shorter.

THE TEST OF TIME

When I was twenty-two, I was as driven as they come. That's still my default setting, but I recognize it for what it is—a *fault* setting.

We have a twofold 2020 vision at National Community Church. The first half of the vision is twenty expressions—campuses, coffeehouses, and dream centers by the year 2020. The second half is giving $2 million to missions annually.

Now let me let you in on a little secret: I want to get there in 2019 or, better yet, 2018. But nearly twenty years of ministry has taught me to be genuinely grateful for delays and detours. God won't get you where God wants you to go until you're good and ready—He loves you too much to do that to you!

No matter what your *what if* is, I can almost guarantee it'll take longer than you ever imagined. It'll also be harder than you thought it would be. But that's what will make it far more fulfilling. The longer you have to wait, the more you appreciate it. And it's part of the process of making sure that success doesn't lead to failure.

Trust me, you don't want your gifts to take you farther than your character can sustain them. That's a precarious place to be, and your success will be short-lived. If National Community Church had grown larger and faster, I'm not sure my pride could have sustained it. Looking back, I'm glad we were slow and steady. I used to get frustrated that we didn't grow faster, but I now see an upside to what I thought was a downside.

Our growth curve as a church facilitated my growth as a writer. If we had grown faster, I wouldn't have had time to read, which was critical to my evolution as a writer. During our first few years, I averaged more than two hundred books per year. You may question my ability to read that many books, but I was only pastoring twenty-five people; I had time on my hands! And if I hadn't had time to read, it would have stunted my growth as an author.

Just as there are trained musicians who read music and self-taught musicians who play by ear, there are trained writers and self-taught writers. I fall into the latter category. In seminary, I scored very low on an aptitude assessment for writing. The way I compensated for that lack of natural ability was reading everything I could get my hands on.

I didn't just read the words; I studied the style. To one degree or another, every writer becomes a unique combination of their favorite authors. Mine include the modern-day mystic A. W. Tozer; the master of truisms Oswald Chambers; and Malcolm Gladwell, whose ability to cite a scientific study and then come in for the punch line is a writing rope-a-dope.

Now here's my point: I read three thousand books before I wrote one.

Technically speaking, the act of writing that first book only took forty days. But it was the cumulative effect of thirteen years of reading books and living life. It took time, and I'm glad it did. If I'd written a book at twenty-two, I probably would have had to write a sequel to retract what I'd written.

Simply put, writing a book is an exercise in patience. But the more time it takes to accomplish something, the greater the likelihood that it will stand the test of time. And that's my goal.

Allow me an observation.

Most of us know next to nothing about our great-great-grandparents. We might know their names and perhaps a story or two. But that's it. I think one of my great-great-grandparents had the surname of Kimmerly. The only thing I know about him is that he was a train conductor. Only one little piece of family folklore has survived the generational gap.

The backyard of the Kimmerly home bordered the train tracks, and when my great-great-grandfather went by, he'd blow the train whistle. It was a signal to my great-great-grandmother to set the dinner table because he was almost home.

That's it.

That's all I've got.

I want my great-great-grandchildren to know what I lived for. I want them to know my hopes and dreams. I want them to know my story line so they can figure out theirs. I want them to know my *if onlys*, my *as ifs*, my *what ifs*, and my *no ifs, ands, or buts about it*. That's why I write.

To me, a book is a time capsule to the next generation. I want my books to have a long shelf life, and that means lots of life has to go into them. I want them to stand the test of time, and that takes time. And that's true of every *what if*.

Fifty Years

We live in a culture that celebrates fifteen minutes of fame. In God's kingdom, it's all about a lifetime of faithfulness. You know what I respect more and more? Someone who has simply done the right thing, the same thing, for a really long time. You know who the real heroes are? Those who have been married for fifty years. Now that's a lifetime achievement award.

Occasionally, I speak at ordination events where the mantle of ministry is placed on newly ordained pastors. I love that moment because it's full of promise, but there is a moment I love even more. In my church tradition, we celebrate the seasoned veterans who have faithfully served God for fifty years. It always brings tears to my eyes! Most of them can barely walk down the aisle, but I imagine the cloud of witnesses giving a standing ovation in heaven.

A few years ago, I had a *what if* idea. As much as I love innovation, I grew tired of going to conferences to hear the latest and greatest. I'd rather sit at the feet of someone who's been there and done that. So I invited four city fathers to share their story and their hearts with DC area pastors. Between the four of them, they represented a combined 147 years of ministry! And they are still going strong. One hundred fifty DC area pastors attended that first gathering, and God is using it to unify the church in Washington, DC, across racial and denominational lines. My prayer is that its effects will be felt by the next generation.

What if takes time.

Then it takes even more time!

But nothing is more inspiring than a long obedience in the same direction.

One of my dreams is to pastor one church for life. I've got almost two decades under my belt, and I started young enough that I've got a shot at fifty years. I don't think I'll be in a lead role that entire time. At some point, I know I'll get in the way if I don't get out of the way.

I also know that what R. T. Kendall said is true: "The greatest opposition to what God is doing today comes from those who were on the cutting edge of what God was doing yesterday."[7] I'm bound and determined that that won't be me! Success is succession, and God will give me the wisdom to know when to hand off the baton. But even after I hand it off, I'll keep running in the lane right behind whomever I hand it off to, cheering them on as long as my tired old legs can keep up.

AND IT CAME TO PASS

There is a little phrase repeated 436 times in the King James Version of the Bible that I've come to love. It might seem like nothing more than a segue, but I think it's one of the most hopeful statements in all of Scripture.

And it came to pass.

If you can't seem to let go of an *if only* regret, remember, it's not here to stay. It came to pass! And if you're still holding out hope for a *what if* dream, hang in there, it will come to pass!

In his biography, *God in My Corner*, the two-time world heavyweight champion George Foreman tells a story about an elderly woman who was asked her favorite Scripture verse. There are lots of amazing choices, including a few in the Great Eight. But she didn't go with "all things work together for good" or "I can do all things through Christ." Her favorite verse? "And it came to pass." And she explained why: "I know that whenever a trial comes, it doesn't come to stay; it comes—to pass."[8]

Now, that's some good theology right there! And, of course, you can flip the coin. "He who began a good work in you will carry it on to completion."[9] In other words, He'll bring it to pass! Either way, God always finishes what He starts.

A proverb was popularized by the English poet Edward Fitzgerald in an 1852 work titled *Solomon's Seal*. A sultan is said to have asked King Solomon for a sentence that would be true no matter what the circumstances, good or bad. The wisest man in the world said, "This too shall pass." It was that truism to which Abraham Lincoln anchored himself during the depths of the Civil War. "How much it expresses," Lincoln said. "How chastening in the hour of pride! How consoling in the depths of affliction!"[10]

If you're living in the land of *if only* regrets, this too shall pass!

If you're exercising *as if* faith, it will come to pass!

Wait for it . . . wait for it . . . wait for it.

The best is yet to come!

What if you started living in day-tight compartments?

165

18

Narrow Framing

He who searches our hearts knows the mind of the Spirit.

Romans 8:27

On September 14, 1964, the freighter *Al Kuwait* capsized in the harbor of Kuwait City. An estimated one million ships have sunk in the world's waters, but this one created a unique problem because its cargo consisted of six thousand sheep—and the freighter went down near the city's desalinization plant.

Biological toxins from decomposing sheep threatened the city's only source of potable drinking water, and the clock was ticking. The Danish company that insured the *Al Kuwait* gave a Danish engineer, Karl Kroyer, the seemingly impossible task of raising the sunken ship without spilling its cargo. *How do you raise a twenty-seven-ton freighter that is listing at 87 degrees on the floor of the Persian Gulf?*

The nearest floating crane was in Sydney, Australia, so that option was out. But once again, the old English proverb proved true: necessity is the mother of invention.

How the solution was arrived at is the subject of debate. One version credits one of Kroyer's young colleagues, while a far-more-fun version credits a 1949 Donald Duck comic book, in which Donald Duck raises a sunken yacht by filling it with Ping-Pong balls. One way or the other, that's precisely what Karl Kroyer did on the last day of December 1964. The hull of the *Al Kuwait* was filled with 27 million plastic balls weighing 65 tons, and just like Donald's yacht, it floated to the surface.

The cost of saving the ship was $345,000—not a bad return on investment for the insurance company that would have paid out the full $2 million policy. And Karl Kroyer walked away with a $186,000 payday.

Some of the best ideas seem to come out of nowhere, but once again, every idea has a genealogy. Some have interesting origins, like a Donald Duck comic. Others follow a more predictable path, like a college education. One way or the other, I don't believe in accidental ideas. Just as fortune favors the prepared, the best ideas typically come from the most widely and well-used minds. God doesn't bless laziness, including intellectual laziness.

Whether it's the Bible or any other subject matter, we should study to show ourselves approved.[1]

I have a longstanding conviction that dates back to my undergrad days at the University of Chicago: *every* ology *is a branch of* *theology*. In other words, every realm of creation reveals something of the Creator's power, personality, and purpose. That's why my bookshelves are filled with volumes from a wide range of disciplines—theology to psychology, business to biography, neurology to entomology, physics to genetics.

In my experience, breakthrough ideas come from cross-pollination. It's a botanical term that refers to the transfer of pollen from one flower to another, but it can certainly be applied to learning. A little pollen from genetics, for example, heightens our appreciation of Psalm 139.

To fully appreciate how fearfully and wonderfully made we are, a little genetics goes a long way! If your double helix DNA were unraveled, it would stretch 744 million miles—that's long enough to go to the moon and back fifteen hundred times![2] All the *what if* possibilities of your unique personality are preprogrammed within every cell in your body. But no one can unlock those potentialities like the One who knit you together in your mother's womb.

Now let me double back to our side of the sovereignty equation.

Destiny is not a mystery; it's a decision. And how we make those decisions determines our *what if* possibilities. When it comes to decision making, we've got to do our due diligence. But even then, we need the help of the Holy Spirit.

Decision Villain

One of the archenemies of *what if* is narrow framing.

In their brilliant book *Decisive*, authors and brothers Chip and Dan Heath identify narrow framing as one of four decision-making villains.[3] Simply put, it's defining our choices too narrowly. It's only considering two options when there might be a third. It's taking a thin slice of facts into consideration while ignoring the preponderance of evidence.

Sometimes it's turning a blind eye to what's obvious because we want to believe what we want to believe. Sometimes it's because we have blind spots and we don't know what we don't know.

In a fascinating yet disconcerting study of physicians, researchers found that when they reckoned themselves *completely certain* about a diagnosis, they were wrong 40 percent of the time.[4] The obvious implication is this: get a second opinion.

But here's my point: we overestimate our ability to predict the future. Why? Because we think we know more than we know, so we think we control more than we control. Control is an illusion. The reality is, we hardly control anyone or anything, let alone our own thoughts, feelings, and reactions. Does that mean we just leave things to chance? Of course not. Failing to plan is planning to fail. But even the best-laid plans of mice and men need a contingency plan.

Why? Because even the best-intentioned decisions have unintended consequences.

And now that you're paralyzed by fear, let me remind you once again that indecision *is* a decision and inaction *is* an action.

The Heath brothers offer several methods of counteracting narrow framing, including reality-testing your options and attaining distance before deciding. But there's a third method I want to drill down on: widening your options.

For the record, the Bible is the way we do all three. It's the way we reality-test our assumptions against the truth. It's how we attain distance before deciding by getting a God's-eye view. And nothing widens our options like the promises of God. When you read Scripture, you get the perspective of forty authors from three continents and nearly every occupation under the sun, written over a span of two thousand years. Most importantly, each one was inspired by God.

The Sadducees and Pharisees couldn't see the miracles that happened right in front of them because they were using narrow framing. They couldn't imagine the Messiah being born in a stable, healing on the Sabbath, washing feet, or eating with tax collectors. Their religious assumptions created a narrow frame. So despite the preponderance of prophecy and the miracles that happened right before their very eyes, they missed the Messiah.

If you aren't careful, past experience can become a barrier to *what if*. You stop living out of right-brain imagination and start living out of left-brain memory. That's when you stop creating the future and start repeating the past.

Like Peter on the Mount of Transfiguration, we want to pitch a tent and camp there. But Jesus knew there was another miracle waiting for them at the bottom of the mountain.[5] My point? The way you steward a miracle is by believing God for the next miracle—an even bigger and better miracle. In other words, each miracle becomes a high leverage point for *what if*. So as we grow older, our faith gains more and more leverage. There is a compound interest, if you will. So the world doesn't get smaller but gets infinitely larger until "all things are possible."[6]

What got you here might not be what gets you to where God wants you to go next. You can't just climb the learning curve; sometimes you have to jump the curve. No matter how much you've accomplished, you need a new anointing. No matter how old you are, God has new gifts He wants to give you. *What if* demands it.

TWO-DIMENSIONAL WISDOM

"True wisdom has two sides."[7]

That little nugget is my middle C. Or if you prefer, it's my theological tuning fork. Simply put, truth is found in the tension of opposites. Like on a stringed instrument, it's that tension that makes music. Knowledge, by itself, often leads to one-dimensional assumptions. But wisdom, true wisdom, leads to two-dimensional understanding.

The idea of predestination is a good example, and we'll explore it in greater depth in a future chapter. But here's a placeholder: I believe in *both* the sovereignty of God *and* the free will of man. If you don't feel any tension in those counterbalancing truths, you probably have a one-dimensional understanding of something that is two-dimensional. And you probably aren't in proximity to the truth.

Most heresies are the by-product of theological narrow framing. Often it's taking one verse out of context instead of juxtaposing Scripture with Scripture. Sometimes it's giving too much weight to one verse, one practice, or one truth. The result is a theological imbalance that is not unlike a chemical imbalance in the brain. A chemical imbalance can cause a wide variety of mental illnesses, including bipolar disorder. A theological imbalance does the same within the body of Christ. And the resulting divisions can make us seem bipolar to the watching world.

Two-dimensional thinking is thinking outside the box, and the box is the four dimensions of space-time that we exist within. But God exists without. He's not subject to the laws of nature He created. If you make them, you can break them. To the Alpha and Omega, a day is like a thousand years and a thousand years are like a day. To the Omnipresent One, there is no here or there. He is here, there, and everywhere.

It's the Holy Spirit who helps us get outside the box and escape our four-dimensional limitations. Sometimes it's the gifts of the Spirit that take us beyond our ability. Sometimes it's something that could only be revealed by the Spirit of God. Either way, the Holy Spirit widens our options to include any and every *what if.*

SEARCH ENGINE

One of the roles of the Holy Spirit is to search, as in search engine.

The total number of servers Google employs is a well-kept secret, but one recent estimate puts the total at 2,376,640.[8] Using a search algorithm called PageRank, Google crawls 20 billion websites every day and performs over 100 billion searches per month.[9]

Those of us who grew up with the card catalogue system harbor a little resentment toward those who never had to search by subject, author, or title. We also marvel at the internet's capacity to put knowledge at our fingertips. It's one click away! Yet as remarkable as that is, it doesn't hold a candle to the Holy Spirit's search engine. After all, there is nothing He doesn't know.

The Spirit searches all things, even the deep things of God.[10]

The number of hairs on your head.
Every subconscious memory and subliminal desire.

The value of pi to the ten millionth decimal and beyond.

You name it, God knows it.

There is nothing that the Omniscient One doesn't know. And He is searching all things, all the time. Why? There is more than one answer to that question. But the Holy Spirit is searching for one primary reason: to reveal what we need to know, when we need to know it.

That plays out in a wide variety of ways. Sometimes it's a *prompting* to do something, like Philip's divine appointment with an Ethiopian eunuch.[11] Sometimes it's the right word at the right time.[12] And sometimes it's a God idea that seems to come out of nowhere. And it's all one prayer, one click away.

STORM THE GATES

I've always loved Arthur McKinsey's poetic description of problem solving.

> If you think of a problem as being like a medieval walled city, then a lot of people will attack it head on, like a battering ram. They will storm the gates and try to smash through the defenses with sheer intellectual power and brilliance. I just camp outside the city. I wait. And I think. Until one day—maybe after I've turned to a completely different problem—the drawbridge comes down and the defenders say, "We surrender." The answer to the problem comes all at once.[13]

Some problems can only be solved in the presence of God. They require revelation, not education. Go ahead and get an education, but you need the Holy Spirit's help with or without it. Go ahead and set up a counseling appointment, but you need the help of the Counselor one way or the other.

You can't attack heart problems head-on—you must attack them heart-on. That's easier if you're a *feeler* versus a *thinker*, in Myers-Briggs–speak. But either way, it takes an intervention by the Holy Spirit.

He has a solution to every problem.

He has an answer to every question.

He has a breakthrough for every bondage.

The way we storm the gates of hell isn't with a battering ram. Prayer is the difference between us fighting for God and God fighting for us. When we pray, the drawbridge comes down. But once again, it requires a two-dimensional approach.

Planning without praying is a waste of time. Praying without planning is a waste of energy. So once again, we must pray as if it depends on God and work as if it depends on us. It's both/and, not either/or.

And when we do both, *what if* is right around the corner.

JOIN THE CHOIR

For four decades, Art Fry worked as a researcher in the new product development department of Minnesota Mining and Manufacturing. One of the perks of working at 3M was the not one but two golf courses on its 475-acre campus. The powers-that-be at 3M were wise enough to recognize that *recreation* is part of creation.

Art Fry was on the back nine of the Red course when a chemical engineer named Spence Silver mentioned a new adhesive he had developed in the lab—microscopic balls of acrylic that formed a weak bond, leaving no residue after being repositioned. Neither of them could think of a single use, until five years later. Art Fry was singing in his church's choir when the piece of paper he was using as a bookmark fell out of the hymnal. It was Art Fry's *what if* moment. I'm not sure what hymn they were singing, but it led to the invention of the Post-it note.[14]

Here's a counterfactual for you.

What if Art Fry hadn't joined his church's choir? Well, who knows how many things you would have forgotten because the Post-it note wouldn't be there to remind you!

My point? Join the choir! What the heck, play a round of golf. And while you're at it, keep an open mind to new ideas!

This is more than an inventive anecdote. It's a biblical injunction.

> Intelligent people are always open to new ideas. In fact, they look for them.[15]

I love the straightforward nature of the Proverbs. Solomon says it like it is, without mincing words. Keep an open mind—that's how you avoid narrow framing.

I can't help but wonder if this proverb was inspired by Solomon's songwriting father, David. No less than six times, the psalmist exhorts us to "sing a new song." In the spirit of two-dimensional wisdom, go ahead and sing the old hymns. They're classics! But thank God for anointed songwriters who, like the ancient psalmist, couple new lyrics with new melodies.

The songwriters on our team at National Community Church—Kurtis, Chris, Joel, Dan, Lina, and others—produce an album every year. It started with an amazing compilation of songs on the character of God called *The God Anthology*. The latest EP is titled *You Alone*. Those new songs keep us from simply lip-syncing!

God doesn't just want to be worshiped out of left-brain memory. He wants to be worshiped out of right-brain imagination too. Few *what ifs* are more powerful than worship!

What if you started praying like it depends on God and working like it depends on you?

19

Out of Your League

The Spirit intercedes for God's people in accordance with the will of God.

Romans 8:27

When I woke up on the morning of August 16, 2014, I had no category for what God would do that day. It surpassed my wildest *what if*.

Before detailing what happened, let me rewind eighteen years.

I never thought our church would own property. Never, as in, *ever*! Land goes for more than $10 million an acre in our neck of the woods. No kidding! So we thought rented facilities would be our only avenue for growth; thus our multisite strategy of meeting in movie theaters around the metro DC area.

Then God started pulling off one real estate miracle after another.

Our first foray into real estate was a Capitol Hill row house that was converted into our church office. That property wasn't even for sale! A Spirit-led, Spirit-timed phone call resulted in a lease with the option to purchase, which we exercised for $225,000. It now appraises for nearly $1,000,000.

The second miracle was right next door—a crack house that we turned into Ebenezer's coffeehouse. The original asking price was $1,000,000, but we got it for $325,000 despite the fact that four parties offered more money for it than we did.

In 2010, we purchased an $8 million piece of property that fronts Interstate 695. We also annexed the oldest commercial building on Capitol Hill, right next door.

Finally, we acquired a century-old theater from the People's Church two blocks away, right at the epicenter of historic Capitol Hill.

Now let me add a very significant footnote. The genesis of all of those real estate miracles was a *what if*—a 4.7-mile prayer walk on August 16, 1996. I felt the Lord prompting me to pray a perimeter around Capitol Hill after I read the promise in Joshua 1:3: "I will give you every place where you set your foot."

It was a *what if* moment.

Now here's the amazing thing—each of those properties is right on the prayer circle! Coincidence? I think not. I don't believe in coincidence. I believe in providence. I believe that God is preparing good works in advance, and I love it when they come with a street address attached to them.

Now, please hear my heart. It's not about buildings! A church that stays within the four walls of a church building isn't a church at all. But if those buildings serve God's purposes, so be it. And let me state the obvious—the Promised Land was *land*. God doesn't just own the cattle on a thousand hills; he owns the hills too! And that includes Capitol Hill.

National Community Church now has seven campuses in the DC area, a coffeehouse on Capitol Hill, and a café in Berlin, Germany. And we're one permit away from building our Dream Center in Washington's Ward 7.

Again, our 2020 vision is twenty expressions—a mix of campuses, coffeehouses, and dream centers. So we're not going to get bored anytime soon! But just when we thought we were dreaming big, God did something we didn't even have a category for. And it took the entire inventory of properties we own to position us for the biggest miracle yet.

INSANE COURAGE

"Sometimes all it takes is twenty seconds of insane courage."

That line from the 2011 film *We Bought a Zoo* ranks as one of my most quoted. I love it because it's so true—twenty seconds of insane courage can change the trajectory of your life!

I also love it because it encapsulates what happened on August 16, 2014. We didn't buy a zoo, but we did buy a castle! And it took twenty seconds of insane courage, plus some cold, hard cash!

Built in 1891 by the Washington and Georgetown Railroad Company, the Blue Castle is one of the most iconic buildings in Washington, DC. It was one of four car barns built to service street-cars at the turn of the nineteenth century. That 100,000-square-foot building sits on 1.64 acres, encompassing an entire city block.

To be honest, my vision wasn't that big. I certainly didn't have a category for its $29.3 million price tag. I knew it would take a miracle, or two, or three!

The first miracle was getting the contract, because we were up against some stiff competition, including an investment firm that offered cash. The second miracle was getting a loan, because banks don't like financing churches—no one wants to foreclose on God. The third miracle was coming up with a deposit in sixty days, and a $4.5 million gift put us in position to do just that.

Now let me share a lesson and one more footnote.

The lesson is this: sometimes faith can be measured in dollars.

Make no mistake about it, it takes $1,000 worth of faith to tithe on $10,000; it takes $10,000 worth of faith to tithe on $100,000; and it takes $100,000 worth of faith to tithe on $1 million.

In the same vein, each of the real estate miracles God has done have required a measure of faith. It took $2.7 million worth of faith to turn a crack house into Ebenezer's coffeehouse. It's taking $3.8 million worth of faith to turn a dilapidated apartment complex into our Dream Center. And it took $29.3 million worth of faith to buy a castle and turn it into a church campus. But that's how God stretches our faith. And because of the value of the air rights above the Castle, I have a holy hunch that this miracle might just pay for itself.

Please don't get distracted by the numbers.

Stewardship isn't about how many zeroes there are in your salary or your savings. It's about stewarding every penny, no matter how little or how much you have. I remember well when our total church income was $2,000 a month and it cost $1,600 to rent the DC public school where we met. That left $400 for my salary, plus all other expenses. Yet long before we were self-supporting as a church, we started investing in missions with a $50 check. It was our way of putting our money where our faith was. And that $50 *what if* has multiplied into the $1.7 million we invested in missions last year.

TO THE DAY

When I did my 4.7-mile prayer walk around Capitol Hill in 1996, I rounded the corner at 8th and M Streets SE—the corner where the Blue Castle sits. That is no geographical coincidence, and neither is the chronology. The letter of intent was signed eighteen years *to the day* from the day I prayed that circle. It would be just as amazing if it had been the day before or the day after, but sometimes God puts an exclamation mark on His answers!

Our real estate agent would point to August 16, 2014, as the day we entered into a contractual agreement, but I point to August 16, 1996. When you pray in the will of God, it doubles as a binding contract. You may still have to circle it for weeks or months or years, but the same God who began a good work will bring it to closing. It took eighteen years for us to exercise the option, but this I know for sure: the Holy Spirit was interceding for us every single day in between.

Your dream may seem like it's a million miles, a million years, or a million dollars away. But don't despise the day of small beginnings. If you do little things like they're big things, someday God will do big things like they're little things!

The Castle was way out of our league, but so was Ebenezer's coffeehouse a decade ago. We had no business going into the coffeehouse business, but that didn't keep us from asking *what if*.

God's anointing is no substitute for a solid business plan, but a solid business plan can't substitute for the anointing either. Before we opened Ebenezer's coffeehouse, we anointed the doors and prayed that people would sense the presence of God when they walked in. Our success is because of His anointing—no ifs, ands, or buts about it. I think it makes the coffee taste a little better too!

OUT OF YOUR LEAGUE

When I don't know how to pray, I take heart in the fact that the Holy Spirit is interceding for me. Prayer is a team sport, a tag-team with the Holy Spirit. The Spirit of God isn't just praying *for* us. He is praying *through* us. And it usually happens in moments when we're asking for something that is way past our pay grade.

That's what happened when we submitted our offer for the Blue Castle. After we got the contract, we discovered that the sellers had at first decided to award the contract to another bidder. I didn't know it at the time, but on that very same day, I felt an incredible compulsion to pray. It was so strong that I couldn't focus on anything else, so I spent the next couple of hours on the rooftop of Ebenezer's, my favorite prayer perch, pacing and praying.

I didn't know exactly what to pray or how to pray. Then I felt this right-field impression that I needed to pray that the God who changed the mind of Pharaoh would change the minds of those making the decision. I prayed for the decision makers by name. Every way I knew how, I prayed that God would change their minds. That's my only explanation for how we got the contract. I don't think the sellers even understood why they decided to give us the contract, and I know the real estate agent was surprised. Why give a contract to a church when an investment firm offers cash?

When it came to negotiating for the Blue Castle, we were way out of our depth. But when you tag-team with the Holy Spirit, you're never out of your league. You're in league with the Holy Spirit. No one can network or negotiate like the Holy Spirit—He knows everyone, knows everything. And He is interceding for our God-ordained *what ifs*.

Sometimes it's divine revelation. Sometimes it's a divine appointment.

The Holy Spirit is both inspiring and conspiring.

Not long ago, a staff member told me she was specifically praying for divine appointments that were out of her league. I had been preaching on the second miracle in John's Gospel, where Jesus heals a royal official's son. One of the subplots in that story is the simple fact that the royal official was in a position of political power over Jesus, yet he submitted to Jesus' spiritual authority.

I stated the obvious in my message: *if you follow Jesus, royal officials will come knocking on your door.* And that's what this woman prayed for. Just a few days later, there was a knock on her door late at night. If she hadn't been praying for a divine appointment that was out of her league, she may not have even answered the door.

While I'm not at liberty to identify her visitor, he is someone who holds a position of great influence. He was preparing for a speech and needed someone to pray for him. He happened to drive by my friend's home and noticed a light on. This friend ended up sharing some Spirit-inspired thoughts that made it into this man's speech.

Who is out of your league?

What is out of your depth?

The answer is no one and nothing. Not when you have the Holy Spirit on your side, on the inside.

Our prayers are limited by our lack of knowledge—we don't know what we don't know. That's why I trust His intercession more than my intuition. That's also why I often preface my prayers with a preamble: *Lord, I want what you want more than I want what I want.* I first heard that prayer from one of our campus pastors, Dave Schmidgall, when he and his wife were making an offer to buy their first home. That prayer is the way they put the ball back in God's court.

Prayer must be in alignment with the will of God or it's null and void. It's not like turning your back to Trevi Fountain and throwing a penny over your left shoulder. If it's not God's will, you're not going to get whatever you ask for. God loves you far too much to spoil you in that way.

But if it is God's will, God will make a way.

Even if it's out of your league!

NO CATEGORY

One of my daily disciplines is journaling. I try to do it every single day, without fail. It's part *gratitude* journal—I literally count my blessings by numbering them. It's part *dream* journal—it's where I write down some of the God ideas I'm not ready to verbalize just yet. It's part *prayer* journal—it's full of people and promises that I'm circling. And it's part *journal* journal—I take notes during sermons, during meetings, during hikes through the woods.

At the end of every year, one of my annual rituals is rereading every journal entry. Few exercises are more meaningful. It screams, "God is faithful!" It connects the dots between prayers asked and prayers answered. And it resurfaces some of the lessons God has taught me throughout the year.

One of those themes originated with our pastor of prayer, Heidi Scanlon. During a staff devotional one day, she said something that made it into my aforementioned journal: "God has blessings for us in categories we don't even know exist."

That's a paraphrase of the promise in Ephesians 3:20: God "is able to do immeasurably more than all we ask or imagine." I didn't have a category for a castle, but God did. Evidently, I was dreaming too small. Then God, the One who creates out of nothing, came out of nowhere and gave us something we didn't have a category for.

During our most recent staff planning retreat, I was reviewing our strategic plans from the last decade. I laughed a few times and blushed a few times. Those plans were our best effort at the time, but God had a surprise around every corner!

I'm not omniscient, which means I don't have a 360-degree perspective. I can't see all the way around every situation. I can't even see around corners, including the corner of 8th and M Street, where the Castle sits!

On my best day, I see a very thin slice of reality. But here's some good news: long before you woke up this morning and long after you go to sleep tonight, the Holy Spirit is interceding for you in accordance with God's will.

If that doesn't give you a holy confidence, nothing will. You still have to do your due diligence because God doesn't bless negligence. But you also need to trust God. He has wisdom beyond your knowledge, power beyond your strength, and favor beyond your ability. And He has them without measure. So maybe, just maybe, you should relax.

God's got everything under control. Even better, He's got blessings for you in categories you don't even know exist yet.

So sit back, relax, and enjoy the ride!

*What if everything in your past is God's way
of preparing you for something in your future?*

20

The Kingdom of
Unintended Consequences

All things work together for good.

Romans 8:28 NKJV

In 1936, Harvard professor Robert K. Merton published a paper titled *The Unanticipated Consequences of Purposive Social Action*. One of the founding fathers of modern-day sociology, Merton coined the concepts of "role model" and "self-fulfilling prophecy."

But his most famous and most enduring contribution was spelled out in his groundbreaking thesis on "the law of unintended consequences." Simply put, the outcome of our actions have unintended consequences that are beyond our ability to control, beyond our ability to predict.

Those unforeseen consequences fall into three categories. On the positive side of the ledger, there are added bonuses called *unexpected benefits*. On the negative side, there are *unexpected drawbacks*, like the side effect of a medicine that cures a condition while causing complications.

Finally, there are *perverse results*. This is when your original intention bites you in the back. It's also dubbed the cobra effect because of the way a bounty for killing cobras backfired in British India by creating a perverse incentive to breed cobras.[1] The attempted solution backfired, making the problem worse.

Parents instinctively keep babies from eating things that are dirty. After all, they might get sick. But according to the hygiene hypothesis, bacteria actually help spur the development of a healthy immune system. And worms, believe it or not, autocorrect the immune system, helping it fight a wide variety of autoimmune disorders.[2] So by protecting our children from getting sick, loving parents actually disable their ability to fight disease later in life. I'm certainly not suggesting that you add dirt to their diet, but perhaps we should reemploy the five-second rule!

While Robert K. Merton popularized the idea of unintended consequences, it didn't originate with him. John Locke expressed his concern about the unintended consequences of raising interest rates in a letter to Sir John Somers, a member of the British Parliament, in 1691.[3] And I remember reading about it in the writings of the Scottish philosopher-economist Adam Smith when I was a freshman at the University of Chicago. I remember it because I didn't get it, and thanks to Smith, the unintended consequence of his writings was a dip in my GPA.

The reality is, the concept of unintended consequences has a much longer genealogy than that. It traces all the way back to one of history's greatest moral philosophers, Joseph. He expounded it this way in Genesis 50:20:

> You intended to harm me, but God intended it for good to accomplish what is now being done, the saving of many lives.

Joseph's brothers sold him into slavery. Their *intended* purpose? To harm their brother! The unexpected benefit? The saving of many lives seventeen years later, including their own! I love the little phrase "but God." It's the most amazing conjunction in Scripture! The sovereignty of God overrides our intentions, good or bad. He can take the cruelty of Joseph's selfish brothers and leverage it to save two nations from famine!

Only God.

THE CROOKEDEST ROAD

One of San Francisco's most famous destinations is a one-block section of Lombard Street, between Hyde and Leavenworth Streets. It's the crookedest street in the world, with eight hairpin turns. It's a little nauseating, but without that zigzag, it'd be hazardous to drive up or down the 27 percent grade. Even with the switchbacks, I double pumped my brakes a few times!

This little stretch of the Romans 8 Road, verse 28, is a little like Lombard Street. It's the crookedest road in the Bible, full of twists and turns. There are blind corners, dangerous intersections, and multiple-lane roundabouts. It's not easy to navigate, but the good news is, God wants us to get where God wants us to go more than we want to get where God wants us to go. And He's awfully good at getting us there! Even when we make a wrong turn, He reroutes.

Every decision we make has a million consequences, very few of which we can predict. Every action we take has a million ramifications, very few of which we can control. But that's where the Sovereignty of God comes into play. There is no contingency the Omniscient One has not taken into account.

When things go from bad to worse, as they did for Joseph, I know it's tough to trust God. All you see is the perverse result, which in this case study was unfair imprisonment. It would take seventeen years for the unexpected benefit to come into play, but the Lord of Unintended Consequences proved faithful once again.

Trust me, every moment was cross-indexed and calculated ad infinitum before the creation of the world.

The proverb puts it poetically,

> The mind of man plans his way,
> But the Lord directs his steps.[4]

Go ahead and plan. Again, failing to plan is planning to fail. But God has ulterior motives, and they are far better than anything you could ask or imagine. We originally moved to Washington, DC, to lead an inner-city ministry, not to pastor National Community Church. NCC didn't exist. But God was setting us up, like a chess grand master who foresees the move after the move after the move.

Even if your StrengthsFinder says you're futuristic, your finite mind can only factor in a few contingencies. The Grand Master? He works backward from checkmate.

In chess, sometimes you have to take a step back in order to take a step forward, lose a piece in order to gain a piece. If our church plant in Chicago had not failed, our church plant in Washington, DC, would have never succeeded. My point? You don't want your plan to succeed if God has a better one!

What does that have to do with the Great Eight?

It promises unexpected benefits, even in the worst of circumstances. Romans 8:28 is the New Testament version of Genesis 50:20. It's Genesis 50:20, version 2.0. It's not an immunity card—bad things still happen to good people. But it does promise an unexpected benefit—God works all things together for good, with an emphasis on *all*.

That's our trump card. It might take months or years or decades for them to work together. And in some instances, time won't tell. Only eternity will reveal that there are no exceptions to this promise. When our logical minds object otherwise, it's because there are unintended consequences we haven't taken into consideration.

My grandmother had a unique saying. I honestly have no idea where she got it from, and I'd never heard anybody outside of our extended family say it until I published it. I don't know if she coined it or got it from someone else, but here it is: "You can't never always sometimes tell." It was her unique way of saying, "You never know." And that's the beauty of God's sovereignty. You do your job, which is obedience. And God will do His job, which is everything else!

He'll prepare good works in advance. He'll order your footsteps. And He'll make all of the unintended consequences work together for your good and His glory!

MATCH.COM

When my first book was published nearly a decade ago, I recruited a team of intercessors to pray that my books would get into the right hands at the right time. Millions of books and thousands of letters later, the sovereignty of God never ceases to amaze me. It doesn't matter whether it's a member of Congress circling the Capitol in prayer, the coach of a top-ranked football program challenging his players to go all in, or a convicted felon chasing a lion.

Each one is an answer to prayer.

Each one is an unexpected benefit.

One of my favorite stories involves a Hollywood starlet, Megan Fox. Shortly after *The Circle Maker* released, someone sent me a link to *People* magazine online. They instructed me to scroll down and take a close look at the photograph of Megan coming off an escalator at the airport in Rio de Janeiro. In the photo, paparazzi are waiting for her at the bottom, and Megan is shielding herself with a book—my book. Now, is that why I wrote it? To shield a Hollywood actress from the paparazzi? No, no it's not. And I sure hope she read it on the way to Rio. But hey, if it doubles as an invisibility cloak for a Hollywood celebrity, so be it.

One of the joys of writing is unintended consequences.

When I hit Save and Send on the final edit, the book isn't just out of my hands and in the hands of my publisher. It's in the hands of God. And I trust Him to put it into the right hands at the right time.

In one of His parables, Jesus likened the kingdom of God to a mustard seed:

> Though it is the smallest of all seeds, yet when it grows, it is the largest of garden plants and becomes a tree, so that the birds come and perch in its branches.[5]

Why did the farmer plant the mustard seed in the ground?

My best guess is that he liked mustard on his hot dog—it was a culinary-motivated decision. This I'm sure of: it had absolutely nothing to do with birds finding a place to nest. That thought never crossed the farmer's mind. But when you plant your seed of faith, you never know where it will branch or who it will bless. It's beyond your consequential capacity to even hazard a guess. But I promise you this—there will be unexpected benefits beyond your ability to ask or imagine.

That's the exponential nature of faith. God uses our seeds of faith to accomplish things we didn't even set out to do.

That's who our sovereign God is.

That's what our sovereign God does.

If you asked me why National Community Church was started, I could offer the textbook answer. We exist to help people become fully devoted followers of Christ. But what amazes me most about NCC are the things God has done that we didn't set out to do. We never intended to be a dating service, of that I'm sure. But with a single population greater than 50 percent at NCC, we've arranged hundreds of marriages!

The church wasn't started so that my brother-in-law, Joel Schmidgall, could meet and marry a Capitol Hill staffer named

Nina Krig. That was an unexpected benefit that parlayed into three more unexpected benefits—two of the cutest nieces on the planet, Ella and Renzi, and a fist-bumping nephew named Zeke.

We didn't start NCC so that John Hasler could propose to Steph Modder after recording one of our live albums at the Lincoln Theater, then move to Germany after getting married and open our café in Berlin.

We didn't start NCC so that Bethany Dukes could meet a drummer named Ryan and change her last name to Strumpell. We didn't start NCC so that Heather Sawyer could meet another Ryan and change her last name to Zempel. And that's just a small cross-section of staff members.

Forget Match.com.

Try Theaterchurch.com!

Few things bring me greater joy than dedicating a baby whose mom and dad met and married at NCC. That baby is a second-generation unexpected benefit! Is that why the church was started? Uh, no! But that's the beautiful thing about the Kingdom of Unintended Consequences—you can't never always sometimes tell.

OH, THE PLACES YOU'LL GO

During Parker's first semester of college at Southeastern University, Lora sent a little care package filled with lots of food. That's his love language. She also included a copy of the Dr. Seuss classic *Oh, the Places You'll Go!* It's not exactly college reading material, but it's so good. It was a whimsical way of reminding Parker how much we believe in him.

Forgive me for this strange juxtaposition, but I always think of the Great Commission when I hear *Oh, the Places You'll Go!* In a day and age when the average person didn't travel outside a thirty-mile radius of their birthplace, Jesus sent His disciples to the edge of the ancient world. "Go and make disciples of all nations."[6] And oh, the places they went. According to Eusebius, the second-century church historian, Peter sailed to Italy, John went to Asia, James the son of Zebedee traveled to Spain, and even Doubting Thomas made his way to India.

Hold that thought.

Let me thin slice our church. But before I do, God is no respecter of persons. And neither are we. God has called us to reach the up-and-in, the down-and-out, and everybody in between. That's enabled us to reach across the political divide and the racial divide at National Community Church.

On a recent weekend, I was greeting people after one of our services, and I couldn't help but smile at the diverse cross-section. I congratulated a newly elected United States Senator and his family. I fist-bumped a homeless friend who is one of our most faithful attenders. I shook hands with a local news anchor, met a Georgetown professor, and said hi to the CEO of a networking organization for entrepreneurs. I met a girl from Kenya who attended NCC as a student six years ago and just moved back to the city. I met a rapper, a DC public school teacher, and a documentary filmmaker. I said hi to the director of FCA in northwest metro Atlanta, who was visiting NCC while on vacation. I met a pastor who needed a place to heal and get whole before jumping back into the game. Last but not least, there was a woman who had been trafficked for nearly two decades, had several children during those years, and was invited by one of them to church.

That's a normal weekend at NCC, and it's nothing less than miraculous.

Honestly, we didn't start NCC for any of those birds. We simply planted a mustard seed of faith in the ground. Then God grew our branches so the birds of the air could build nests in them.

I was walking out of church a few months after Boko Haram kidnapped three hundred schoolgirls from Chibok, Nigeria. Emmanuel, a Nigerian attorney and advocate for religious freedom, stopped me and introduced me to one of the girls who had escaped. Here she was, half a world away, at NCC.

Then there's the debate team from Rwanda that recently toured the United States, staying with a family that attends our church. Did I write *The Circle Maker* so that a member of that Rwandan debate team named Yvan could pick it up after one of our services, read it on the way back to Rwanda, translate it into Kinyarwanda, and challenge every member of his church to pray every day of their lives? That never crossed my mind. I'm not sure I could even point to Rwanda on an African map!

But God can, and God does. He cares for all the birds of the air. How? He turns the smallest of mustard seeds into the largest of garden plants that reach all the way to Rwanda.

At the end of an email to me, this Rwandan debater-turned-prophet said,

> The most important thing I want to tell NCC is that you can't know every person that enters your church or where they're from, but one thing is sure: you are on the verge of completely changing humankind even when you don't know who entered the service.

Don't tell me God isn't ordering footsteps! He's doing it all the way from a remote village in Rwanda to a church in Washington, DC.

Don't tell me God isn't preparing good works in advance! He's orchestrating divine appointments half a world away. And He's doing it in ways we could have never dreamed of nineteen years ago. Our podcast got hundreds of thousands of plays in 144 countries this past year—some of which are closed to the gospel. It's a digital branch that reaches to places we can't go to.

At NCC, our *immediate* family members are those who physically attend one of our campuses. But podcast listeners are part of our *extended* family—they nest in our branches!

And it all started with *what if*.

Where it ends, only the Lord of Unintended Consequences knows!

THE POWER OF A SEED

If I were to show you a mustard seed without telling you what it was, you'd have no clue what it could become—unless you're a horticulturist, but that's cheating. It's a small round seed less than two millimeters in diameter that comes in three primary varieties—yellow, black, and white.

It seems so simple, yet it's amazingly complex. Within that single seed is a remarkable nutritional profile, including vitamins A, B6, B12, C, E, and K. It's also a source of calcium, iron, magnesium, phosphorus, potassium, sodium, and zinc, just to name a few. It has anti-inflammatory and anti-cancer properties, and it tastes fantastic on pretzels!

In my opinion, seeds rank as one of God's most amazing creations. We know oak trees come from acorns, but how does a thimble-sized acorn turn into a one-hundred-foot oak that can live for two hundred years? While we're on the subject, how does a little black seed become a beautiful green watermelon?

William Jennings Bryan, famous for his role in the Scopes Monkey Trial, once used the watermelon as a metaphor for the mystery of God:

> I have observed the watermelon seed. It has the power of drawing from the ground and through itself 200,000 times its weight. When you can tell me how it takes this material and out of it colors an outside surface beyond the imitation of art, and then forms in it a white rind and within that again a red heart, thickly inlaid with black seeds, each one of which in turn is capable of drawing through itself 200,000 times its weight—when you can explain to me the mystery of a watermelon, you can ask me to explain the mystery of God.[7]

Since we're on the subject, anyone can count the number of seeds in a watermelon. Only God can count the number of watermelons in a seed.

We waste way too much worry on consequences we cannot control. Quit focusing on the outcome—the increase is God's responsibility. Our job is planting and watering seeds of faith. And if we sow mustard seeds of faith, God will turn those *what ifs* into a thousand unexpected benefits.

What if you sowed a seed
at your point of need?

21

The Rosetta Stone

To those who are called according to His purpose.

Romans 8:28 NASB

Long before Batman and Robin, there was Pierre-François Bouchard and Jean-François Champollion.

Bouchard was an engineer in Napoleon's Grande Armée that occupied Egypt in 1799. While overseeing the demolition of a wall in the ancient city of Rosetta, he uncovered a 1,676-pound slab of black granite stone with ancient writing on it. If Bouchard had demolished that stone—the Rosetta stone—much of Egyptian history would remain a mystery.

But the army engineer recognized it as something special and saved the ancient artifact. That's where Champollion comes into play—wonder twin powers activate![1] The French academic was a linguistic locksmith who spoke a dozen languages. It took two years to line up letters with letters, thereby deciphering the three ancient languages—hieroglyphics, demotic script, and Greek. But

194

when Champollion broke the code, it unlocked the ancient civilization of Egypt.

The twenty-eighth verse of the eighth chapter of Romans is the Rosetta stone of Scripture. Without it, much of life makes no sense whatsoever. With it, we're able to decipher our experiences.

To many, it's the greatest verse in the greatest chapter. Few things are more comforting or more exhilarating than knowing that God is the One putting together the jigsaw puzzle of your life.

It was a London cartographer, John Spilsbury, who is credited with commercializing jigsaw puzzles around 1760. During the Great Depression, they were popularized in America as a cheap form of entertainment. Puzzles come in all shapes and sizes, including the latest and greatest—3D spherical jigsaws. But the method of assembly has not changed in hundreds of years. It requires the fitting together of oddly shaped, interlocking and tessellated pieces.

The key, of course, is the picture on top of the box. Without it, good luck. And that's why many of us feel helpless and hopeless at times—because the pieces of our lives don't seem to fit together, and we can't see God's vision for the whole. But the Rosetta stone, Romans 8:28, promises that God will make every piece fit in the most efficient, effective, and beautiful way possible!

Just as the Rosetta stone unlocked three ancient languages, 8:28 unlocks the mysteries of life. There will still be experiences that won't make sense until we get to heaven, no doubt about it. And let me be as explicit as possible: there is nothing *good* about the bad things people do. Let's call sin, sin. Evil is evil. If you've been the victim of injustice or betrayal or abuse, this doesn't negate that. It does, however, promise to recycle it, redeem it, and use it for your good and God's glory.

Bad things happen to good people, but the fight is fixed. In the end, we win. So let's stop playing not to lose. Don't let your mistakes, or someone else's, put you on the defensive. Play offense with your life. It's okay to mourn the bad things that have happened, but don't throw a pity party. No matter what you've experienced, you are not a victim. You are more than a conqueror.

NEEDLEPOINT

When I was five years old, our family went to see a movie called *The Hiding Place*. It proved to be one of the defining moments of my life. After watching that film, I asked Jesus into my heart.

The movie documents the story of Corrie ten Boom, whose family hid Jews during the Nazi invasion of the Netherlands. When a Nazi spy discovered their secret room, the entire family was arrested. Corrie's eighty-four-year-old father, Casper, was offered asylum because of his age—as long as he promised not to cause any more trouble. He courageously refused, was shipped off to prison on a Nazi Holocaust train, and died ten days later.

Corrie ended up in Ravensbrück, a concentration camp for women. Despite brutal mistreatment and inhumane conditions, she did more than survive. After her miraculous release, Corrie shared her horrific experiences with audiences all around the world, and she did so with amazing grace.

Corrie would often look down while she talked, but she wasn't reading notes. She would sometimes work on a needlepoint while speaking and use it as an illustration when she finished. Holding up the back side, which was a jumble of threads with no discernible pattern, Corrie would say, "This is how we see our lives." Then she'd turn it over to reveal the design, saying, "This is how God views your life, and someday we will have the privilege of viewing it from His point of view."

In the meantime, we need to trust 8:28.

Corrie could have questioned why she had to suffer in a Nazi concentration camp or how God could let her father and sister die in such camps. It was unjustifiable. But God used the suffering of a woman named Corrie ten Boom to touch the heart of a five-year-old Mark Batterson thirty years ex post facto. I feel bad for what Corrie ten Boom had to endure, but I'm the beneficiary of her unanswerable questions and unexplainable experiences. Her suffering led to my salvation.

Some of your earthly experiences won't make sense this side of eternity. And I cannot promise you a painless existence. But in God's economy, your temporal pain can result in someone else's eternal gain.

Is there anything nobler than that?

While I'm not sure what road you've traveled, it always starts at the cross. Every salvation story starts with the agony Christ endured at Calvary. The cross is history's greatest injustice—the Creator nailed to a tree by His creation. But even that, God used for good. He turned the ancient symbol of a torturous death into the symbol of eternal hope for humankind.

And if God can do that with the cross, He can redeem your pain, your failures, your fears, and your doubts. The cross is the missing piece in the middle of every puzzle. Without it, we're helpless and hopeless. With it, the puzzle is solved.

THE BEST ADVICE I EVER GOT

Nantucket Nectar changed my life. Well, sort of. It wasn't the beverage itself. In fact, I can't even remember what flavor I was drinking. It was the saying inside one of the bottle caps:

If every day were a good day, there would be no good days.

A few years ago, I was invited to participate in a book project titled *The Best Advice I Ever Got*.[2] The editors asked a wide swath of people to share life's most important lessons. It was incredibly difficult to narrow it down to one piece of advice, but I picked the bottle cap. At first, it sounds like a Jedi mind trick. But if you really think about it, it's the bad days that help us appreciate the good days. Without them, we'd have no comparison point.

Try these on for size.

If you woke up this morning with more health than illness—you are more blessed than the million who will not survive this week.

If you have never experienced the danger of battle, the loneliness of imprisonment, the agony of torture, or the pangs of starvation—you are better off than five hundred million people in the world.

If you can attend a church meeting, or not attend one, without fear of harassment, arrest, torture, or death—you are more blessed than three billion people in the world.

If you have food in the refrigerator, clothes on your back, a roof overhead and a place to sleep—you are richer than 75 percent of this world.

If you have money in the bank or in your wallet, or spare change in a dish someplace—you rank among the top 8 percent of the world's wealthy.

If you can read this book—you are more blessed than over two billion people in the world who cannot read at all.

So count your blessings and remind everyone else how blessed we all are!

In case you didn't notice, each of those scenarios starts with *if*.

I promise you this, there is always someone who is worse off. That doesn't mean you play some kind of sadistic game where you revel in other people's misery. It ought to heighten Christlike compassion.

My point is this: *It can always be better, but it can always be worse.* And our reference point is critical. When I'm going through a difficult circumstance, I sometimes remind myself that at least it's not a concentration camp. That puts everything into perspective.

"All you have to do is go to the hospital," noted famed psychologist Abraham Maslow, "and hear all the simple blessings that people never before realized were blessings—being able to urinate, to sleep on your side, to be able to swallow, to scratch an itch."[3]

THE CONTRAST EFFECT

A fascinating study was conducted a few years ago at the University of Wisconsin–Milwaukee.[4] The focus of the study was the relationship between perspective and satisfaction.

A control group was shown pictures of extremely harsh living conditions in Milwaukee around the turn of the nineteenth century. The imaginative exercise in deprivation resulted in a measurable increase in levels of satisfaction. Why? Because compared to how things used to be, it's not so bad now!

Now juxtapose that with this.

In a similar experiment at the State University of New York at Buffalo, subjects were asked to complete the following sentence:

I'm glad I'm not a _____.

After five repetitions of that exercise, there was a measurable increase in levels of satisfaction. Another group of subjects was asked to complete this one:

I wish I were a _____.

The net result was a measurable decrease in levels of satisfaction.[5]

Psychologists call this phenomenon the contrast effect. Simply put, how you see anything depends on your reference point. One way or the other, your focus will determine your reality.

If you get into a hot tub after swimming in a cold pool, it will seem even hotter. And of course, if you get into a cold pool after chilling in a hot tub, it will seem even colder. It's the contrast effect. If you lift a really heavy weight, then lift a lesser weight, it will seem even lighter.

So what does that have to do with Romans 8:28?

When you believe that all things work together for good, it redefines the bad things that happen in your life. The worst day of your life can turn into the best day. There is a silver lining to every storm cloud, and every downside has a potential upside.

When you interpret life through the prism of 8:28, it gives you a quiet confidence that everything is going to be all right. In fact, it reassures you that the best is yet to come.

> Aoccdrnig to a rscheearch at Cmabrigde Uinervtisy, it deosn't mttaer in waht oredr the ltteers in a wrod are, the olny iprmoetnt tihng is taht the frist and lsat ltteer be at the rghit pclae. The rset can be a total mses and you can sitll raed it wouthit a porbelm. Tihs is bcuseae the huamn mnid deos not raed ervey lteter by istlef, but the wrod as a wlohe.

There is an element of interpretation in every experience. Our Rosetta stone is 8:28. It's the keyhole, the wormhole. Even when your life seems like a jumbled mess, you trust that the same God who created order out of chaos will make your life make sense.

THIS IS GOOD

There is an old African folktale about a king and his friend who grew up together and did everything together. The king's friend had a saying. In every circumstance, he would say, "This is good."

One day, the king and his friend were out hunting. The friend loaded the firearm for the king, who fired it, but it exploded, blowing off the king's thumb. As was his habit, the friend said, "This is good."

To which the king replied, "This is *not* good," and had his friend thrown in prison.

A year later, the king was out hunting, without his friend, when he was captured by cannibals. The king was taken back to their village and tied at the stake. He thought to himself, "This is not good."

But just before lighting the fire, one of the cannibals noticed that the king's thumb was missing. According to tribal tradition, they would never eat anyone who wasn't whole. So they untied the king and let him go.

When the king realized that his missing thumb was what spared his life, he immediately thought of his best friend whom he'd sent to prison. He said to his friend, "You were right. It is good that my thumb was blown off. I'm sorry for sending you to jail. This is not good."

To which his friend said, "No. This *is* good."

The king still didn't understand. "What do you mean, 'This is good'? I sent my best friend to jail for a year!"

The friend insisted, "This is good. If I hadn't been in jail, I would have been with you. And my thumb's not missing!"

I'm not smart enough to know what's good for me and what's bad for me. Sometimes I get it right. But more often than not, I get it wrong. What we think is good is sometimes bad. And what we think is bad is often good.

The key is making a distinction between *immediate* good and *ultimate* good. I don't believe 8:28 promises immediate good all the time. Jesus said, "In this world you will have trouble."[6] The 8:28 guarantee is this: God will use even the worst things that happen for your ultimate good—and His eternal glory.

There is an old expression repeated in many Christian traditions:

> God is good, all the time.
> All the time, God is good.

We like to say it when things are going good, but if it's not true when things are going bad, then it's not true at all.

It doesn't mean bad things are good. That's sadistic. It does mean that no matter how bad things are, God can *use* them for good.

When Candy Lightner lost her thirteen-year-old daughter to a hit-and-run drunk driver, there was nothing *good* about it. Candy got mad. Then she formed MADD, Mothers Against Drunk Driving. Since its founding in 1980, MADD has helped save countless lives. But the genesis of her lifesaving efforts was a tragic death.

Where have you been wounded? That is often where God uses us to help others. In fact, that is part of the healing process. Our pain is leveraged for someone else's gain. And somehow, someway, God turns *if only* into *what if*.

What if you let God leverage your greatest
failures and deepest disappointments?

22

Bold Predictions

For those whom He foreknew, He also predestined.
Romans 8:29 NASB

The 1932 World Series between the Chicago Cubs and the New York Yankees was tied, one win apiece. Game three was tied, four runs to four. That's when, in the top of the fourth inning, Babe Ruth stepped into the batter's box.

It was a classic showdown between baseball icons. Charlie Root was, and still is, the winningest pitcher in Chicago Cubs history. Babe Ruth was, well, The Babe. Ruth took strike one from the right-hander. When he took strike two, the fans at Wrigley Field started heckling him. That's when Babe Ruth stepped out of the batter's box and pointed his bat to center field. Then he hit the next pitch 440 feet to the place where he pointed. The Babe called his shot.

That home run won game three, and the Yankees went on to win the 1932 World Series. Like many legends, this one has taken on a life of its own over the years. But legends are born of bold predictions, and it's those bold predictions that change the course of history.

On May 25, 1961, John F. Kennedy stood before a joint session of Congress at a critical juncture in the space race. The Soviet Union had launched Sputnik into Earth's orbit a few years before. They had a significant head start, but President Kennedy confidently declared that we'd win the space race. In his inimitable Bostonian accent, he said, "I believe that this nation should commit itself to achieving the goal, before this decade is out, of landing a man on the moon and returning him safely to the Earth."[1]

JFK's *what if* became reality on July 20, 1969, the day Neil Armstrong took one small step for man, one giant leap for mankind.

If history turns on a dime, the dime is bold predictions. They've got to be backed up with bold actions. And if it's the space race, some cold hard cash too. But it starts by pointing a bat toward center field. It starts by making a speech, setting a deadline, and then backing it up with a $531 million budget.

What if starts with bold predictions.

It's Martin Luther posting ninety-five theses on the doors of the Castle Church in Wittenberg, Germany, on October 31, 1517.

It's Dr. Martin Luther King Jr. delivering his "I Have a Dream" speech on the steps of the Lincoln Memorial on August 28, 1963.

In my case, it was vowing to write my first book by my thirty-fifth birthday. That's not as epic as the history-changing moments I've referenced, but it was a game changer for me. It was one of my *what if* moments.

SMALL BEGINNINGS

I felt called to write as a twenty-two-year-old seminary student, but I didn't self-publish my first book until thirteen years later. Dreams without deadlines usually turn into *if only* regrets. I had half a dozen half-finished manuscripts on my computer, but I couldn't tie off the umbilical cord. As the years passed, I stopped celebrating my birthday and started despising it. My birthday became an annual reminder of a dream deferred. Writing books was my *what if*, but all I had to show for it was *if only*.

I'm not sure where the idea came from, but I decided to throw down the gauntlet. I made a bold prediction forty days before my thirty-fifth birthday, vowing that I wouldn't turn thirty-five without a book to show for it. It would be my gift to myself, and somehow I pulled it off. It's certainly not my best-written book, and I had to foot the bill to self-publish it. But I proved to myself that I could do it.

I made another bold prediction when I was twenty-two. I had totally forgotten all about it until Lora recently reminded me of it. When I felt called to write, I didn't just tell Lora that I was going to write a book. I told her I was going to write a book that sold a million copies.

Knowing what I know now, it sounds a little naïve. After all, 97 percent of books don't sell five thousand copies total. What makes it even crazier is that I had just taken that occupational assessment revealing my low aptitude for writing. But I fanned into flame the gift of God by reading thousands of books before I wrote one. I honed my skills by manuscripting sermons and writing blog posts. Finally, I self-published *ID: The True You*. It only sold 3,641 copies, a far cry from one million. My first royalty? $110.43. But that bold prediction was fulfilled when my sixth book, *The Circle Maker*, became my first book to cross the million mark.

What bold prediction do you need to make?

Maybe it's time to throw down the gauntlet. Pray a bold prayer! Dream a God-sized dream. After all, if you are big enough for your dream, your dream isn't big enough for God.

But one word of caution. You can't just make a bold prediction, then sit back and hope it happens while twiddling your thumbs. No matter how big your dream is, you have to prove yourself faithful with a few things. But again, if you do little things like they're big things, then God will do big things like they are little things!

I believe that you are destined, predestined. But don't turn it into a theological crutch or an excuse for less effort. I want to hear God say, "Well done, good and faithful servant."[2] I want an A for effort. God is setting up divine appointments, but you have to keep them. God is the gift giver, but you have to fan them into flame. God is calling, but you have to answer. God is ordering your footsteps, but you have to keep in step with the Spirit. And God is preparing good works in advance, but you need to carpe diem.

It doesn't matter whether it's sports history, space race history, or your history—it's bold predictions backed up by bold actions that change history. And no one made bolder predictions than the Ancient of Days. He didn't just predict who would betray Him, how He would be tortured, His method of execution, or His resurrection, right down to the day—He made some bold predictions about your life!

WORLD FAMOUS

Everybody needs somebody who believes in them more than they themselves do. One of those people in my life has been Bob Rhoden.

Even though we started out with a core group of only nineteen people at National Community Church, I was still underqualified because I had zero experience. The only thing on my résumé was a summer internship at my home church, and all I did was manage the men's softball league.

Well, I guess there was a failed church plant too. But that wasn't an asset; it was a liability. Still, Bob Rhoden saw something in me that I didn't see in myself. A decade later, he invited me to join him as a trustee of a charitable foundation. I still don't get it, but I'm grateful. What a joy and privilege giving grants to kingdom causes!

One of the most important and most underrated skill sets of a Christ follower is the ability to spot potential. It doesn't matter whether you're a GM on draft day, making a political appointment, or coaching Little League. Few things will shape your future more than the ability to see possibilities where others see impossibilities—it's called faith.

No one was better at this than Jesus. He wasn't afraid to put self-righteous people in their place with a well-worded rebuke. He once said to Peter, "Get behind me, Satan!"[3] But long before that He also saw *Peter* in Simon. Then He turned an ordinary fisherman into a fisher of men.

The prediction no one saw coming involved a prostitute. Even the disciples gave her a hard time when she anointed Jesus. But Jesus made his boldest prediction yet:

> Truly I tell you, wherever this gospel is preached throughout the world, what she has done will also be told, in memory of her.[4]

If you interpret this literally—and I do—this one takes the cake! Come on, what are the chances? There were seventy-seven Roman Caesars, and you can't name five of them unless you majored in ancient Roman history or watch way too much *Jeopardy!* There were 332 pharaohs, and the only one you can name is King Tut or the one in *Night at the Museum.*

The who's who of history are long forgotten. No matter how famous these figures may have been, only a select few are remembered a hundred years later. So what are the chances of a Jewish prostitute being remembered two thousand years later? I'd say slim and none, and slim just left town.

Even fifteen minutes of fame seems unlikely, but here we are two thousand years removed, and you're reading about her right now. If this book follows the same path as others, you're reading about her in dozens of languages, all around the world. And each time her story is read, that bold prediction is fulfilled one more time!

It's Never Too Late

It's never too late to become who you might have been.

It was true for this prostitute.

And it's true for you.

I have a friend who pastored one of the largest churches in America. Then he made a mistake and lost just about everything. He lost his church, lost his health plan, and lost his retirement. The toughest thing? Telling his wife and kids what he'd done. He didn't have an affair, but he went too far on Facebook.

What he did was wrong, and he's the first to admit it. But you know what grieves me? Even when someone genuinely repents, we sometimes shoot our wounded. After a two-year restoration process, I asked him if he'd share his story at NCC. It was one of the rawest messages I've ever heard. And his courage to openly confess opened the door for others to confess their secret sins.

We went out to dinner after church, and I felt like God gave me a word for him from Scripture:

> Instead of your shame
> you will receive a double portion.[5]

When those words left my mouth, tears rolled down his cheeks. It was the very same verse his sister-in-law had given him a few days before. How appropriate that a promise about a double portion would be confirmed twice!

I have no idea how big a mistake you've made or how badly you've messed up, but God has not given up on you. How do I know this? You're still breathing. Putting our faith in God is wonderful, powerful. But God warrants our faith. Isn't it far more amazing that God puts His faith in fallible people like you and me?

My friend will live with the emotional, relational, and spiritual scars of his mistake for the rest of his life. But God is using his brokenness to heal the wounds of others. And just like our physical scars, they tell a story of healing.

I have quite a few scars, but the most prominent is a cut from my sternum to my belly button. It used to be embarrassing to me. I felt like a freak show when we went to the beach. Now? I'm proud of it. That cut saved my life! It marks one of the worst days of my life, but I now consider it one of the best things that has ever happened to me.

God has made some bold predictions about you—they're called *promises*. And you can take them to the bank. Why? Because the One who made those promises always delivers. The resurrection is the down payment on every promise. If God made good on that prediction, what are you worried about?

God does not overpromise or underdeliver.

If we meet the conditions, He always exceeds expectations.

What if you quit making excuses,
quit playing it safe,
and quit hedging your bets?

23

The Pavlovian Effect

Predestined to be conformed to the image of his Son.

Romans 8:29

I have a friend who works for the Metropolitan Police Department. One day he pulled me over, and it wasn't to say hi.

Before I confess, here's the circumstantial evidence. I was driving our 1997 Honda Accord with 250,000 miles on it. Just about everything has gone wrong with the car, but it takes a licking and keeps on ticking. Several years ago, the radio mysteriously died, so my phone became my radio.

Right after one of our Saturday night services, a few blocks from our Capitol Hill campus, I came to a stoplight at the corner of 6th and Pennsylvania Avenue SE. Just as I tapped on my ESPN Radio app, my officer friend tapped on the window. He was patrolling by bike that day, and he spotted me fingering my phone. Well, evidently friends don't let friends drive distracted.

The $100 ticket was one thing; the awkwardness was another. I honestly had no idea what to say. "Hey Leo, good to see you." No, not really! Not under these circumstances!

To make matters worse, I was just a couple of blocks from church, a couple of minutes after the service. There must have been a dozen NCCers who drove by! I didn't know what to do, and neither did they. Do you smile? Wave? Not fun. At all. I got quite a few text messages and even a few photographs from my "friends."

Now here's my point.

Every time I get to the corner of 6th and Pennsylvania—which is just about every day—I feel a twinge of residual guilt. It feels as if I'm getting a $100 ticket all over again. It's my least favorite light in DC. And I instinctively keep an eye out for local law enforcement. That physiological reflex is known as the Pavlovian response.

Around the turn of the nineteenth century, a Russian physician named Ivan Pavlov won a Nobel Prize for his experiments with dogs. He had more than forty of them. For the dog lovers out there, I'll mention that Mirta, Norka, Jurka, Rosa, and Visgun were a few of their names.

All of them had one thing in common—like any normal dog, they salivated around food. But Pavlov wanted to find out if salivation could be caused by another stimulus. As you may remember from a psychology class, Pavlov conditioned the dogs by ringing a bell before feeding them. Eventually the dinner bell caused salivation, even if food wasn't served. Pavlov referred to this learned relationship as a conditioned reflex.

To one degree or another, we're all Pavlovian. We have been consciously and subconsciously conditioned our entire lives. And much of our behavior is dictated by those conditioned reflexes. Over the course of time, we acquire an elaborate repertoire.

Some of these reflexes are minor idiosyncrasies such as a forced laugh, a fake smile, or biting your lower lip when slightly embarrassed. Others become major personality traits, such as a critical spirit or contagious joy.

Some conditioned reflexes are as normal and natural as a blush. Others are as destructive as drinking to drown your sorrows. But conscious or subconscious, harmless or harmful, one thing is certain: we are far more conditioned than we realize. And one dimension of spiritual growth is being reconditioned by the grace of God.

"You have heard that it was said . . . but I say unto you."

Jesus uses that couplet over and over again.[1] What was He doing? He was uninstalling Old Testament applications and reinstalling New Testament truths. It was no longer "an eye for an eye." Jesus upgraded it to "turn the other cheek,"[2] and it required reconditioned reflexes.

I've said it many times, but it bears repeating: it's much easier to *act* like a Christian than it is to *react* like one. Reactions are conditioned reflexes, and they must be reconditioned by the grace of God. In my experience, they are often the hardest thing and last thing to get sanctified.

PREDISPOSITION

Nature or nurture?

It's the age-old debate. So which is it? Well, it's a combination of both, not unlike the interplay of the free will of man and the sovereignty of God. And both forces are at play in Romans 8:29. The "predestined" part hints at nature, and I certainly believe in predisposition and predestination. But we also have a choice in the matter!

The "conformed" part hints at nurture, which requires work. The tension between these two ideas is resolved by both/and thinking. A good example is the oft-repeated maxim, pray like it depends on God and work like it depends on you. If you only do one or the other, it'll result in half-baked spirituality.

Philippians 2:12 says, "Work out your salvation with fear and trembling." Salvation is a gift from God, so you can't work *for* it.

But you can work *on* it. So how do you work it out? Well, the same way you work out your muscles. If you want to get into good shape, you've got to exercise! And the more you work out, the stronger you become. You've got to take your faith to the gym and bench press it. It will involve some trembling—that's what muscles do when they are pushed to their limit. But that's how you grow stronger!

I recently did a little experiment with a phrase from the Psalms:"from strength to strength."[3] This is embarrassing to admit, but I could barely do twenty-five push-ups at a time.

But I wondered how many I could do if I simply added one push-up per day. We have a staff member who moonlights as a trainer, and he told me the concept is called linear progression. I got up to one hundred push-ups, and then quit for several months.

When I picked it back up, I wasn't all the way back at twenty-five— my new baseline was fifty. Spiritual growth is a lot like that. Today's faith ceiling will become tomorrow's faith floor. It won't happen in a day, but it will happen someday if you keep working out your salvation.

ROUGH RIDER

Teddy Roosevelt is my favorite president for a wide variety of reasons. One of them is that he was a man's man. He's the Rough Rider who courageously charged Kettle Hill and helped win the Battle of San Juan. Roosevelt went on African safaris for months on end. He set up a boxing ring at the White House, much to the chagrin of the Secret Service, sparring with anyone brave enough to get into the ring with him. He actually lost sight in his left eye from one of those fights, but he never bothered to tell anyone about it.

My favorite Roosevelt legend involves his campaign stop in Milwaukee on October 14, 1912. A would-be assassin shot Roosevelt at point-blank range. The .32-caliber bullet lodged two inches deep in his chest, but that didn't keep him from giving his speech. He informed the audience he'd been shot, then, in apologetic fashion, said, "The bullet is in me now, so that I cannot make a very long speech." Evidently, that meant fifty-three minutes! By the time he finished, he was standing in a pool of his own blood.[4]

That's a man's man, but here's the rest of the story. By all accounts, Teddy Roosevelt was once a mama's boy. He was also sickly, suffering from a severe case of asthma. But Roosevelt made a defining decision that his physical disposition would not deter his dreams.

He set out to remake his body through regular exercise. It took both physical exercise and the exercise of willpower. But the hundred-pound weakling turned into a barrel-chested man you didn't want to mess with.

Don't use your predisposition as an excuse.

Don't use your disability as an alibi.

You are not a victim. You are more than a conqueror. And with Christ's help, there is nothing you cannot do, nothing you cannot become. Will it take hard work? Harder than you can imagine! But if you keep working out your salvation, you'll fulfill your destiny—to be conformed to the image of Christ.

One footnote.

Another reason I love Roosevelt is the insatiable curiosity he had about everything. He read five hundred books per year while fulfilling his duties as president, studying every subject under the sun. He also taught a Sunday school class on the side. And oh, he *still* had time to play a game of hide-and-seek with his kids in the White House as heads of state waited.

Few people have exuded or embodied *what if* like Teddy Roosevelt. It was that *what if* spirit that resulted in the Panama Canal, lots of national parks, and Union Station.

I'm sure Roosevelt thought he was building a train station when he signed that bill of Congress on February 28, 1903. But there was an unintended consequence: Roosevelt was also building our

church. For thirteen wonderful years, NCC met in the movie theaters at Union Station.

What if has a way of ricocheting like that!

ALBEDO

Our destiny has far less to do with what we do than it does with
who we become. Simply put, our destiny is to be conformed to
the image of Christ. And God can use any circumstance, good or
bad, to accomplish that objective.

> Do everything without complaining or arguing, so that you may
> become blameless and pure, children of God without fault in this
> crooked and depraved generation in which you shine like stars in
> the universe.[5]

Paul likens us to shining stars, and the word *shine* means to reflect. The scientific term is *albedo*. It's a measurement of how much
sunlight a celestial body reflects. The planet Venus, for example,
has the highest albedo at .65. In other words, 65 percent of the light
that hits Venus is reflected. Depending on where it's at in its orbit,
the almost-a-planet Pluto has an albedo ranging from .49 to .66.
Our night-light, the moon, has an albedo of .07. Only 7 percent
of sunlight is reflected, yet it lights our way on cloudless nights.

In a similar sense, each of us has a spiritual albedo.

The goal? One hundred percent reflectivity.

> We, who with unveiled faces all reflect the Lord's glory, are being
> transformed into his likeness with ever-increasing glory, which
> comes from the Lord.[6]

You cannot produce light.

You can only reflect it.

And that's what it means to be conformed to the image of
Christ. We become a mirror image of the Invisible One. We think

like, talk like, feel like, and act like Him. Our reflexes become conditioned by His grace.

Destiny is not an accomplishment; it's a reflection. It's not competency as much as it is character—the character of Christ being formed in you until you reflect His love, His power, His patience, His joy.

PROGRESSIVE REVELATION

My mother-in-law recently pulled out a photo album that was nearly forty years old. I saw baby pictures of my wife that I'd never seen before. But the remarkable thing was seeing Lora's mom in Lora—it was like a time-stamped reflection. We could also see family resemblances in the extended family. My nieces are the spitting image of Lora as a toddler, which means they are bound for beauty.

Now let me zoom out.

A relationship with God involves progressive revelation. Like a marriage tempered by time, we get to know the nuances of God's character. Some dimensions of God's character can only be discovered in decades, not days.

His faithfulness, for example, takes time. The longer I follow Christ, the more meaningful "Great Is Thy Faithfulness" becomes. I sing it differently than I did twenty years ago. I might not sing it any better in terms of pitch, but I sing it with far more conviction.

In my experience, as the pastor of a church whose majority is made up by twentysomethings, most of our stress is caused by circumstantial questions. Should I go here or there? Major in this or that? Should I do it now or later? And the big one, *Is this person the one?*

We pray as if the will of God is primarily geographical, occupational, or relational. It's not. The will of God has already been revealed—that you be conformed to the image of Christ.

That's your destiny and pre-destiny! And you can do that here or there or anywhere! You can do that no matter what job you have or who you marry. Too often our prayers revolve around changing our circumstances, when sometimes those circumstances are the very thing God is using to change us.

The ultimate *what if* is *who*.

Who can you become in Christ?

> *What if the circumstances you're asking*
> *God to change are the very circumstances*
> *God is using to change you?*

24

Change Agents

And those he predestined, he also called.

Romans 8:30

On August 26, 1910, Anjezë Gonxhe Bojaxhiu was born in Skopje, Albania. And you thought it was hard learning to spell your name! At the age of seventeen, Anjezë devoted her life to God's service while praying at the shrine to the Black Madonna.

After joining the Sisters of Loreta, Anjezë was first stationed at Loreto Abbey in Rathfarnham, Ireland. After taking her religious vows as a nun, she chose to be named after Thérèse de Lisieux, the patron saint of missionaries. We know her as Mother Teresa.

Shortly after taking her vows, she shared her *what if* with her mother superiors. "I have three pennies and a dream from God to build an orphanage."

Her superiors said, "You can't build an orphanage with three pennies. With three pennies you can't do anything."

Mother Teresa smiled and said, "I know. But with God and three pennies I can do anything."[1]

For fifty years, Anjezë worked among the poorest of the poor in the slums of Calcutta, India. In 1979, she won the Nobel Peace Prize. And nearly two decades after her death, the ministry she started, Missionaries of Charity, consists of 4,500 sisters serving in 133 countries.

How does such a "little flower," the meaning of her birth name, become one of the most recognizable and revered women in the world? How does a woman with three pennies inspire billions of dollars given to charity?

The answer is *what if*.

Never underestimate someone on a mission from God.

CHANGE AGENTS

A few years ago, a handful of Colombian farmers cut down their cocaine fields in a guerilla conflict zone after hearing the gospel. They risked their lives and their livelihood to grow coffee beans instead of coca plants.

Santiago Moncada, a native of Colombia, saw an opportunity to come alongside the good work God had already begun. Santi brought back five pounds of coffee beans and a dream called Redeeming Grounds. As with any dream, it took some financial equity and some sweat equity.

But that dream is now a reality because Santi had the courage to ask *what if*. Ebenezer's coffeehouse has partnered with Redeeming Grounds, selling 285 bags year-to-date. This year they'll purchase 16,000 pounds of coffee beans. I don't think Starbucks needs to worry just yet. But even the biggest of dreams has small beginnings.

And if you don't despise the day of small beginnings, the God who began a good work will carry it to completion. Why? Because it's not your vision; it's His. It's not your business; it's His. It's not your job; it's His. It's not your cause; it's His.

Someone may have hired you to do your job, but make no mistake about it, they didn't call you. Only God can call us. You may have been elected to your position, but make no mistake about it, your constituents didn't call you; God did. No matter where you work or what you do, you are called by God.

Your job is your sermon.

Your colleagues are your congregation.

That sense of calling turns Monday morning into *what if*.

The mission arm of National Community Church is called A18, as in Acts 1:8. During our annual missions series this year, we used latitude and longitude coordinates as the series theme because we wanted to remind our congregation that no matter where you are, you are *on mission*. We'll take thirty-four mission trips this year, but you don't have to go halfway around the world to be on mission.

That's why we had seven NCCers from seven domains of society share TED-style talks about how they leverage their jobs into callings.[2]

Erica Symonette is a self-proclaimed fashionista. She has leveraged her passion for fashion into an online store called *Pulchritude*. "The world doesn't need another boutique," Erica admitted. "But it does need more kingdom businesses." Her store is a manifestation of Isaiah 61:10: "he has clothed you with garments of salvation." Erica uses net profits to help victims of sex trafficking.[3]

Joshua DuBois feels called to the political arena. He is the former head of the Office of Faith-Based and Neighborhood Partnerships in the executive office of the White House, but even if you report to the president, you still answer to a higher authority! "I went to policy school, not seminary," Joshua said. Yet for seven years, he functioned as a prophet to the president, sharing a daily word of encouragement with POTUS.

Kate Schmidgall was voted Young Entrepreneur of the Year by the DC chamber of commerce in 2013. Her design firm, Bittersweet, turns stats into stories, awareness into action. Kate unapologetically says, "Nonprofits are *for* profit." If you don't make a profit, the business model isn't sustainable. The difference? Bittersweet uses those net profits to cast a net for kingdom purposes.[4]

Finally, Shajena Erazo teaches at one of DC's toughest public schools. Her high school has a history of making the news for all the wrong reasons. No matter how many security guards or metal detectors they put in place, they couldn't seem to keep crime out. That school is Sha's mission field. "I see myself as a youth pastor," she says. "I just don't report to church. I report to my principal." Sha is every bit as called to teach high school English as I am to preach the gospel. After reading *The Circle Maker*, she started circling her high school. Sha anoints students' desks with oil; she prays with fellow teachers; and by the end of every school year, her journal is filled with pages of prayers for each of her students.

In their own unique way, each of these change agents is asking *what if*. They refuse to be paralyzed by statistics. They are making a difference one person, one project, one class at a time. They know God has called them and has anointed them.

It doesn't matter what domain of society you work in or where you are on the org chart. You are called and commissioned by God. You are right where God wants you to be—even if you're not where *you* want to be. Sometimes the greatest sermon is doing a good job at a bad job or doing a thankless job with a grateful heart.

ON MISSION

I have a few convictions when it comes to calling. They are keys to unlocking *what if*.

1. God doesn't call the qualified. He qualifies the called.

There is a high likelihood that God will call you to do something you're not smart enough, good enough, or strong enough to pull off. By definition, a God-ordained dream will always be beyond your ability and beyond your resources. Why? So that you have to rely on God every single day!

I'm keenly aware of the fact that in my current state of spiritual maturity, I'm not capable of leading National Community Church two years from now. I need to keep growing, keep learning. And that's the way it should be. Nothing keeps you on your knees in raw dependence upon God like a God-sized dream.

2. Criticize by creating.

In my opinion, criticism is a cop-out for those who are too lazy to solve the problem they are complaining about. Instead of criticizing movies or music, produce a film or an album that is better than whatever it is you're complaining about. The most constructive criticism is called creativity.

At the end of the day, we should be more known for what we're *for* than what we're *against*. Anybody can point out problems. We're called to solve them by writing better books, starting better schools, and drafting better legislation.

3. The anointing is for everyone.

It doesn't matter whether you're a teacher, a doctor, a lawyer, or a barista. From the top of the organization chart to the bottom, God wants to anoint you to do whatever it is you're called to do.

If I need legal help, I certainly want an attorney who has been to law school. But I also want an attorney who is anointed by God.

If I need surgery, I certainly want a doctor who has been to med school. But I want more than that: I want a doctor whose hands are anointed by God.

If I need dirty chai with two shots of espresso—well, you get the point. The anointing of God knows no limits when it comes to position or portfolio.

4. Live for the applause of nail-scarred hands.

Whatever it is that you feel called to do, do it as if your life depended on it. That's 1 Corinthians 10:31 in a nutshell: "So whether you eat or drink or whatever you do, do it all for the glory of God."

The key word is *whatever*. It doesn't matter what you're doing; do it to the glory of God. "It is inbred in us that we have to do exceptional things for God," said Oswald Chambers, "but we have not. We have to be exceptional in the ordinary things."[5] And when we are, we put a smile on God's face.

MUNDANE TASKS

Richard Bolles, author of the classic bestseller *What Color Is Your Parachute?*, makes a profound observation: "The story in the Gospels of Jesus going up on the mount and being transfigured before the disciples is to me a picture of what calling is all about. Taking the mundane, offering it to God, and asking Him to transfigure it."[6]

Taking mundane tasks and figuring out how to transfigure them. That's what calling is all about.

More than a decade ago, I gave the eulogy at a memorial service in the Caucus Room of the Russell Senate Office Building. Some of the most important hearings in our nation's history have been held in that room. If those walls could talk!

Yet here we were to honor the life of a woman with no rank. Jayonna Beal was the administrative assistant in charge of constituent correspondence for fourteen years. That isn't the position people are fighting for on the hill, but Jayonna did it with grace. She didn't have position or power, but that room was packed with the who's who of Washington.

I spoke right after her boss, who would run for president a few years later. He, along with countless others, shared stories of how Jayonna's small acts of kindness made a big difference in their lives. Jayonna baked cookies, sewed buttons, and showed interns the ropes. And she did it all in the name of Jesus. Jayonna practiced that old adage, "Share the gospel every day; if necessary, use words."

It's the little *ifs* that change the world.

In the words of Dr. Martin Luther King Jr.,

> If a man is called to be a street sweeper, he should sweep streets even as Michelangelo painted, or Beethoven composed music, or Shakespeare wrote poetry. He should sweep streets so well that all the hosts of heaven will pause to say, "Here lived a great street sweeper who did his job well."[7]

I know a great street sweeper. Her name is Val, and she is a custodian who cleans like it's nobody's business but God's. She inscribed *SDG* on her mop handle, just like Johann Sebastian Bach did on his symphonies. It stands for *Soli Deo Gloria*. It's a reminder that she cleans for the glory of God.

Believe it or not, Val drove all the way from Canada to clean our offices at National Community Church. I know that sounds strange, but I think it falls into the category of *strange and mysterious*. She was profoundly impacted by our podcast, and she wanted to repay her debt of gratitude the best way she knew how. So she drove all the way to DC to clean our offices.

Who does that?

I'll tell you who. Someone who knows God has called them. Back home, Val is the custodian for the school district. It's often a thankless job, the job no one else wants to do. And it isn't always easy. "My prayer last year was that God would get me off the third shift," Val told me. "But now I have changed my prayers. I want to be taught by God what I need to learn."

There might be educators in her district smarter than her, but I dare say that no one is more teachable than the custodian. And that's what really counts in God's kingdom.

Being a third-shift custodian isn't most people's dream job. But *what* you do isn't as important as *how* you do it and *whom* you do it for. So no matter what you do, do it like Michelangelo painted, Beethoven composed, Shakespeare wrote poetry, and Val cleans bathrooms.

Whatever you do, don't settle for *what*.

Imagine *what if.*

> *What if money weren't an object*
> *and you knew you couldn't fail—*
> *what passion would you pursue?*

25

I Dwell in Possibility

If God is for us, who can be against us?

Romans 8:31

On any given day, 23,000 scheduled flights take off and land at American airports.[1] At any given time, 5,000 of those airplanes are simultaneously airborne. That means that approximately one million people are flying 300 mph at 30,000 feet at any given moment. Kind of crazy to think about, isn't it? A hundred years ago, this was the stuff of science fiction. Then two brothers, Wilbur and Orville, turned science fiction into science fact.

As you can probably guess by now, it all started with *what if*.

The Wright brothers' dream of flying traces back to an autumn day in 1878 when their father, Bishop Milton Wright, brought home a rather unique toy. Using a rubber band to twirl its rotor, a miniature bamboo helicopter flew into the air. Much like our mechanized toy helicopters, it broke after a few flights. But instead of giving up on it and going on to the next toy, the Wright brothers made their own. And the dream of flying was conceived.

A quarter century later, on December 17, 1903, Orville himself went airborne for twelve gravity-defying seconds in the first powered, piloted flight in history.

It's almost impossible to imagine life as we know it without airplanes. But like every innovation, every revolution, every breakthrough, someone had to imagine the impossible first.

Every dream has a genesis moment—a moment when *possibility* pulls off a coup d'état and overthrows impossibility. It usually starts small—as small as a toy helicopter. It takes time and patience for the genesis to become revelation. But the chain reaction of faith defies gravity, defies the imagination. Without knowing it, the Wright brothers were creating the airline industry, the FAA, and the TSA. I'm sure it never crossed their minds, but their flying faith is the reason why a million people are speeding through the troposphere right now.

The next time you take off in a Boeing 747, remember that it's *what if* that enables our dreams to take off. It was two pastor's kids, Wilbur and Orville, who punched your ticket with their possibility thinking.

POSSIBILITY

A decade after the Wright brothers took flight at Kitty Hawk, a young nurse's aide in Toronto was caring for dying soldiers returning from the warfront. During breaks, Amelia took her mind off the grave circumstances by watching planes take off at a nearby airfield.

On a snowy day in 1918, the backwash from an airplane's propellers threw freezing snow into her face. It woke her up to *what if.* "It was the finest cold shower ever imagined," she later reflected. "I determined then and there that I would someday ride one of these devil machines, and make it blow snow to my will."[2]

Amelia Earhart did just that, becoming the first woman to fly solo across the Atlantic Ocean. She died just a few time zones short of her dream of flying around the world, but not before inspiring a generation of women to pursue their *what ifs*.

A century before Earhart's trip around the world, an introverted poet named Emily Dickinson took flight with words. Fewer than a dozen of her 1,800 poems were published during her lifetime, but one of them ranks as my all-time favorite: "I Dwell in Possibility."

That title encapsulates my personality.

According to the StrengthsFinder assessment, my top five strengths are Strategic, Learner, Futuristic, Ideation, and Self-Assurance. Those talents combine into one StrengthsFinder label: trailblazer. Simply put, I see possibility behind every bush—every bush is a burning bush where God might show up and show off His glory!

That combination of characteristics is perfectly captured by Dickinson's one-liner: I dwell in possibility. I love it so much that I have an artist's rendering of those four words, *I dwell in possibility*, prominently displayed in my office. I've even named my office after Dickinson's poem. Hey, people name boats. Why not offices? So when you walk into my office, you walk into *Possibility*.

It's not just where I go to work; it's where I dream of ways to change the world. I'm a possibility thinker. Is there a downside to that type of personality? Undoubtedly! For starters, I'm easily bored. If it's not challenging, I check out.

Another downside, as our team will attest, is indecisiveness. Frankly, I like keeping options open until the last second. The upside is that I have an eye for opportunity. In fact, I see opportunity everywhere I look. I'm like Dug, the talking dog in the Pixar classic *Up*. Every time he sees a squirrel, well, he says, "Squirrel!" and his attention is 100 percent diverted from whatever it was on. In my case, the squirrel is named *opportunity*.

I think it's why *if* is my first instinct and *what if* is second nature. *If* is the way I'm wired, but no matter what your personality type, I believe it's a biblical imperative. *If* God is for us, then *what if* isn't optional. My prayer is Søren Kierkegaard's plea:

If I were to wish for anything I should not wish for wealth and power, but for the passionate sense of what can be, for the eye which, ever young and ardent, sees the possible. Pleasure disappoints, possibility never. And what wine is so sparkling, what so fragrant, what so intoxicating as possibility?[3]

WE PUT A MAN ON THE MOON

One of the highlights of this past year was doing a chapel for the Green Bay Packers. I've done quite a few NFL chapels, but it's a little different doing a chapel for the team you pulled for, yeah even prayed for, as a kid. In fact, I used to cry when they lost, which was quite often in my formative years!

I'm not sure my message had anything to do with it, but the Packers put up 42 points in the first half of that game! And we had front row seats for the Lambeau Leaps! A friend texted me during the game, "You're living the dream right now, aren't you?" That's when it dawned on me, *yes, yes I am!* It was one of those "pinch me" moments.

The day of the game, I spent some time with the team's chaplain and pastor of Green Bay Community Church, Troy Murphy. He gave me the nickel tour of their building, and I picked up a very cool idea. Hanging outside every team member's office was a sign revealing their personality profile and strengths.

The cheat sheets also listed dos and don'ts, followed by a one-liner. I loved the "don't" on Troy's sign: "Don't say I can't." We must be cut from the same cloth. When someone tells me why something can't be done, it drives me crazy! I usually remind them that we put a man on the moon! So don't tell me it can't be done!

All things are possible.

Nothing is impossible.

That covers all bases, doesn't it? But just for good measure, we can do all things through Christ who strengthens us![4] To an infinite God, all finites are equal. That's the essence of *what if.*

Where others see problems, *what if* sees solutions.

Where others see impossibility, *what if* sees opportunity.

IT ALL STARTS WITH *IF*

During the first-ever college football National Championship Game with the playoff format, the Ohio State Buckeyes faced off against the Oregon Ducks. The Buckeyes won the game, but the Ducks won the commercial. No offense, but the Buckeyes commercial was absolutely forgettable.

The Ducks commercial was as unique as their uniforms. Here's a remix of that spot, "Explore the Power of 'If.'" The spot began by asking: "What if there was no *if*?"[5]

> Deep in the woods, *if* sparks a revolution. . . .
> *If* searches and researches. . . .
> *If* opens doors. . . .
> Goes for it on fourth down.
> *If* doesn't care about yesterday. . . .
> Just two simple letters, right?
> Wrong.
> *If* sleeps never. And goes for extra credit. . . .
> It all starts with *if*.
> Because *if* becomes *when*, and when becomes *now*.
> And now becomes *how*, and how becomes . . . *wow*.
> *If* will change your stance.
> *If* will change the game.
> *If* will change the world.[6]

Their tackling could have been better, but not their tagline: "We *if* at the University of Oregon." Bravo, Oregon, bravo! Maybe it's because I'm an *if* fanatic, but that ad is pure brilliance.

When it comes to *if*, my point of reference is Romans 8:31. It's where possibility is conceived. It's where opportunity is perceived. And it always starts with God. If God is with you, for you—it's game on, it's game over.

In the beginning, God created us in His image. And we've been creating God in our image ever since! The technical term is *anthropomorphism*. What you end up with is an idol that is a mirror image of yourself. In the words of A. W. Tozer, "a God who can never surprise us, never overwhelm us, nor astonish us, nor transcend us."[7]

That's not the God I believe in.

That's not the God of the Bible.

I believe in a God who is omnipotent, omniscient, and omnipresent. I believe in a God who is high and exalted. I believe in a God who is able to do immeasurably more than all I can ask or imagine.[8] I believe in a God whose thoughts are higher than my thoughts, whose ways are higher than my ways.[9] I believe in a God whose love I can't possibly comprehend, whose power I can't possibly control, whose mercy I can't possibly deserve. I believe in the God who exists outside of the four dimensions of space-time He created. I believe in the God who can make and break the laws of nature.

His name is Wonderful Counselor, the Mighty God, the Everlasting Father, and the Prince of Peace. And He shall reign forever and ever![10]

"How much happier you would be, how much more of you there would be," said G. K. Chesterton, "if the hammer of a higher God could smash your small cosmos."[11]

God is able.

That is the first and last tenet of my theology—my a priori assumption, my fallback position, my default setting.

THE KERNEL

I recently upgraded my iPhone by downloading the latest and greatest version of Apple's operating system. Again, I'm no Apple genius, but the operating system or OS is the interface between your hardware and software applications. The applications, from

Angry Birds to Instagram, run by obeying rules preprogrammed into their OS. And the key code is called the kernel.

The kernel provides the most basic level of control over all of the hardware devices. It manages input and output requests; it's responsible for memory allocation; and it establishes priorities.

Occasionally computers will experience what is called a priority inversion. Humans do too! Simply put, a high priority task is preempted by a low priority task, thus inverting the relative priority of the two tasks. It's the kernel that keeps that from happening. It establishes what are called preemptive priorities. When you're multitasking, the kernel determines which application takes precedence.

If you think of your brain as an OS, we all have a kernel. The key code is your default settings—it's your core beliefs, your core convictions. It's the most buoyant values that always rise to the surface when you have difficult decisions to make. Maybe you've never thought of them as preemptive priorities, but that's what they are. It's the truest thing about you.

One of our core convictions at National Community Church is that the church ought to be the most creative place on the planet. There are ways of doing church that no one has thought of yet. To us, everything is an experiment. We're more afraid of missing opportunities than making mistakes.

All of that to say this: we *if* at NCC.

It's our kernel code.

PERHAPS

"Perhaps the LORD will act in our behalf."[12]

That may be my favorite sentence in the Bible, outside the Great Eight.

It tells me everything I need to know about Jonathan. It's his one-sentence mission statement; his default setting; his OS; his MO.

Perhaps is Jonathan's *why not*, Jonathan's *what if*.

And *perhaps* causes him to do something crazy—climb a cliff and fight the Philistines who outnumber him ten to one. I don't know about you, but I want better odds than that. But his one act of courage saved a nation: "So on that day the LORD saved Israel."[13]

How? How did the Lord save Israel? One man's *what if*, plus an armor bearer who was crazy enough to *if* with him.

This one verse, one kernel, doubles as our philosophy of ministry at NCC. You know the old adage, *Ready, set, go*? We reversed it. You'll never be ready! If you wait until you're ready, you'll be waiting till the day you die. And you'll never be set. Sometimes you need to just go for it.

Now listen, you certainly need to count the cost. Count twice! But don't just count the actual cost, count the *opportunity* cost.

Honestly, I think many people operate out of the opposite mentality, thinking, "Perhaps the Lord *won't* act in our behalf." They let fear dictate their decisions. They get stuck maintaining the status quo. They live as if the purpose of life is to arrive safely at death.

Change your sequence! *Go. Set. Ready.* Why? Because if God is for us, who can be against us?

I recently spoke at a retreat for Senator James Lankford and his staff. We first met when he served in the House, and he shared his remarkable story with me over a cup of coffee. I profiled his unlikely rise to political power in day one of *Draw the Circle: The Forty Day Prayer Challenge*.[14] He was a Christian camp director when he felt God calling him to run for Congress.

After serving two terms in the House, he had another *what if* moment when a Senate seat opened up. But when he threw his hat in the ring, a mutual friend told me that some of the political powers-that-be threw their weight and their resources behind his opponent.

Then my friend said in a very matter-of-fact manner: "But nothing can come against him, if God is for him." He won the primary convincingly, and then he won the election overwhelmingly. And I'm not sure he's reached the top rung of his political ladder just yet.

It was Frederick Douglass who said, "One and God make a majority."[15] I would add a little amendment, since we're on the subject of politics: one and God make a supermajority! If God is for us, nothing can stop us!

There are no odds He cannot overcome.

There is no obstacle He cannot overwhelm.

As Abraham Lincoln so famously and aptly said, "My concern is not whether God is on our side, but whether we are on *His* side."[16]

The issue is not whether or not God is on our side. That question was answered at the cross! God is *for* us. The only question that remains is this one: Are we on His side? God has cast His vote for us, Satan has cast his vote against us, and we must cast the deciding vote.

God is for you—no ifs, ands, or buts about it.

The only question is: Are you for God?

What if you were more afraid of missing opportunities than making mistakes?

26

Monogrammed Blessings

He who did not spare his own Son, but gave
him up for us all—how will he not also, along
with him, graciously give us all things?

Romans 8:32

Our family recently discovered one of the most beautiful places
on the planet, Cabo San Lucas. Situated at the southern tip of
the Baja California Peninsula, Cabo is nestled between the Sea of
Cortez and the Pacific Ocean.

The very last rock formation that juts out of the ocean is called
Land's End, and it does in fact feel like the end of the earth. Some
friends invited us to vacation with them at an oceanfront villa over
New Year's. Hey, that's what friends are for!

And just an observation: sunny and 80s feels even better when
you know it's below freezing back home!

We ate our daily quota of guacamole and watched spectacular
sunsets, but the hands-down highlight was a glass-bottomed

boat trip. We saw sea lions sunbathing on the rocks and exotic yellowtail fish swimming right beneath our boat, which was awesome.

But then we saw something in a category by itself. Our tour was supposed to stay by the shoreline, but Captain Carlos saw some larger boats congregating a few hundred yards offshore. So Carlos headed straight out to sea, jumping waves like the flying fish leaping from the water on the starboard side of the boat. Then we saw it—a humpback whale breached right off our bow.

Have you ever been within a hundred feet of a forty-ton whale in the wide-open ocean? It's both frightening and exhilarating at the same time. The largest land animal is the African elephant, weighing in at 14,000 pounds. That's how much a whale's tongue weighs. Its heart is the size of a compact car. And a humpback is as long as a five-story building is high.

Its cousin, the blue whale, is twice that long. Humpback whales are most famous for their songs, which span oceans.[1] According to Dr. Christopher Clark, director of the Bioacoustics Research Center at Cornell University, their songs can travel 1,800 miles underwater.[2]

Have you ever wondered why God made whales? I didn't give it much thought until we came within a hundred feet of one. The psalmist reveals the answer:

> There go the ships,
> and Leviathan, which you formed to play in it.[3]

God made whales to *play*. There you have it. But wait, shouldn't they serve some higher purpose than *play*? Nope! When they play, they are fulfilling their eternal purpose. Whales certainly play a vital role in the ocean's ecosystem too, but their primary purpose is to play. Maybe that's why it's so wonderful watching one flap its fins or blow its hole.

Is it possible that we have underappreciated the sanctity of play?

This psalm is a peephole into the playful side of God's personality. Parents, is there anything that brings you more joy than watching your kids play sports or play music? Or perform a role in the school play? Or even play with Legos?

Play is an innate expression of *what if*. It's also one of life's simplest and purest forms of enjoyment. And if it brings so much joy to us, why are we surprised that it brings joy to our heavenly Father? When we commend the playful accomplishments of our kids with "Good job," we're echoing God's original "It is good."

That moment when the whale breached in front of our boat was nothing less than a sacred gift from God. I can say that definitively and authoritatively because the Great Eight says so. God has graciously given us *all things*.

That sure sounds all-inclusive to me, so it must include breaching whales.

ONE HUNDRED BLESSINGS

Gratitude is one of four Batterson family values, and it's an art form. I'm always trying to find new ways, better ways to express gratitude. But I haven't come up with any ideas that are any better than a good old-fashioned gratitude journal. I've been keeping one off and on for a decade, but I turned it into a deliberate practice this past year. I started counting my blessings by numbering them, and it made a qualitative and quantitative difference.[4]

I got to 567 "gratitudes" last year, and I'm aiming for one thousand this year. That might sound like a lot, but an observant Jew says a bare minimum of one hundred blessing prayers each day! Every blessing starts with the Hebrew formula, *Baruch Atah Adonai*. Then the blessing is nuanced and pronounced.

Practicing Jews bless God when they see a comet, put on new clothes, or experience something for the first time. They bless God for smells and tastes. And if something is pleasurable, they bless

God. Married couples, when was the last time you blessed God after sex? It was His idea, after all.

If you enjoy something without saying a blessing, according to the Talmud, it's as if you have stolen it. How many blessings have we shoplifted?

I recently got a rather unique gift in the mail—half a hog. No kidding. It was delivered on dry ice from a farmer in Illinois whose ministry is butchering hogs and shipping them to pastors. Well, hallelujah! Now that's a calling and a blessing.

But I wasn't just grateful for forty pounds of pork. I nuanced it. I'm grateful for each and every cut of meat—pork chops, pork loins, sausage links, and last but not least, thick-cut slices of bacon. I stewarded that gift the same day by putting some in a frying pan and setting off our smoke detector!

The more nuanced you become in offering gratitude, the more joy is multiplied. It becomes a gratitude game. How can I thank God in a new way for something I've tasted, touched, smelled, seen, or heard a thousand times?

I did that recently with one of my favorite cookies, a German classic called springerle. It's most common in the Christmas season, but it's good all year round. What makes a springerle unique is a licorice-flavored spice called anise. It's so good, and so awkward if you pronounce anise the wrong way! My point? Don't settle for generic gratitude. Nuance it in new ways.

WHAT THE WHAT?

"All these blessings shall come upon you and overtake you."[5]

If I had to describe my life in a single verse, it might be that one. I have off days, like everyone else. But if you time-lapse my life, it looks like Deuteronomy 28:2. The blessings of God are overtaking me, and they are doing so with greater frequency and magnitude.

That doesn't mean I don't have issues; I do. And the truth is, the blessings of God will complicate your life! Just as sin complicates our lives in negative ways, the blessings of God complicate our lives in positive ways.

Like every promise, this one comes with the conditional clause: *if.* You have to meet the condition, which in this case is to "diligently obey the voice of the LORD."[6] But *if* you meet the condition, it comes with a *what if* warranty, and there is no expiration date!

The blessings were pronounced by the elders of Israel from the top of Mount Gerizim, one of the highest peaks on the West Bank. They were first pronounced in BC 1406, but they are still under warranty 3,421 years later. By my calculations, it's 5,879 miles from Mount Gerizim to Washington, DC. But even if you are farther from Mount Gerizim than that, you are well within the coverage area.

This past year, both a car and a boat were given to our family. And as if for special effect, they were given to us on the same day! The amazing thing is that we weren't asking for or expecting either of them. It was a *what the what?* moment. Now, the boat is a forty-year-old johnboat worth a few hundred dollars, but still, it floats. And the car had more than a hundred thousand miles on it, but that was a hundred thousand miles less than the one I was driving!

When you meet the conditional clause of God's promises, you better buckle your seat belt. Crazy stuff happens. You never know how or when or where His blessings will overtake you. But not unlike His mercy and goodness, which follow us all the days of our lives, the blessings of God are tracking you down like a heat-seeking missile. They're hot on your trail. And someday, one day, they're going to overtake you.

Now please hear my heart.

God doesn't bless us so we can raise our standard of living. God blesses us so we can raise our standard of *giving.* The greatest blessing of a blessing is the ability to bless others because of it.

FLIP THE BLESSING

Where have you been blessed?

That's where you need to *flip the blessing*.

Where has God shown you favor?

That's where you need to *return the favor*.

This has become a way of life for Lora and me. We love blessing people in the way God has blessed us. This might seem like a trivial example, but during our first few years of marriage, we couldn't afford a vacation. I know, there are much greater hardships.

Back when Lora was putting me through seminary and we didn't have a nickel to spare, we heard about a cabin in Galena, Illinois, that was free to seminary students.

What a blessing!

Over the years, gracious and generous people have let us use their lake homes, their log cabins, and even a chateau for free. And they all fit within our budget—free ninety-nine!

Some of our most treasured family memories are the by-product of people's generosity and hospitality. And because we've been blessed in that way, we love to flip that particular blessing. Sometimes it's offering a night away at a hotel for a couple with kids that just needs to get away and enjoy the blessing, double entendre intended. Sometimes it's someone like we were, who we know can't afford a vacation.

If it's within our means, we try to help them make some memories. Now here's the crazy thing: the more we flip the blessing, the more blessings seem to come our way. Just as you cannot out-give God, you cannot out-bless Him either. But it sure is fun trying!

We've discovered that there is no greater joy than being on the giving end of a gift. Isn't that what Jesus said? It's more blessed to give than to receive.[7] I love getting a gift as much as anyone else, but I've never received a gift that came close to the joy of giving one.

And maybe that's why God enjoys nothing more than graciously giving us all things.

$100,000 BLESSING

A few years ago, I was speaking at Covenant Church in Dallas, Texas. Right after I said amen, Pastor Mike Hayes got up and said, "We're going to raise $100,000 in five minutes to bless National Community Church." I wasn't expecting it, and quite frankly, I'd never heard anyone say anything like that before.

The remarkable thing is that we had purchased an old apartment building that day that would become our DC Dream Center. But Mike didn't even know about it. Mike and Kathy Hayes pledged $5,000 and asked five people to join them by a show of hands. Five hands went up in five seconds. Then he asked twenty-five people to give $1,000. Boom. Done. And finally, he asked one hundred people to give $500. I'll never forget the sight of hands going up all over the place, like a kindergarten classroom. I'd known Mike all of fifteen minutes! We met for the first time before the service started, yet they raised $100,000 in five minutes flat.

A few months later, we raised $3.3 million in three months flat to build our Dream Center in DC. I believe it was that $100,000 gift that planted the seed and set the stage. But that isn't even why I bring it up. Let me tell you the thought that fired across my synapses when Mike made that announcement.

I certainly thanked God for the gift, but I marked the moment with a prayer: *Lord, give us the privilege of doing for someone else what's just been done for us.* In other words, help us return the favor! It was humbling being on the receiving end, but I want to be on the *giving* end. We're doing our best to flip the blessing. And that's at the heart of *what if*.

One of our sermon series this past year was "I Like Giving." The title of the series is the title of a must-read book by my friend Brad Formsma. During that series, we felt impressed to bless a dozen churches in the DC area. It was our way of saying, it's not about the name over the church door; it's about the Name that is above every name! If a church is preaching and practicing the gospel, we're on the same team.

So we took an offering for those churches and raised more than $50,000 in one offering. Part of the inspiration for that offering was the simple fact that other churches helped NCC survive during its first few years. So we flipped the blessing.

We haven't hit $100,000 with one offering yet, but we will. If we keep giving to missions and caring for the poor in the city, I'm absolutely confident that God will take care of our bottom line. Why? Because when God gives a vision, He makes provision!

God did it once again on the last day of last year—our one-day donations on December 31, 2014, were more than our entire first year's income in 1996. Actually, twice as much!

Translation: God is providing more in *one day* now than He did in *one year*, eighteen years ago. His cumulative blessings are overtaking us, and they compound interest for eternity!

MONOGRAMMED BLESSING

There are hundreds of blessings in Scripture, and each one has your name on it. If you are *in Christ*, the blessings belong to you. In fact, they belong to you twice—once by birthright, twice by inheritance.

I was on the receiving end of some rather interesting gifts this past year. Certainly none tasted better than forty pounds of pig. And the car was over the top! But the most personalized blessing was thanks to Dave Ramsey.

Dave convened a gathering of pastors to converse on the subject of stewardship in Nashville, Tennessee. On the opening night he rented the Country Music Hall of Fame for a private concert. Red Solo cup, I lift you up! Then he topped it off in unforgettable fashion by giving each of us a very cool handmade leather saddlebag made in the USA by Colonel Littleton. And it was monogrammed.

Every promise has your monogram on it.

It belongs to you by birthright; by inheritance.

And your claim ticket is the cross.

"No matter how many promises God has made, they are 'Yes' in Christ."[8]

If that isn't a catalyst for *what if*, I don't know what is.

Where has God blessed you? You need to identify the blessings, including the blessings in disguise. That's the way you steward them. If you don't share them, the blessings can actually become curses. Then, once you identify when and where and how God has shown you His favor, return the favor!

Count the blessing.

Flip the blessing.

Repeat.

What if you increased your standard of giving instead of your standard of living?

No Ifs, Ands, or Buts about It

If you're looking for an excuse, you'll always find one.
The same is true of opportunity.
God-ordained opportunities are all
around you, all the time.
Of course, many of them come disguised as problems.
Despite what the old adage says,
opportunity doesn't knock.
Sometimes you have to ask for it, seek it, and knock on it.
But don't seek opportunity first and foremost.
Seek God.
If you do, opportunity will seek you.

27

The Cornerman

Christ Jesus who died—more than that, who was raised to life—is at the right hand of God and is also interceding for us.

Romans 8:34

Because I have thousands of books in my library and I've written a few of my own, I often get the question, "Who is your favorite author?"

That's an impossible question to answer, but I quote A. W. Tozer more than most. I read his classics, *The Pursuit of God* and *The Knowledge of the Holy*, at a formative stage in my life, and they still rank as some of my all-time favorites. Nearly every other sentence is underlined, but one statement has underscored my theology more than any other:

> What comes into our minds when we think about God is the most important thing about us.[1]

That's a sweeping statement, but it's the spiritual sweepstakes. How you see God will dictate how you see yourself, see your future, see your life. It's your trademark, your watermark. And any astigmatism in how you see God will distort your vision of everything else.

When you close your eyes, what snapshots of God are developed in the darkroom of your mind? Is God smiling? Or frowning? Or laughing? Is He standoffish? Or is He warm and welcoming, with arms wide open?

When I think about Jesus, two pictures come to mind. One is Jesus as the Good Shepherd. It's Gentle Jesus, with a lamb draped around his neck. The other is Jesus standing at an old wooden door, about to knock—an artist's rendering of Revelation 3:20. Those are the two pictures that come to mind first, because those are the first pictures of Jesus I saw as a child. Both of them hung in my grandparents' home. Now they hang in my mind.

While I can't back this up with any kind of study, I think it's safe to say that the predominant portrait of Christ in our culture is Christ on the cross. And it is the timeless snapshot of God's amazing grace, so please don't misinterpret what I'm about to say. We desperately need a vision of the crucified Christ, but that isn't where Jesus is.

Jesus is seated at the right hand of the Father, in power and glory. And that's what we need a vision of—the resurrected Christ, the ascended Christ. We also need a high-definition understanding of what He is doing.

Are you ready for this? The Advocate is interceding for you. Now consider the implications—you don't just have one member of the Godhead interceding for you. You have two!

It's a divine double-team.

CORNERMAN

You might not know the name Angelo Dundee, but you've undoubtedly heard of Muhammad Ali. For more than two decades, Angelo Dundee was in Muhammad Ali's corner, literally. He was Ali's cornerman! He's the one who made Ali float like a butterfly and sting like a bee. He also trained fifteen other world boxing champions.

Angelo Dundee described his job as a cornerman this way: "When you're working with a fighter, you're a surgeon, an engineer and a psychologist."[2]

I can't think of a better description of our Cornerman, Jesus Christ.

In 1 Timothy 6:12, Paul exhorts us to "fight the good fight." Listen, you're going to get knocked down a time or two. But you've got a Cornerman who once went three rounds with death itself. He got knocked down at the cross, and the devil thought it was a knockout. But Jesus got back up three days later! He walked out of the tomb, winning the fight against sin and death. Where is He now? He's at the right hand of the Father, interceding for you. In other words, Christ is in your corner! And He's not the only one.

Jesus called the Holy Spirit the *Paraclete*, which translates as *comforter* or *counselor* in English. But I like Cornerman even better. Paraclete is a military term, referring to Roman soldiers who would fight back-to-back when they got into hand-to-hand combat. They protected each other's back side, blind side. And that's what the Holy Spirit does.

The Holy Spirit has got your back. And Christ is in your corner. The prophet Isaiah calls Him our rear guard:

> The LORD will go before you,
>   the God of Israel will be your rear guard.[3]

He's the God who goes before and the God who comes after. He's the God who is with us through thick and through thin.

IN YOUR CORNER

"In your corner."

That is one of my favorite taglines when I text my kids. It's my way of reminding my kids, "I'm with you. I'm for you. And no matter what, I'm in your corner!" In a sense, I'm their corner-man—when they have a winning round and when they have a losing round.

The cross was God's way of saying, "I'm in your corner." No ifs, ands, or buts about it. I don't mean 99 percent. If you are only 99 percent certain of God's good intentions, that 1 percent margin of error will undercut your complete confidence. So let me up the ante. God isn't 100 percent for you; He's *200 percent* for you. And it's not just that we have two advocates.

Follow my logic.

You don't belong to God once; you belong to Him twice. Once by virtue of creation, twice by virtue of redemption. That means you don't owe God one life; you owe Him two. That's why 110 percent effort isn't enough. You owe God 200 percent. After all, isn't that what God gives us? Jesus or the Holy Spirit could get the job done singlehandedly, but both of them are interceding for you day and night, night and day.

That double-team is our double blessing.

God isn't just *for* you once—He is *for* you twice!

Add the heavenly Father to the equation, and it's thrice!

If you don't believe God is 100 percent for you, it might be because you aren't 100 percent for God. My advice? Quit projecting! Is it possible that because you're holding out on God, you think God is holding out on you? Go *all in* with God. Then hold on to this paraphrased promise: if you don't hold out on God, God won't hold out on you.[4]

This is important, so let me come at it from one more angle.

During one game in the 1990 NBA season, Michael Jordan dropped 69 points on the Cleveland Cavaliers. After the game, a reporter asked Stacy King how he would remember that epic performance.

Stacy King had watched most of it from the bench. He was a role player, but he was a role player with a sense of humor. Stacy only scored one point that game, and that is what made his response an instant classic. Stacy King said, "I'll always remember this as the night Michael Jordan and I combined for 70 points!"

For the record, Stacy King rode Michael Jordan's coattails all the way to the NBA championship—not once, not twice, but three times! All thanks to MJ!

When it comes to salvation, we want to be part of the stat line—even if it's one point. But you don't show up in the box score, except for turnovers! The sinless Son of God went to the cross solo, and it was your sin that nailed Him there.

But don't go berating yourself because of the box score.

Celebrate the fact that Jesus settled the score once and for all.

Final Score? Jesus 1, Death 0.

ON YOUR SIDE

When our extended family gets together for holidays or vacations, we enjoy a good game of mafia. Three people are chosen as mafia, and they start killing off the townsfolk. I won't explain the rules, but it's hard to know who is telling the truth. In my experience, the best liars usually win. I rarely win, which I guess is good.

I'm not sure how to say this, because my extended family reads my books, but it takes a day or two for me to fully trust them again. I know it's just a game, but it's hard not to harbor residual feelings of distrust.

I think we struggle with the same subliminal feelings toward God. We cognitively know all things work together for good but when all hell breaks loose, it's difficult to disengage our feelings of distrust.

This goes all the way back to the Garden of Eden. The enemy planted seeds of doubt in Adam and Eve's spirit: *Perhaps God is holding out on you.* If the enemy can get you to distrust God's goodness, it's game, set, match. He's mafia, and he sits on a throne of lies![5]

Growing up, many of us had no clue what our parents did forty hours a week. We might have known where they worked, but we weren't altogether sure what they did. Of course, I live in a city where some people can't tell you what they do or they'd have to shoot you.

In much the same way, most of us don't really know what Jesus does all day. And our lack of holy confidence stems from that very fact. So let me tell you what Jesus does all day, every day: He is pleading your case, pleading your cause. All you have to do is *plead the blood*.

That phrase has fallen out of circulation in some circles, in part because of its misapplication. Let me see if I can revive it. Pleading the blood is not some superstition, like not stepping on a crack to preserve your mother's back. And it's not an abracadabra. It's an awareness of your authority in Christ. It's an understanding that your forgiveness has already been paid for in blood money. It's coming to terms with the fact that we overcome the enemy by the blood of the Lamb.[6]

Christ is in your corner, which means you have the full backing of the King and His kingdom. His full blessing, His full authority! And it goes back to our core identity. If you are a child of the King, that makes you a prince or princess. And the biblical reality is that someday the King of Kings will crown your head. We'll immediately place that crown at the feet of Jesus, *no ifs, ands, or buts about it*. But what a moment that will be!

So maybe we should quit begging like a pauper with no power, no plea.

Christ Himself is pleading your case!

Christ is in your corner, on your side.

That makes every *what if* possible.

———

What if you approached every person,
every situation, every challenge as
if Christ were in your corner?

28

The Event Horizon

Who shall separate us from the love of Christ?
Shall trouble or hardship or persecution or
famine or nakedness or danger or sword?

Romans 8:35

Kay Kostopoulos teaches a class called "Acting with Power" at the Stanford Graduate School of Business.

At the beginning of each semester, her first assignment sets the stage for the class. She pairs off students randomly, then instructs them to stare at each other for three minutes without saying a word.

As you can imagine, the first few seconds are quite awkward. It's one thing staring into the eyes of someone you know, someone you love. It's quite another thing doing a three-minute stare-down with a complete stranger.

But Kostopoulos has found that something almost mystical happens during the exercise. After a few seconds, students lose self-consciousness as they focus their full attention on the face of the other person. They discover that this stranger's face tells a story. It exposes whether they've consistently used sunscreen or not. It's easy to tell if someone has had acne or a case of the chicken pox. Then there are the scars, which raise questions. And, of course, the smile lines, frown lines, and worry lines that reveal a thin slice of history and personality.

If you did that exercise with Jesus, what would it reveal?

That day is coming when we will see our Savior face-to-face. The first thing we'll notice, I think, will be the scars spanning His forehead. Like a barbed wire tattoo, the crown of thorns left its hallmark. It also erased any question mark about His love for us. Jesus wore that crown of injustice so that we could be crowned with righteousness.

When we gaze into His eternal eyes for the first time, we'll see that our Savior's scars are the most beautiful thing about Him because they reveal the physical pain He was willing to endure for our eternal gain. We'll also see smile lines and laugh lines. He carried the weight of the world on His shoulders, shouldering the cross to Calvary, but it didn't rob His joy or diminish the sparkle in His eye.

We'll also see fire in those eyes, the same fire that drove the moneychangers out of the temple with His homemade whip.

There is one more thing we'll see—the same look He gave Peter after Peter's greatest failure. That look is a split second in the crucifixion plotline, but it's an inciting incident for Peter. Right after the rooster crowed, Jesus turned and looked straight at Peter.[1]

When you want your kids to tell the truth, the whole truth, nothing but the truth, what do you tell them? *Look me in the eyes*, right? Why? Because it's much harder to lie that way! Eye contact is a powerful thing, and not just as a truth serum. When you're in love, words aren't necessary. You get lost in each other's eyes.

So Jesus—the Truth, the Whole Truth, Nothing But the Truth— leveraged the power of eye contact with Peter at a critical moment.

If you had just denied Jesus three times, wouldn't you think your career as a disciple was over with? Peter would have given up on himself, save a look. It was *the look* that changed his life. I know I'm reading between the lines, but there wasn't one wink of condemnation.

After all, Jesus could have simply called him out. If He had used words, He would have outed Peter, and Peter probably would have ended up on a cross next to Him! So Jesus gave him a look—a look of utter love, a look of absolute forgiveness. With one look, Jesus said, "I forgive you, I love you—I'm still in your corner." Without saying a word, Jesus said it all. No ifs, ands, or buts about it.

That's how He looks at you.

We have a mistaken notion that God is keeping His eye on us for all the wrong reasons—to catch us doing something wrong. We think he's like Ben Stiller's future father-in-law in *Meet the Parents*. The former CIA counterintelligence officer, played by Robert De Niro, points to his eyes, then points to Greg. In other words, *I've got my eye on you*. And it wasn't for the right reasons.

God has His all-seeing eye on you. In fact, He never takes His eyes off you. But it's not because He's some cosmic killjoy who wants to catch you doing something wrong. He can't take His eyes off you because you're the apple of His eye. He loves you too much to look away!

No Turning Back

In the realm of general relativity, an event horizon is the point of no return. It's the point at which gravitational pull becomes so great that it's impossible to escape. The most obvious example is a black hole—a celestial object so massive that light can only enter but never exit its gravitational field. The escape velocity of a black hole is greater than the speed of light, which is impossible to exceed. So once you cross its horizon, there is no turning back.[2]

255

Hold that thought.

One of the defining moments of my childhood was a Billy Graham crusade at Milwaukee's County Stadium. I invited friends to go with me, hoping they'd go forward when the altar call was given.

To be perfectly honest, I knew it would probably be my only opportunity to stand on the baseball field where the Brewers played. Sure enough, my friends walked the aisle, and I got to stand right where Gold Glove winner Sixto Lezcano played right field. Of course, I was even more excited about my friends responding!

I remember singing a simple chorus as we went forward:

> I have decided to follow Jesus,
> No turning back, no turning back.

It was an event horizon. The love of God entered their hearts, and there was no escaping it. The moment they put their faith in Christ, they passed the point of no return. They crossed the threshold of faith—from "the wages of sin is death" to "the gift of God is eternal life."[3]

God is love.

Such a simple descriptor, but the implications of that one statement will take all of eternity to unpack. Here's what I know now: nothing pulls stronger or longer than God's love. Love is the event horizon, and once you cross over, you can't get back. And who would want to?

Now here's the catch-22: logic won't get you to God's love. His love is beyond logical—it's *theo*logical. The only way to receive the love of God is via revelation, because the love of God surpasses knowledge:

> And I pray that you, being rooted and established in love, may have power, together with all the Lord's holy people, to grasp how wide and long and high and deep is the love of Christ, and to know this love that surpasses knowledge—that you may be filled to the measure of all the fullness of God.[4]

If you've read his epistles, you know that Paul is the patron saint of run-on sentences. This one sentence comprises three verses. But those run-on sentences hint at something that cannot be captured with words. The love of God can't be spelled with twenty-six letters of the English alphabet. And punctuation marks don't come close to doing the trick. So Paul often turns to geometric shapes, cardinal directions, and spatial dimensions.

The point? The love of God, like the power of God, is measureless. It doesn't fit in a box, not even a box the size of the universe. And if the universe isn't big enough to circumscribe the love of God, that love certainly won't fit within the confines of your logical left-brain. So how do we get it in our hearts, in our minds?

God uses the side entrance, the secret entrance called revelation. And much like a black hole, revelation is all but impossible to explain.

SUMMA THEOLOGICA

Thomas Aquinas was one of the most prolific writers and thinkers of the Middle Ages and one of only thirty-three Doctors of the Church. His magnum opus, *Summa Theologica*, is one of history's most exhaustive and enduring theologies. But Aquinas never finished it because something happened on December 6, 1273, that caused him to quit writing. It was his *no ifs, ands, or buts about it* moment.

"All that I have written seems to me like straw," Aquinas said, "compared to what has now been revealed to me."[5] Exactly what was revealed remains a mystery, but that one revelation surpassed all the knowledge he'd acquired.

No matter what your IQ, that's what you need. No one is smart enough to reason their way to God. We need the spirit of wisdom and revelation. In the meantime, we rely on analogies to draw kindergarten-quality paintings of God's love.

Nothing will define your life, change your outlook, or even alter your personality like a revelation of God's love. But it's so diametrically different from the way we give and receive love on a human level that it demands delineation.

First of all, His love is unconditional. There is nothing you can do to make God love you more or less because He already loves you perfectly, eternally. Even when we don't reciprocate His love, it doesn't deter, deflect, or diminish His love. It accentuates it.

While we were still sinners, Christ died for us.[6]

It's easy to love someone when they're at their best. When they're at their worst? Not so much. But that's the test of true love. Our love tends to be reactive, but God's love is proactive. It doesn't reciprocate; it procreates. He loves us when we least expect it and least deserve it. And even when we're at our worst, He's at His best.

The closest I can come to understanding the love of the heavenly Father is thinking about it as an earthly parent. Being a parent to our three children has taught me more about God's love than three graduate degrees in theology. Nothing compares. Yet no matter how high and wide and deep and long our love for our children is, it's still measured in years.

God's love is forever and a day!

QUESTION MARK

By the time we get to the event horizon in the Great Eight, the apostle Paul is making closing arguments. And when Paul really wants to make a point, he doesn't just use run-on sentences. He often employs a question mark as his exclamation point.

In the span of five verses, he asks seven questions. They are loaded questions—the kind of question trial attorneys ask when they already know the answer, the kind of question that will break a case wide open. In my humble opinion, the leading question is the one we've already answered: "If God is for us, who can be against us?"[7]

If you get that one wrong, nothing will be right. If you get it right, nothing can go wrong. It's *the* question. But the question in verse 35 is a close second:

What shall separate us from the love of Christ?

The answer, of course, is *nothing*. And the chapter would end there, but Paul spells it out as best he can. He comes up with a laundry list of worst-case scenarios—from trouble to danger and anything in between. And he's not blowing smoke. As Paul pens these words, each one conjures up memories. When Paul writes *hardship*, he's back on the Mediterranean Sea during a terrible typhoon. *Persecution* pings his memory of being stoned at Lystra and left for dead. *Trials?* Paul stood trial before Nero himself. He also went without food, got bit by a poisonous snake, and had the clothes stripped off his back so he could be flogged.

Nor did this happen once or twice. Five times he received the maximum sentence—forty lashes minus one. Paul's back was whiplashed and crisscrossed with 195 scars.

Hardship has one of two effects: it either hardens or softens our hearts. And it's that hardening or softening that makes us or breaks us. I've seen some marriages come apart at the seams when tough times hit, but I've also seen hardship form a bond like no one's business. It can turn men into a band of brothers, and women into a ya-ya sisterhood.

The love depicted in the Great Eight isn't a sentimental love. It's not in the same category as "I love Thin Mint Girl Scout cookies," "I love Washington, DC," or "I love the lake." It's a hard-fought, hard-earned love.

It's a love that is bound by blood, sweat, and tears.

It's a love tempered by fifty years of marriage.

It's a love that has endured a miscarriage, the death of a parent, or even an affair.

It's a love that has been knocked down—but gotten back up every time.

Like a fine wine or fine cheese, love goes through an aging process. And that's why aging should be embraced as one of God's greatest gifts.

When I worship, I don't just sing in the present tense. I sing out of my past-tense memories and future-tense dreams. I sing out of the sum total of my life. So a song isn't just five minutes of praise. For me, it's more than four decades of worship. Each song spans our lifespan, so the older we get, the more capacity we have to worship God. And not only does my song span my lifespan, it also spans the heavens, hitting the eardrums of God Almighty.

I don't think I'll ever know the kind of persecution Paul endured, but each of those experiences was an event horizon that revealed more of God's love, more of God's grace.

If you're in a tough place, a place where it's hard to even ask *what if*, take heart. No one likes tough times in the present tense, but those tests add tenor to our testimony. And those are often the memories we cherish the most. Our great-grandparents loved telling stories about adding water to ketchup to make tomato soup during the Great Depression, using the outhouse in subzero temperatures, and walking through a foot of snow to a school that was uphill both ways.

We look back on challenges with a touch of nostalgic pride. According to one poll of Londoners, 60 percent of those who survived Germany's blitzkrieg during World War II remembered it as the happiest time of their lives. It's the tough times—trouble, hardship, persecution, famine, nakedness, danger, and sword—that test our love. But that's also how it's proved.

The love of Christ wasn't proved by His miracles, as impressive as those miracles were. His love was proved on a Roman cross. And it has proven to be failproof.

The cross is God's way of saying, "Over my dead body."

No matter what trouble, hardship, or persecution you face, this too shall pass. More importantly, Jesus is *with you* and Jesus is *for* you. And no matter what has died at the hands of sin or Satan, Jesus can roll away the stone.

What if you fully surrendered your life
to Christ, right here, right now?

29

More than Conquerors

No, in all these things we are more than conquerors through him who loved us.

Romans 8:37

Remember the 1977 power ballad "We Are the Champions"? It
was the traditional encore at the end of performances by the British band Queen. While it never hit number one on the charts, a
team of scientific researchers dubbed it the catchiest song in the
history of pop music.

Maybe it's the unique combination of jazz chords—major and
minor 6th, 7th, 11th, and 13th harmonies. Or perhaps it was the
male high C, in falsetto, belted out by lead singer Freddie Mercury.

Regardless, once it gets in your head it's tough to get it out.
Nearly three decades after the original recording, it was voted the
world's favorite song in a worldwide music poll.[1]

If the Great Eight were an album, "More than Conquerors"
would be the title track. The whole thing is a power ballad. The

melody starts with "no condemnation" and ends with "nothing can separate us from the love of Christ." The bass line is "all things work together for good." But the high falsetto is "more than conquerors."

"We are the champions, my friend. And we'll keep on fighting to the end." Freddie Mercury is no theologian, but this song is a pretty good paraphrase of the Great Eight. Well, except for the part about no time for losers. Jesus would have been awfully lonely if He hadn't done that, and so would we!

This is our soundtrack. It might not feel that way on a bad day. But even if you've failed a thousand times, you're still more than a conqueror. And to think of yourself as anything less than who you are in Christ is false humility.

In my experience, it takes time to take on a new identity. Like a new pair of shoes, you've got to break it in. When I first started pastoring, I didn't feel like a pastor, and I didn't look like one either. It took a few years to take on that mantle. When I wrote my first book, I felt funny calling myself an author. It took a few books for it not to feel like a fake passport.

The same is true with this identifier. But even if you're losing more battles than you're winning, you're still more than a conqueror. Why? Because the battle isn't yours to win or lose. The battle belongs to the Lord. And Christ has already conquered. No ifs, ands, or buts about it.

SWOOSH

On October 7, 1916, Georgia Tech defeated Cumberland College by a record-setting score of 222-0. It still ranks as the most lopsided victory in college football history. Much like in today's ranking system, margin of victory mattered back then too. So Coach John Heisman, after whom the Heisman trophy is named, ran up the score.

Hey, it could have been worse! Cumberland College did block one extra point using a human pyramid. According to the final box score, Cumberland gained, or maybe I should say lost, negative 28 yards.[2]

That's a convincing victory!

You might even call it *hupernikao*.

The three-word phrase "more than conquerors" comes from that one Greek word. It's a rare compound that means to hyper-conquer, over-conquer, or conquer with success to spare.[3] It's more than a *W*; it's a defining *W* that demoralizes your opponent.

That's where the word *Nike* comes from. In Greek mythology, she was the goddess of victory. Both in battle and in sport, *Nike* personified and epitomized victory. So the apostle Paul redeems that word and uses it to describe us.

I still remember asking my parents for my first pair of Nike shoes. I pronounced it with one syllable, not two. And I made it plural, *Nikes*. But even in the second grade, it was a status symbol. Next to Coca-Cola, the Nike swoosh may be the most recognizable logo on the planet.

Romans 8:37 is our *swoosh*!

When I introduce myself to people, I don't say, "Hi, I'm a hyper-conqueror." I typically use my birth name, Mark. But that's my birthright as a child of God. And when we look in the mirror, that's who we should see. Sure, I see my imperfections too. But my truest reflection is the image of God. And in Christ, I'm more than a conqueror.

When I was interviewing for ministerial credentials as a twenty-two-year-old seminary student, a wise pastor asked me a profound question: "If you had to describe yourself in one word, what would it be?"

How would you answer that question?

By the way, if you want to get to know someone really well, really fast, that's a pretty good question!

I've written about my answer elsewhere, so I won't expound. But the twenty-two-year-old me said *driven*.

Truth is, you can't be reduced to a one-word descriptor. Not even a hyphenated word. But biblically speaking, I can't think of a better answer than *hupernikao*. I think it comes as close as any word. That's who you are in Christ. It's your truest identity, your surest destiny.

God is preparing good works in advance.

God is ordering your footsteps.

God is working all things together for good.

All of those promises translate into one moniker: *more than a conqueror*.

TAPE DELAY

Let me reveal an idiosyncrasy.

It's a piece of my personality that my inner circle knows all about, and it has to do with how I watch sports. It might seem irrelevant or insignificant, but not when you watch sports with as much passion as I do. So here's the scoop on my TV-watching habits—after a bit of historical backdrop.

I grew up in Chicago during the Michael Jordan era, so it felt like poor stewardship to miss a single game. If the game coincided with church, we would record it on something called a VCR. Well, that happened quite frequently back then because anything less than three services a week was backsliding! During the playoffs, I hoped against hope that the games wouldn't fall on a Sunday or Wednesday because we had church.

Quite honestly, it was hard to concentrate on the message if the Bulls were playing. All I could do was pray for Michael Jordan, which might explain six championships!

Now here's the idiosyncrasy. We'd tape the game, then make a beeline for the exit just as church finished. The benediction was our "Star-Spangled Banner" and "Play ball!" Sometimes I'd cover my ears on the way out so I wouldn't inadvertently hear the score. And we would never, ever turn on the radio on the way home. Then we'd watch the game as if it were live, and if the phone rang, we wouldn't answer it, because it might contain information pertaining to the game. That would be impermissible and inadmissible.

Then, when the fat lady finally sang, we'd know the final score about three hours after everyone else in the Chicagoland area. It worked like a charm until one occasion when the game went into overtime.

We ran out of VHS tape with two minutes to play, in a playoff game!

It was close to midnight, and we couldn't just google it back then. So we desperately dialed friends' numbers, trying to find out whether or not we'd won. It was the longest five minutes of our lives!

Fast-forward twenty-five years, and my routine has changed. I still DVR an occasional game, but I now check the score before watching. If my team lost, why subject myself to three hours of pain and suffering? If they won, I enjoy the game even more. Sure, the element of surprise is lost, but there is far less stress!

I actually enjoy every play because I know the final outcome. And even if we're losing, I'm not worried about it, because I know we're going to win.

What if we approached our lives the same way?

Read the box score in the book of Revelation. We win!

Do we still have to fight the good fight? Absolutely! And we might get knocked down a time or two, but the fight is fixed. It's no contest. Yet judging by the demeanor of some Debbie Downer Christians, you'd think the outcome was in doubt. Come on! He's the God who saves us, from the guttermost to the uttermost.

When Jesus died on the cross, the enemy thought it was game over. But that wasn't the final buzzer. The game went into overtime. And when Jesus walked out of the tomb three days later, the final score was posted. The victory was signed, sealed, and delivered two thousand years ago. Now we just need to live like it.

A 22-POINT COMEBACK

My best friend in high school, Rick Workman, recently sent me a newspaper clipping dated February 22, 1988. The title read: "Wolfe, Batterson Bomb Redskins to Title." I hadn't seen it in twenty-five years, but it ranks as the most memorable game of my basketball career, and there isn't a close second.

With the conference title on the line, we trailed our crosstown rivals, the Naperville North Huskies, by 22 points with 5:35 remaining. That's an insurmountable deficit by high school standards, but we hit six three-pointers in the fourth quarter, including a buzzer-beater to tie the game. Then we completed the comeback with a two-point victory in overtime.

Did we try to fall that far behind? Of course not! But that's what made the victory so sweet. No one likes a setback, but how else can you experience a comeback? And the bigger the setback, the greater the comeback!

Maybe you're battling cancer, going through a difficult divorce, or drowning in debt. If so, please hear me. When you experience a setback, you may take a step back, but God is already preparing your comeback.

It was the setback of the cross that set up the greatest comeback in human history, the resurrection of Jesus Christ. As Tony Campolo is famous for saying, "It's Friday, but Sunday's coming." And remember, without a crucifixion, there is no resurrection.[4]

I could tell you a thousand stories of setbacks experienced by God-fearing, Bible-believing, Christ-loving people. While the circumstances may differ, the story line is the same. Through Christ, we overcome.

It's no coincidence that the word testimony begins with *test*. Pass the test, get a testimony.

There is no addiction so strong that God's power cannot deliver.

There is no failure so final that God's grace cannot forgive.

There is no wound so deep that God's love cannot heal.

No matter how bad it is, His grace is sufficient. And no matter how good it is, the best is yet to come.

THE LAMB HAS CONQUERED

I have a favorite sweatshirt.

It was a gift from David Perkins, the founder of the Desperation movement in Colorado Springs, Colorado. I was speaking at their annual conference where thousands of teenagers throw down in worship and seek God with reckless abandon. It's a sight to behold.

I happened to spot a very cool sweatshirt with the image of a lamb on the front, and David was kind enough to give me an XL. Encircling the lamb is a saying,

The Lamb Has Conquered.
Follow the Lamb.

In the eighteenth century, Count Ludwig Nikolaus von Zinzendorf founded a group called The Order of the Mustard Seed. The members of that group included such notables as the king of Denmark, the Anglican Archbishop of Canterbury, the secretary of state of Scotland, and an eighty-seven-year-old Creek Indian chief named Tomochichi.

The members solemnly pledged to be true to Christ, to be kind to people, and to take the gospel to the nations. They also pledged all of their wealth and influence to the cause of Christ. Most significantly, they started a prayer meeting in 1727 that would pray around the clock for one hundred years! The aftershocks of that *what if* were still felt 277 years later when David Perkins visited Herrnhut, Germany, the birthplace of that Moravian revival.

David knelt at the grave of Count von Zinzendorf and wept. God birthed a *what if* in his spirit—what if he came back to Colorado Springs and started an around-the-clock prayer meeting like the Moravians?

It's that prayer meeting that has turned into a movement called Desperation. Their logo? A conquering lamb—the same symbol the Moravian Church emblazoned on the front of their victory flag, now emblazoned on my sweatshirt.

Their mission statement? The rallying cry of the Moravians: *The Lamb Has Conquered. Follow the Lamb.*

What makes us more than conquerors? The blood of the Lamb—the Conquering Lamb.[5]

TO HIM WHO OVERCOMES

A friend of a friend is an NFL chaplain. In fact, his team won the Super Bowl a few years back. He wasn't on the 53-man roster or part of the coaching staff. And like most chaplains, he raises financial support to do what he does. But the head coach so valued the chaplain's investment that he gave him a Super Bowl ring.

If you're in Christ, you get a ring. Even if you don't play a single down, you get a ring. Even if you have a bad game, you get a ring. Even if you're the ball boy, you get a ring. Why? Because you're *in Christ*, which means you're on the team. It's that simple.

Never have the odds been more stacked against someone than they were the day Christ was betrayed, arrested, flogged, and crucified. But Jesus overcame the odds, and that makes us the overcomers! And He gives us a ring.

> "On that day," declares the LORD Almighty, "I will take you, my servant Zerubbabel son of Shealtiel," declares the LORD, "and I will make you like my signet ring, for I have chosen you."[6]

A signet ring was a king's official seal, symbolizing his royal authority. Once invoked, it could not be revoked. That's you. You are God's signet ring.

When the Green Bay Packers won Super Bowl XLV, I was there. Despite being a shareholder, I did *not* receive a ring. After the game, I heard about the bold move made by Coach Mike McCarthy the night before the game. He had his players sized for Super Bowl rings!

You've already been sized, and not just ring size. Hat size too! You get to wear the ring now, plus there is a crown in heaven with your name on it.

Seven times the book of Revelation refrains: "To him who overcomes." It's the same word that's used in the Great Eight, *hupernikao*. And a promise is attached to all seven. They include the right to eat from the tree of life, a white stone with a new name on it, and the right to sit on the Father's throne.

These seven refrains raise the question, How do we overcome? The answer is simple: *in Christ*. It's the only way—the Way, the Truth, and the Life.

You are more than a conqueror, and to think of yourself as anything less is false humility. And false humility is worse than pride! Pride is believing something about yourself that isn't true. False humility is *not* believing something about yourself that is true. Here's the truth: *you are more than a conqueror.*

No ifs, ands, or buts about it.

*What if you stopped thinking of yourself
as anything less than who you are
in Christ—more than a conqueror?*

30

Keep Calm and Carry On

> For I am convinced that neither death nor life, neither
> angels nor demons, neither the present nor the future,
> nor any powers, neither height nor depth, nor any-
> thing else in all creation, will be able to separate us from
> the love of God that is in Christ Jesus our Lord.
>
> Romans 8:38–39

The first air raid siren sounded over London in September of 1939.
For anyone who lived in the city during World War II, it's a sound
that will echo forever. The German blitzkrieg dropped a hundred
tons of explosives on sixteen British cities. More than a million
homes were destroyed, and forty thousand civilians lost their lives.

Hitler thought the blitz would demoralize the British into surrendering. He thought wrong. The blitzkrieg backfired, steeling
the Brits' resolve to fight, even if it meant fighting to the death.

During the darkest days of the war, Prime Minister Winston
Churchill visited Harrow School, the same school where he had

spent four of his most formative years. It had been half a century since he had won the school's fencing championship. But it seems fitting that Churchill would deliver one of his most famous speeches at the school where he recited poetry and competed in debates.

Fifty years of flashbacks must have fired across his synapses as he stood to speak on October 29, 1941. His words were fit "for such a time as this,"[1] but they ring true in peacetime as well as war. His speech wasn't as punctual as some have made it seem, but his words proved more powerful than the German blitzkrieg.

> Never give in, never, never, never—never, in nothing great or small, large or petty—never give in except to convictions of honor and good sense. Never yield to force; never yield to the apparently overwhelming might of the enemy.[2]

It's a powerful rule of thumb: never give in. But the exception to the rule is even more powerful: except to your convictions.

There is an old adage: let your conscience be your guide. Let me one-up it: let your *convictions* be your guide. If you want to accomplish something for the kingdom, you can't conform to culture. That's how you fit in, not stand out. If you want to make a difference, live according to your convictions. Of course, you have to identify them first.

I have a handful of core convictions, my kernels of truth. With each repetition, they become more and more engrained, like a memory trace. The one I repeat most often is probably, "Pray like it depends on God and work like it depends on you." But there are others, such as, "Criticize by creating," "Thou shalt offend Pharisees," and "Catch people doing something right."

I also believe that "Playing it safe is risky," "There are ways of doing church that no one has thought of yet," and "When God gives a vision, He makes provision." If you reverse engineer Mark Batterson, those core convictions are my key code.

What are your core convictions?

If you want to build a hundred-story skyscraper, you need a ten-story foundation. In much the same way, big dreams require deep convictions. The heights of your accomplishments will never exceed the depth of your convictions.

If you don't know what your convictions are, you don't really know *who* you are. I know that's blunt, but your convictions are the truest thing about you. You are your convictions. Or more accurately, you become your convictions.

For better or for worse, your deepest held beliefs will define who you become. For Paul, it was the fact that nothing can separate us from the love of Christ. It wasn't just the foundation upon which Paul built his life. He banked all of eternity on it.

CORE CONVICTIONS

Let me make a distinction between *core convictions* and *core values*.

I don't want to degrade core values in any way, shape, or form. In fact, our family has four words, four values that we aspire to: humility, generosity, gratitude, and courage. But those values had to crystallize into convictions over time.

The value is generic *humility*, but the conviction is deeper and stronger. It's more nuanced than a one-word value. *If you stay humble and stay hungry, there is nothing God cannot do through you.* The emphasis is on *if.* I believe that as much as I believe anything, which is what makes it a core conviction. It's a truth that you can take to the bank, take to the grave, or even take home to meet the in-laws.

The problem with most value statements is that they are written with ink on paper. Some of them are beautifully designed, including our family coat of arms. We even translated the four values into Latin. Fancy, I know. But it's still ink.

Convictions are written with blood, sweat, and tears. And the font is often written in our flesh. Paul wrote his letter to the Romans on parchment, but in reality, it was written with a whip, in prison blocks, and hanging on to a piece of ship that had shipwrecked and shattered on the rocks. Each of those experiences steeled his conviction that nothing can separate us from the love of Christ.

Convictions are lessons learned from experiences we'd never want to go through again, but we wouldn't trade for anything in the world. They can't be learned in a lecture hall. They are taught by life's toughest teachers—pain, grief, disappointment, and failure. If you've gotten a graduate degree in grief or taken a test procured by Professor Pain, you know what I'm talking about.

Convictions come at a cost, but the value added is inestimable. And that's why the words at the end of the Great Eight carry so much weight. It's like a change in air density when you get to the last verses in the greatest chapter.

They aren't just poetic parallelisms. They strike a dominant chord in our spirits. When all else fails, it's all we need to know. Even death, our mortal enemy, cannot separate us from the love of Christ.

So let me ask again: What are your core convictions? What are you willing to go to the grave for? What will you stake your reputation on?

Those are your *no ifs, ands, or buts about it* convictions.

THE SWAN SONG

"I am convinced."[3]

That's a powerful little phrase. It's Paul's core conviction. And there are no ifs, ands, or buts about it. Paul doesn't just know; he knows that he knows. Not a hint of doubt. Absolute certainty.

Here's my point: the Great Eight isn't a chapter; it's a conviction. It starts with the conviction that *there is no condemnation.* Ironically, the key to that conviction is responding to the conviction of the Holy Spirit. The underlying conviction that *all things work together for good* is the heart of the Great Eight.

Then there's the game changer: *If God is for us, who can be against us?*

By the end, *we are more than conquerors*. Then there is one last conviction. It's the swan song. *Nothing can separate us from the love of Christ*. What a crescendo! When everything goes wrong, this one conviction makes everything right. It's the happily ever after.

Before drilling down on this conviction, let me add one more layer of history.

Before the blitzkrieg began, the British Department of Information designed three "Home Publicity" posters. They weren't dissimilar from the Uncle Sam "I Want You" or Rosie the Riveter "We Can Do It" posters. Each of the posters used the Tudor Crown as its watermark.

The first said, "Your Courage, Your Cheerfulness, Your Resolution Will Bring Us Victory."

The second said, "Freedom Is in Peril."

The third and most famous said, "Keep Calm and Carry On."

To date, more than nine million parodies have been made of that original maxim, most of them trivializing that truth. But in its original form and original context, it was the quintessential rallying cry.

Now, here's the irony. While 2.45 million posters were printed, they were never publicly displayed. That motto had all but vanished from Britain's consciousness when a bookstore-owning couple in Alnwick, Stuart and Mary Manley, discovered an original copy of the poster at the bottom of a box of old books.

Keep Calm and Carry On

If you can get past all the parodies, it's an enduring sentiment. In fact, it has biblical undertones. He who began a good work will carry it to completion. We can do all things through Christ who strengthens us. All things work together for good to those that love

God and are called according to His purpose. Every promise is *yes* in Christ. And nothing can separate us from the love of Christ.

So keep calm and carry on!

BETWEEN A ROCK AND THE RED SEA

The most difficult and perhaps the most important sermon I ever preached was on October 11, 2009. It wasn't a matter of life or death, but it was my "Never Give In" speech.

Six days before, I'd gotten an unexpected phone call informing me that the movie theater at Union Station, where National Community Church had met for thirteen years, was shutting down. To make matters worse, the manager told me that the next Sunday would be our last Sunday! We numbered in the thousands, not millions, like the Israelites. But I still felt a little bit like Moses, who must have wondered how he'd pull off the road trip from Egypt to Canaan with two million people in his caravan.

The news was devastating to me. So much of our history and identity as a church was wrapped up in where we met. Honestly, it was probably unhealthy, but it was reality. I secretly wondered if our best days were behind us. But one thing was certain: I knew I needed a word from God that weekend. And I got one.

The Holy Spirit quickened Exodus 14. Moses found himself between a rock, which was the Egyptian army, and a hard place, the Red Sea. It was an impossible circumstance, but God gave Moses very specific instructions:

> Do not be afraid. Stand firm and you will see the deliverance the LORD will bring you today. The Egyptians you see today you will never see again. The LORD will fight for you; you need only to be still.[4]

Sounds an awful lot like *keep calm and carry on*, doesn't it?

What would be the hardest thing to do if Egyptian chariots were charging straight at you at full speed? The hardest thing to do would be to do what God told them to do: stand still.

When we find ourselves in this sort of situation, we want to *do* something—*anything*. We have a nervous energy that tries to solve the problem as quickly as possible. But these are the tests that reveal trust. No one wants to find themselves between the Egyptian army and the Red Sea, but that is where our convictions are tried and tested.

Sometimes God leads us to a place where we have nowhere to turn but Him. This is that moment for the Israelites. And that's how I felt when the movie theaters at Union Station shut down. It would be two long years before we'd figure out where God was taking us. I've never felt more helpless as a leader, but I've also never felt more energized. I knew that God was giving us Exodus 14 as a promise to stand on. I knew we needed to stand still, stand firm.

I very candidly said to our church, "I don't know what we're going to do, but I know exactly what we're *not* going to do. We're not going to panic! We're going to stand still. And we're going to see the deliverance of the Lord!"

I have stopped categorizing things as good and bad. Why? Because all things work together for good. That's my conviction. I'm not saying they are good when they happen, but there is nothing that God cannot redeem and recycle for His purposes. And sometimes it's the bad things that turn out to be the best things that have happened to me.

When the theaters closed, I thought it was the worst thing that could happen to us. But that one domino led to another, and now we own a castle! When Union Station closed, our net assets were a negative number. We had more debt than equity. In the five years following, God gave us one piece of Promised Land after another until our balance sheet shows somewhere around $30 million in net assets.

Honestly, I don't even know exactly how it happened. But the numbers don't lie. And those real estate acquisitions started with something that we perceived as bad.

In nearly twenty years of pastoring through the ups and downs, I've learned to *keep calm and carry on*. The same is true in marriage and in raising children. It's true in business and it's true in politics. Keep doing the right things day in and day out; exercise a long obedience in the same direction. There will certainly be some Red Seas along the way, but what seems like a dead end might just turn into your defining moment.

One thing is certain: God will never leave you nor forsake you. And there are no ifs, ands, or buts about it.

JESUS LOVES ME, THIS I KNOW

In 1962, the Swiss theologian Dr. Karl Barth did a lecture tour of the United States. Barth is regarded by many within the Protestant tradition as the greatest theologian of the twentieth century. He also made his mark outside the church, hitting the cover of *Time* magazine on April 20, 1962.

One of his lecture stops that year was the University of Chicago. That invitation alone is remarkable to me because I was a student there several decades later, and I can't imagine a theologian being invited, much less esteemed.

After Barth delivered his lecture at Rockefeller chapel, a student asked him if he could summarize his whole life's work in a single sentence. That's not an easy question for someone as prolific as Barth, whose résumé included more than six hundred works. His magnum opus, *Church Dogmatics*, was written over a thirty-five-year span. The eight-thousand-page, thirteen-volume set is a library unto itself.

Barth responded to the question in no uncertain terms. He went old school, citing the words of a song he learned at his mother's knee:

> Jesus loves me, this I know,
> for the Bible tells me so.[5]

More specifically, the Great Eight tells me so.
It's high-definition, high-resolution.

It's 24 frames per second, 24-bit RGB, 1080p.

The apostle Paul has already painted a picture, but now he adds the finishing touch. Like reinforced concrete, these verses add tensile strength to God's love. And there is no failure point. Paul's sweeping parallelisms cover all the bases.

It starts with our mortal enemy, *death*. Then Paul throws in anything *life* can throw at us. Those bookends, life and death, would seal the deal. But wait, there's more. By citing *angels* and *demons*, Paul includes the paranormal. God's love isn't natural; it's supernatural.

And it certainly can't be confined to three tenses of time. Just as nothing can surprise the One who knows all things, no *present* predicament or *future* contingency can change His unconditional love one iota.

But wait, there's more! No *powers*, plural, can overpower His love.

And just for good measure, one more set of bookends: *height* and *depth*.

The furthest galaxy discovered by spectroscopy is z8_GND _5296.[6] No, that's not an old AOL screen name. It's a galaxy that is 13.8 billion light-years old, or 13.8 billion light-years away. Spatially speaking, it's the highest height. The deepest depth is the Challenger Deep, part of a trench 6.85 miles beneath the U.S. Territorial Island of Guam.[7]

From the zero gravity of space to the 1,000-times atmospheric pressure of the deep seas, God's love is present and accounted for. You can't escape it, even if you could escape time and space. His love goes beyond the borders of space, beyond the boundaries of time. It cannot be measured nor manipulated.

The only thing that can frustrate the grace of God is your refusal to receive it. But even before you accept His saving grace, His common grace has been in every breath you've taken.

The last thing on the list? Any created thing, which would include everything. What a wrap!

LOVE YOU MORE

Jesus doesn't just love you. His love is deeper than the Challenger Deep. His love is truer than the truest color, purer than the purest sound. His love is smaller than the smallest subatomic particle and larger than the largest galaxy. His love is more beautiful than an angel, more powerful than a demonic stronghold. At some point, just like Paul, we run out of analogies. And that's when God's love has just begun. Even if we could look through the Hubble Space Telescope, it would be but a peephole into God's infinite love.

I love the catchphrase "love you more." It caught on in our family when Lora and Summer started saying it to each other. We even got a wall hanging with those words on it for Summer.

I know they both mean it when they say it, but like any parent, Lora is able to say it more authoritatively. After all, she gave birth to Summer. She's loved Summer longer than Summer can remember. She's loved Summer more than Summer can imagine.

And if that's true of us as earthly parents, just imagine how much the heavenly Father loves you.

Actually, you can't imagine it, because it's beyond what you can ask or imagine.

And perhaps that's Paul's point after all.

God loves you more.

No ifs, ands, or buts about it.

What if you committed yourself to long obedience in the right direction?

Epilogue

Forty Years Hence

In his brilliantly conceived book *Life Verses*, F. W. Boreham shares the favorite passages of famous personages. It's a fascinating prism through which to view a person's biography. In many respects, our lives become caricatures of our most cherished verses. Those Scriptures become the script of our lives.

In Harriet Beecher Stowe's history-changing book *Uncle Tom's Cabin*, her favorite verse is revealed vicariously through Uncle Tom. As he draws his dying breath, Old Tom murmurs, "Who, who—who—who shall separate us from the love of Christ?" The Great Eight was the pillow of faith upon which he fell asleep one last time.[1]

When John Bunyan had a revelation of this verse, he said, "Surely I will not forget this forty years hence"![2] It was the anchor for his soul, and perhaps the inspiration for *Pilgrim's Progress*.

But my favorite story is that of John Bruce, a federal judge appointed by Ulysses S. Grant. On his deathbed, he instructed his daughter to "Fetch the book."[3] He told her to turn to the eighth chapter of Romans and said, "Put my finger on these words," and quoted:

> For I am persuaded, that neither death, nor life, nor angels, nor principalities, nor powers, nor things present, nor things to come,
> Nor height, nor depth, nor any other creature, shall be able to separate us from the love of God, which is in Christ Jesus our Lord.[4]

When his daughter found the words, John Bruce told her to hold his finger there. He passed away with his finger on that promise.[5] What a way to enter heaven, the eternal *what if*.

My advice, at the end of this book, is to fetch *that* Book. Put your finger on the Great Eight, and anchor your soul to its promises.

In time, your *if only* regrets will fade to black.

In eternity, your *what if* dreams will come to light.

No if, ands, or buts about it.

Notes

Chapter 1 The Power of *If*

1. Howard Schultz and Dori Jones Yang, *Pour Your Heart into It: How Starbucks Built a Company One Cup at a Time* (New York: Hyperion, 1997), 63.

2. "Starbucks Coffee: How Many Cups of Coffee Does Starbucks Sell Each Year?" Quora query answered by Ali Ahmed, January 17, 2011, http://www.quora.com/Starbucks-Coffee-How-many-cups-of-coffee-does-Starbucks-sell-each-year. Accessed March 18, 2015.

3. "15 Facts about Starbucks That Will Blow Your Mind," *Business Insider*, http://www.businessinsider.com/15-facts-about-starbucks-that-will-blow-your-mind-2011-3?op=1#ixzz3Uki21JWv. Accessed March 18, 2015.

4. Neal Roese, *If Only: How to Turn Regret into Opportunity* (New York: Broadway, 2005), 48.

5. Robert Cowley, ed., *What If?* (New York: Putnam, 1999), xi.

6. John Piper, "Greatest Book, Greatest Chapter, Greatest Joy," Desiring God, September 28, 2014, http://www.desiringgod.org/conference-messages/greatest-book-greatest-chapter-greatest-joy. Accessed March 18, 2015.

7. "Vorrede auff die Epistel S. Paul: an die Romer," in *Martin Luther: Die gantze Heilige Schrifft Deudsch 1545 aufs new zurericht* vol. 2, ed. Hans Volz and Heinz Blanke, trans. Bro. Andrew Thornton (Munich: Roger & Bernhard, 1972), 2254–68.

8. William Tyndale, *Doctrinal Treatises and Introductions to Different Portions of the Holy Scriptures*, ed. Henry Walter (Cambridge: University Press, 1848), 484.

9. Douglas J. Moo, *Romans 1–8*, Wycliffe Exegetical Commentary vol. 1., ed. Kenneth Barker (Chicago: Moody Press, 1991), 499.

10. Romans 8:1.

11. Romans 8:38–39.

12. Romans 8:28 KJV.

13. Romans 8:37.

14. Romans 8:31.

Chapter 2 The Most Terrifying Fact

1. "National Prayer Breakfast," CSPAN transcript, February 2, 2012, http://www.c-span.org/video/?304149-1/national-prayer-breakfast.

2. Ibid.

3. See "The Lever: Introduction," http://www.math.nyu.edu/~crorres/Archimedes/Lever/LeverIntro.html. Accessed March 18, 2015.

4. See Isaiah 54:17.

5. See 1 John 4:4.

6. See Philippians 4:13.

7. Oswald Chambers, "Inspired Invincibility," *My Utmost for His Highest*, online daily devotional, April 14, 2015, http://utmost.org/classic/inspired-invincibility-classic/.

8. Malcolm Gladwell, *The Tipping Point* (New York: Little, Brown, 2000), 12.

9. Luke 2:14 KJV.

10. See Psalm 84:11.

11. *Wired*, December 2014, 208.

Chapter 3 Can't Forget

1. Jill Price, *The Woman Who Can't Forget* (New York: Free Press, 2008), 47.

2. Ibid., 3.

3. See Isaiah 61:10.

4. See Zechariah 2:8.

5. John 8:7, 11 NKJV.

6. Joshua 5:9 NLT.

7. See 1 Timothy 1:15.

8. See Romans 3:23.

Chapter 4 Double Jeopardy

1. Rudyard Kipling, "If—" in *Rewards and Fairies* (1910), available online at The Poetry Foundation, http://www.poetryfoundation.org/poem/175772. Accessed March 19, 2015.

2. Romans 8:1.

3. See Deuteronomy 6:4.

4. See 2 Corinthians 2:11.

5. Revelation 12:10 KJV.

6. Horatio Spafford, "It Is Well with My Soul," 1873. See http://cyberhymnal.org/htm/i/t/i/itiswell.htm.

7. See Romans 5:20.

Chapter 5 A $100 Million Fast

1. Isaiah 58:6–7 NKJV.

2. Mohammed Yunus, a Nobel Peace Prize winner for his work on microfinance, later told Tony that the fund had reached more than $500 million.

3. *The Matrix*, directed by The Wachowski Brothers (Warner Bros., 1999).

4. I first encountered this little fact while working out at Results Gym on Capitol Hill. One of the trainers had written it on the chalkboard. I had a great workout that day!

5. Andy Stanley, *Choosing to Cheat* (Colorado Springs: Multnomah, 2003), 10.

6. See Mark 11:12–14, 20–21.

7. In the King James Version.

Chapter 6 Muscle Memory

1. Thanks to our executive pastor, Joel Schmidgall, for this thought.

2. Galatians 6:9.

3. 1 John 2:16.

4. Romans 8:4 KJV.

5. 1 Corinthians 10:23 NIV 1984.

6. Thanks to Jim Collins and his brilliant book *Good to Great* for this little play on words.

7. Thanks to Oswald Chambers and his classic devotional, *My Utmost for His Highest*, for this play on words.

8. Romans 8:4 KJV.

9. Matthew 16:18 ESV.

Chapter 7 Factory Reset

1. See 2 Corinthians 5:17.

2. See Hebrews 8:12.

3. Many articles have been written on this little phrase. One of them is by R. Albert Mohler Jr., "A Bee-Line to the Cross: The Preaching of Charles H. Spurgeon," *Preaching*, November 1, 1992, http://www.preaching.com/resources/past-masters/11567332/.

4. That is, in the King James Version.

5. Exodus 20:8 KJV.

6. Deuteronomy 32:7.

7. Psalm 105:5.

8. Luke 17:32.

9. See Psalm 56:8.

10. Roland H. Bainton, *Here I Stand* (New York: Penguin, 1978), 41.

11. 1 Peter 4:10 NKJV, emphasis added.

Chapter 8 Reaction Time

1. Philippians 2:5 NKJV.

2. John 1:1.

3. Psalm 119:25 KJV.

4. James 1:19.

5. See Numbers 14:40.

Chapter 9 The Anchoring Effect

1. Daniel Kahneman, *Thinking, Fast and Slow* (New York: Farrar, Straus and Giroux, 2011), 123–24.

2. See Hebrews 6:19.

3. Hebrews 11:1.

4. "The American Colony in Jerusalem: Family Tragedy," Library of Congress Exhibition, January 2–April 2, 2005, http://www.loc.gov/exhibits/americancolony/amcolony-family.html. Accessed March 22, 2015.

5. See Philippians 2:12.

6. See Philippians 4:7.

7. Philippians 4:8.

8. Thanks to Ann Voskamp for her brilliant book *One Thousand Gifts*. That's where the idea for numbering originated.

9. See Revelation 12:11.

10. Dan Harris, Felicia Biberica, and Jenna Mucha, "Sunday Profile: Eckhart Tolle," *ABC News World News Tonight*, February 15, 2009, http://abcnews.go.com/WN/CelebrityCafe/story?id=6884584.

11. Steve Bradt, "Wandering Mind Not a Happy Mind," *Harvard Gazette*, November 11, 2010, http://news.harvard.edu/gazette/story/2010/11/wandering-mind-not-a-happy-mind/.

12. "Don't Believe Everything You Think," Cleveland Clinic Wellness, 2012, http://www.clevelandclinicwellness.com/programs/NewSFN/pages/default.aspx?Lesson=3&Topic=2&UserId=00000000-0000-0000-0000-000000000705. Accessed March 22, 2015.

13. See Proverbs 18:21.
14. Jeremiah 1:7 KJV.
15. See Matthew 12:34.

Chapter 10 The Power of Suggestion

1. Charles Allen, *God's Psychiatry* (Grand Rapids: Revell, 1997), 125.
2. Philippians 4:13 NKJV.
3. Romans 8:37.
4. See John 16:33.
5. See Deuteronomy 31:6.
6. See Proverbs 16:9.
7. Mike Aquilina, *The Way of the Fathers: Praying with the Early Christians* (Huntington, IN: Our Sunday Visitor, 2000), 41.
8. "Albert Einstein Quotes," GoodReads.com, https://www.goodreads.com/quotes/987-there-are-only-two-ways-to-live-your-life-one. Accessed April 15, 2015.
9. John Hamm, *Unusually Excellent: The Necessary Nine Skills Required for the Practice of Great Leadership* (San Francisco: Jossey-Bass, 2011), 151.
10. Kris Cole, *The Complete Idiot's Guide to Clear Communication* (Alpha, 2002), 34.
11. Ibid., 83.
12. Galatians 2:20.
13. Luke 9:23.
14. This idea originates with Martin Luther. He used the word *preach*. I substituted the word *live*.
15. This experiment was described, among other places, in John C. Maxwell's article "Encouragement Changes Everything," *Success* magazine, August 2009, 22.
16. Stephen R. Covey, *The 7 Habits of Highly Effective People* (New York: Simon & Schuster, 2013), 407.
17. Matthew 16:23.
18. See John 1:14.

Chapter 11 Cross-Eyed

1. Evan Wiggs, "George Whitefield," Measure of Gold Revival Ministries, http://www.evanwiggs.com/revival/portrait/whitefie.html. Accessed March 23, 2015.
2. John Rinehart, *Gospel Patrons* (Reclaimed Publishing, 2013), 63.
3. Ibid.
4. Ibid.
5. Ibid.
6. Wiggs, "George Whitefield."
7. 2 Corinthians 5:21.
8. Romans 12:1.

Chapter 12 The Scenic Route

1. Mike Marriner, Brian McAllister, and Nathan Gebhard, *Finding the Open Road* (Berkeley, CA: Ten Speed Press, 2005), 21.
2. Galatians 5:25.
3. *Saturday Night Live*, October 9, 1993, transcript available at http://snltranscripts.jt.org/93/93cidiot.phtml. Accessed March 23, 2015.

Chapter 13 The Reckoning

1. "Nick Vujicic: Life without Limbs" (video), CBN TV, http://www.cbn.com/tv/1430455394001, accessed April 20, 2015.
2. Romans 8:18 KJV.

3. Peter Senge, C. Otto Scharmer, Joseph Jaworski, and Betty Sue Flowers, *Presence: Human Purpose and the Field of the Future* (New York: Currency, 2005).

4. Ibid., 25.

5. Ibid., 26.

6. See John 6:1–14.

7. Malcolm Gladwell, *David and Goliath* (New York: Little, Brown, 2013), 49–50.

8. Ibid., 46.

9. "Jim Elliot Quote," Billy Graham Center Archives, Wheaton College, May 31, 2012, http://www2.wheaton.edu/bgc/archives/faq/20.htm. Accessed March 23, 2015.

Chapter 14 Eternal Optimist

1. Helen Keller, *Optimism: An Essay* (New York: T. Y. Crowell and Company, 1903), public domain. Text available online at https://archive.org/details/optimismessay00kelliala. Accessed March 23, 2015.

2. Helen Keller, quoted at BrainyQuote.com, Xplore Inc, 2015, http://www.brainyquote.com/quotes/quotes/h/helenkelle383771.html. Accessed March 23, 2015.

3. Beverly Kirkhart, Jack Canfield, Mark Victor Hansen, Patty Aubery, and Nancy Mitchell Autio, *Chicken Soup for the Cancer Survivor's Soul* (Deerfield Beach, FL: Health Communications, 2012), 85.

4. Norman Cousins, *Healing Heart*, audio edition (Avon, 1984).

5. These lines are from George Bernard Shaw's play *Mrs. Warren's Profession*, act 2.

6. John 16:33.

7. See Romans 8:37.

Chapter 15 Who If

1. Psalm 139:13–16.

2. See 1 Chronicles 11.

3. W. M. Zoba, "The Grandmother of Us All," *Christianity Today* 40, no. 10 (1996): 44–46.

4. Marcus Brotherton, *"Teacher": The Henrietta Mears Story* (Ventura, CA: Regal, 2006), 10.

5. Ibid., 145.

6. See 1 Corinthians 14:25.

7. See Revelation 2:17.

8. Hebrews 13:2.

9. C. S. Lewis, *The Weight of Glory* (New York: HarperOne, 2009), 46.

10. See Hebrews 4:12.

11. Matthew 6:10.

Chapter 16 The Third Wheel

1. I have since heard that there are some five-cylinder vehicles, but I cannot claim prescience.

2. You can't even put your faith in Christ without the help of the Holy Spirit. First Corinthians 12:3 says, "No one can say 'Jesus is Lord,' except by the Holy Spirit."

3. Romans 8:23.

4. 2 Corinthians 1:21–22.

5. See 1 Corinthians 6:19.

6. Ephesians 1:23.

7. See Philippians 4:19.

8. "William Booth," Salvation Army Torrance Corps, 2015, http://www1.usw.salvationarmy.org/usw/www_usw_torrance2.nsf/vw-sublinks/FCD98CD6A8BFB1B68825771D00178DE1?openDocument.

Chapter 17 And It Came to Pass

1. Richard Thaler, "Some Empirical Evidence on Dynamic Inconsistency," *Economics Letters* 8 (1981), 201–207, http://faculty.chicagobooth.edu/Richard.Thaler/research /pdf/Some%20Empirical%20Evidence%20on%20Dynamic%20Inconsistency.pdf.

2. Frank Partnoy, *Wait: The Art and Science of Delay* (New York: PublicAffairs, 2013), 104.

3. Dale Carnegie, *How to Stop Worrying and Start Living* (New York: Pocket Books, 1990), 3.

4. Ibid., 4.

5. Ibid.

6. C. S. Lewis, *The Screwtape Letters* (New York: Scribner, 2009), 77, 79.

7. R. T. Kendall, *The Anointing: Yesterday, Today, and Tomorrow* (Lake Mary, FL: Charisma House, 2003).

8. George Foreman, *God in My Corner* (Nashville: Thomas Nelson, 2007), 132.

9. Philippians 1:6.

10. "This Too Shall Pass," *Wikipedia*, March 23, 2015, http://en.wikipedia.org /wiki/This_too_shall_pass.

Chapter 18 Narrow Framing

1. See 2 Timothy 2:15.

2. "Your DNA Would Reach the Moon," *Wow! Really?* (blog), November 2016, http://wow-really.blogspot.com/2006/11/your-dna-would-reach-moon.html. Accessed March 24, 2015.

3. Chip and Dan Heath, *Decisive: How to Make Better Choices in Life and Work* (New York: Crown, 2013).

4. Ibid., 17.

5. See Matthew 17:1–13.

6. Matthew 19:26.

7. Job 11:6.

8. James Pearn, "How Many Servers Does Google Have?" Google Plus post, January 25, 2012, https://plus.google.com/+JamesPearn/posts/VaQu9sNxJuY. Accessed March 24, 2015.

9. Lalit Kumar, "Google Facts: Amazing Trivia about Google," TechWelkin, September 22, 2014, http://techwelkin.com/google-facts-amazing-trivia-about-google#google -search-facts. Accessed March 24, 2015.

10. 1 Corinthians 2:10.

11. See Acts 8:26–40.

12. See Luke 12:12.

13. M. Mitchell Waldrop, *Complexity: The Emerging Science at the Edge of Order and Chaos* (New York: Simon and Schuster, 1992), 29.

14. "About Post-it Brand," 3M, 2015, http://www.post-it.com/wps/portal/3M/en _US/PostItNA/Home/Support/About/.

15. Proverbs 18:15 NLT 2004.

Chapter 20 The Kingdom of Unintended Consequences

1. See "Cobra Effect," *Wikipedia*, modified February 24, 2015, http://en.wikipedia .org/wiki/Cobra_effect. Accessed March 24, 2015.

2. Jane E. Brody, "Babies Know: A Little Dirt Is Good for You," *New York Times*, January 26, 2009, http://www.nytimes.com/2009/01/27/health/27brod.html?_r=0.

3. See "Unintended Consequences," *Wikipedia*, modified March 23, 2015, http:// en.wikipedia.org/wiki/Unintended_consequences. Accessed March 24, 2015.

4. Proverbs 16:9 NASB.
5. Matthew 13:32.
6. Matthew 28:19.
7. William Jennings Bryan quoted in *The Sabbath Recorder*, vol. 64 (Plainfield, NJ: American Sabbath Tract Society, January 6, 1908), 738; see also William Jennings Bryan, "The Prince of Peace" (a lecture delivered at many religious gatherings), http://thriceholy.net/Texts/Prince.html. Accessed June 15, 2012.

Chapter 21 The Rosetta Stone

1. A reference for cartoon lovers; also a favorite phrase of mine around the office!
2. *The Best Advice I Ever Got: Wit and Wisdom for Graduates* (Grand Rapids: Zondervan, 2007).
3. David G. Myers, *The Pursuit of Happiness* (New York: William Morrow, 1993), 66.
4. Ibid.
5. Ibid., 66–67.
6. John 16:33.

Chapter 22 Bold Predictions

1. President John F. Kennedy, "Special Message to the Congress on Urgent National Needs," May 25, 1961, excerpt quoted at NASA.gov, https://www.nasa.gov/vision/space/features/jfk_speech_text.html. Accessed March 25, 2015.
2. Matthew 25:21.
3. Matthew 16:23.
4. Matthew 26:13.
5. Isaiah 61:7.

Chapter 23 The Pavlovian Effect

1. For five examples, see Matthew 5.
2. Matthew 5:38–39.
3. Psalm 84:7.
4. See Christopher Klein, "Shot in the Chest 100 Years Ago, Teddy Roosevelt Kept on Talking," History.com, October 12, 2012, http://www.history.com/news/shot-in-the-chest-100-years-ago-teddy-roosevelt-kept-on-talking. Accessed March 25, 2015.
5. Philippians 2:14–15 NIV 1984.
6. 2 Corinthians 3:18 NIV 1984.

Chapter 24 Change Agents

1. Quoted in Jack Canfield and Mark Victor Hansen, *The Aladdin Factor* (New York: Berkley Books, 1995), 255.
2. Videos of these stories are available online: "A18: Innovate," National Community Church, November 23, 2014, http://theaterchurch.com/media/a18/aoneeight-innovate.
3. See www.shoppulchritude.com.
4. See www.bittersweetmonthly.com
5. Oswald Chambers, "Direction by Impulse," *My Utmost for His Highest*, online daily devotional, October 21, 2014, http://utmost.org/classic/direction-by-impulse-classic/.
6. Quoted in John Maxwell, *Life@Work: Marketplace Success for People of Faith* (Nashville: Thomas Nelson, 2005), 127.
7. Dr. Martin Luther King Jr., quoted at The King Center online, "Quote of the Week," April 9, 2013, http://www.thekingcenter.org/blog/mlk-quote-week-all-labor-uplifts-humanity-has-dignity-and-importance-and-should-be-undertaken.

Chapter 25 I Dwell in Possibility

1. Matthew Alice, "On an Average Day, How Many Airplanes Are in the Sky across the United States?" Straight from the Hip, *San Diego Reader*, May 17, 2001, http://www.sandiegoreader.com/news/2001/may/17/average-day-how-many-airplanes-are-sky-across-unit/#. Accessed March 26, 2015.

2. "Exploring History," *National Geographic* (Winter 2012): 21.

3. Søren Kierkegaard, *Either/Or: A Fragment of Life* (New York: Penguin Classics, 1992), 14.

4. See Philippians 4:13.

5. University of Oregon, "Explore the Power of 'If,'" YouTube video, posted January 1, 2015, https://www.youtube.com/watch?v=6fvPsoidQmI.

6. Ibid.

7. A. W. Tozer, "God of Glory" (devotional), The Alliance, October 31, 2012, https://www.cmalliance.org/devotions/tozer?id=1346. Accessed April 17, 2015.

8. See Ephesians 3:20.

9. See Isaiah 55:8.

10. See Isaiah 9:6–7.

11. G. K. Chesterton, *Orthodoxy* (Ortho Publishing, 2014), 13.

12. 1 Samuel 14:6.

13. 1 Samuel 14:23.

14. See Mark Batterson, *Draw the Circle: The Forty Day Prayer Challenge* (Grand Rapids: Zondervan, 2012), Day 1.

15. Frederick Douglass quoted in Tryon Edwards, *A Dictionary of Thoughts: Being a Cyclopedia of Laconic Quotations from the Best Authors of the World, Both Ancient and Modern* (Detroit: F. B. Dickerson Company, 1908), 324.

16. As quoted in Joe Carter, "Being on God's Side," *First Things*, December 22, 2010, http://www.firstthings.com/web-exclusives/2010/12/being-on-gods-side-an-open-letter-to-the-religious-right.

Chapter 26 Monogrammed Blessings

1. Molly Bentley, "Unweaving the Song of Whales," BBC News, February 28, 2005, http://news.bbc.co.uk/2/hi/science/nature/4297531.stm. Accessed March 26, 2015.

2. See Andrew Stevenson, "Whale Song and How Far It Carries," Whales Bermuda, http://www.whalesbermuda.com/all-about-humpbacks/whale-behaviour/54-whale-song/136-whale-song-and-how-far-it-carries. Accessed March 26, 2015.

3. Psalm 104:26 ESV.

4. Thanks to Ann Voskamp and her brilliant book, *One Thousand Gifts*. I highly recommend it.

5. Deuteronomy 28:2 NKJV.

6. Deuteronomy 28:1 NKJV.

7. See Acts 20:35.

8. 2 Corinthians 1:20.

Chapter 27 The Cornerman

1. A. W. Tozer, *The Knowledge of the Holy: The Attributes of God: Their Meaning in the Christian Life* (New York: HarperOne, 2009), 1.

2. "Angelo Dundee" (obituary), *The Telegraph*, February 2, 2012, http://www.telegraph.co.uk/news/obituaries/sport-obituaries/9056657/Angelo-Dundee.html.

3. Isaiah 52:12.

4. See Psalm 84:11.

5. Yes, this is an allusion to my favorite Christmas movie, *Elf*, which I happened to watch the night before writing this chapter.

6. See Revelation 12:11.

Chapter 28 The Event Horizon

1. See Luke 22:61.

2. For a basic explanation see "Event Horizon," *Wikipedia*, modified March 16, 2015, http://en.wikipedia.org/wiki/Event_horizon. Accessed March 27, 2015.

3. Romans 6:23.

4. Ephesians 3:17–19.

5. Quoted in Richard Foster, *Longing for God* (Downer's Grove, IL: InterVarsity, 2009), 99.

6. Romans 5:8.

7. Romans 8:31.

Chapter 29 More than Conquerors

1. Lester Haines, "'We Are the Champions' Voted World's Fave Song," *The Register*, September 29, 2005, http://www.theregister.co.uk/2005/09/29/world_music_poll/.

2. "1916 Cumberland vs. Georgia Tech Football Game," *Wikipedia*, modified February 8, 2015, http://en.wikipedia.org/wiki/1916_Cumberland_vs._Georgia_Tech_football_game. Accessed March 27, 2015.

3. John MacArthur, *The MacArthur New Testament Commentary: Romans 1–8* (Chicago: Moody Press, 1991), 514.

4. Thanks to John Ashcroft for this little line. I first heard it from him.

5. See Revelation 12:11.

6. Haggai 2:23.

Chapter 30 Keep Calm and Carry On

1. Esther 4:14.

2. Winston Churchill, "Never Give In," speech at Harrow School, October 29, 1941, text at The Churchill Centre, http://www.winstonchurchill.org/resources/speeches/1941-1945-war-leader/never-give-in.

3. Romans 8:38.

4. Exodus 14:13–14.

5. See Roger E. Olson, "Did Karl Barth Really Say 'Jesus Loves Me, This I Know . . .'?" Patheos blog, January 24, 2013, http://www.patheos.com/blogs/rogereolson/2013/01/did-karl-barth-really-say-jesus-loves-me-this-i-know/.

6. Elizabeth Landau, "Scientists Confirm Most Distant Galaxy Ever," CNN.com, October 25, 2013, http://www.cnn.com/2013/10/23/tech/innovation/most-distant-galaxy/.

7. "Ocean Facts: How deep is the ocean?" National Ocean Service, http://oceanservice.noaa.gov/facts/oceandepth.html.

Epilogue

1. See F. W. Boreham, *Life Verses* (Grand Rapids: Kregel, 1994), 216–17.

2. Ibid., 222.

3. Ibid., 226.

4. Romans 8:38–39 KJV.

5. See Boreham, *Life Verses*, 225–6.

Mark Batterson is the *New York Times* bestselling author of *The Circle Maker*, *The Grave Robber*, and *A Trip around the Sun*. He is the lead pastor of National Community Church, one church with seven campuses in Washington, DC. Mark has a doctor of ministry degree from Regent University and lives on Capitol Hill with his wife, Lora, and their three children. Learn more at www.markbatterson.com.

Discover resources for individuals and
small groups at

MARKBATTERSON.COM

You will find...

Sermon outlines

Church resources

Printable bookmark, flyer, and more

...

Connect with

MARK
BATTERSON

at
MarkBatterson.com

 @MarkBatterson

Mark Batterson

@MarkBatterson

Connect with National Community Church at
WWW.THEATERCHURCH.COM

New York Times Bestselling Author

MARK BATTERSON

Dares Us to Imagine *What If?*

Perfect Resources for Individuals, Groups,
or Churchwide Campaigns

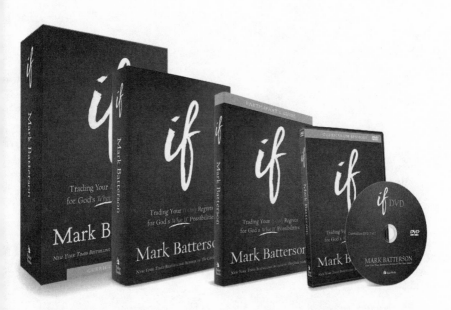

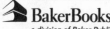

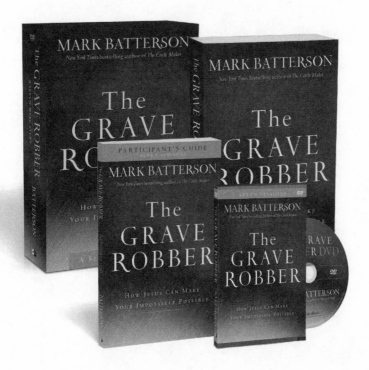

A Challenge to
Choose Adventure

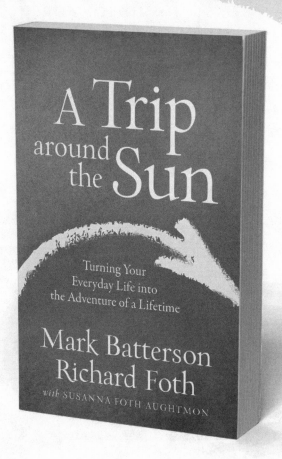

"*A Trip around the Sun* will awaken your hunger to make your life your adventure. If you can read this book without being stirred to life—check your pulse."

—JOHN ORTBERG, senior pastor of Menlo Park Presbyterian Church and author of *Soul Keeping*

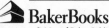